WALKING AMERICA:

A 10,000 Mile Journey
of Self-Healing

Jake Sansing

Contact:
jakedoesamerica@gmail.com
(Pictures available upon request)

Contents

<u>Opportunity</u>

After spending four years in the Army, I purchased a brand-new Nissan Altima and drove across the country from Ft. Lewis, Washington, back to my home state of Tennessee. I then used the money I'd saved during the service to open a recording studio in the town of Humboldt. Of course, Humboldt may not have been the best place for that type of business, but the city's location near the interstate provided me with enough traveling customers to pay the bills. Although I was barely getting by, money wasn't that important to me. I was perfectly content with living in the back of the studio, which was the price I had to pay to afford my dream job. Before I even started the business, I knew that it would probably be a year before I could afford it and a house at the same time.

Fast forward about a year of living and working in that studio, the woman I had been dating for the past six months was eager for us to get a house together. Although I was a bit skeptical, I wasn't entirely against the idea. After all, my business had really taken off by then, and I knew our relationship would require that progression at some point.

One day, my girlfriend walked in and showed me an advertisement for a two-story, Victorian house located in the country. With a few acres of forest land to go with it, I couldn't say no. The only drawback was the location. It was too far for a daily commute, which meant I would have to give up my studio. The plan, however, was to continue working from home as a mixing and mastering engineer. And working from home

7

seemed doable since I had enough customers by then that I felt confident they would continue to use my service.

After meeting with the landlord and looking over the house, we decided to take the risk, and I signed my name on the lease. I then sold all of my recording equipment and had the house fully furnished within two weeks. However, by the second month of living there, I already felt like I'd made a huge mistake. Only a handful of my customers were sending me tracks that needed work. The rest of them had found another studio to work with entirely. These misfortunes were causing me to feel stressed, but I'd always coped well with stress before. I just knew I'd have to find another job to make ends meet, so I began searching.

Over the next month's time, I had put in about twenty job applications but hadn't heard anything back. One evening, I returned home feeling defeated when I discovered a note on the kitchen table. It was a letter from my girlfriend, which stated that she had given up on us and had moved back in with her parents. I couldn't believe it. I had just given up everything for her, and she had walked out on me. I wished I could take it all back, or at least rent another building to get back to work, but I had sunk all my money into our house, and there was no way I could afford to start up another studio. I then realized that I had lost it all and that I was about to become homeless.

Scared to keep hanging on and risk losing more than I already had, I decided to sell all the furniture from my house and began living out of my car. Keeping the unnecessary items seemed pretty much pointless anyway, and I knew I would need the extra money for gas if I planned on finding any work. Although, I did keep my computer and headphones, which I continued to use for engineering.

After parting ways with my house, I spent the next few weeks driving around and applying for all sorts of jobs, regardless if it was full-time or part-time. Although I had obtained a few odd jobs here and there, none of it was amounting to anything. It appeared as though I was finding just

8

enough work to afford a motel room to get cleaned up for another quick buck. The rest of the time, I was sleeping in parking lots, dumpster diving behind stores, and cursing myself for the decisions I had made that led up to these troubling times.

It had been a rough winter, but once spring came around, I made my way to my hometown of Greenfield to visit my parents. I hadn't seen them in a while, so I was sure they wouldn't mind if I stayed with them for a couple of days. Although I felt they were suspicious of me being there, I never told them the struggles I was going through. However, they eventually asked how everything was at the studio. I wondered if rumors had gotten around, and maybe they weren't sure how to bring it up, but I was too embarrassed to admit the truth. I just smiled and told them everything was going great, that I had simply taken a few days off work to relax. I figured they would have no reason not to believe that, and my deterrence appeared to have worked because the conversation ended there.

The first night at my parents', I fell asleep on the couch while pondering at the idea of moving back in with them. While it would mean that I had a roof over my head, that would be about it. My chances of finding a job around there were even slimmer than everywhere else I had been, and I wouldn't want to be a burden on anyone. While I'm sure they wouldn't have cared at first, I knew there would eventually come the point of arguing about it, and I'd rather avoid that because my parents were the last people I wanted to feel were against me.

The next day, while my parents were gone to work, I brought my clothes in from my car's trunk and threw them into the washer. If I had done my laundry while my parents were home, then I was sure it would have made their suspicions grow more than they already had. So, before they got home that evening, I made sure that all my things were tucked away in my car and decided to go for a walk in the woods.

My parents owned several acres of forested land, which I spent a great deal of my younger years. It was nice to be back out there, to just kind of forget the troubles I was going through. The idea of living in the woods even crossed my mind, but I wasn't sure how anyone else would feel about it. It seemed like a good backup plan, but the reality was that everyone else would probably think it was strange. Plus, summer was right around the corner, and I'd probably be miserable once the forest became unbearably hot, a time best left to all the copperheads, ticks, and mosquitos. Although I saw living out there as an option, I decided to keep it as a last resort and made my way back to my parents' house before dark.

During the second night of visiting with my parents, I made my way to my old bedroom, which my mother had converted into somewhat of a gym. I then saw one of my old acoustic guitars they had kept standing in the corner, so I decided to pick it up. I took a seat in the middle of the room and began to gently pluck at the soft nylon strings, trying to play quietly enough not to wake anyone. I must have been sitting there for an hour or so, as time quickly passes when you're under the spell of creating music. I then thought I felt the house begin to shake, which got my full attention. Although it wasn't unusual to feel a slight vibration from the trains passing through the woods behind their house, something about this seemed different. I then lowered my hand to mute the resonating guitar strings, focusing on what was going on outside. Before I had time to figure out what was happening, something came crashing through the house and sent me flying through the wall behind me. I knew something terrible had happened, but I still didn't know for sure. All I knew was that it was now pitch black and that I was underneath a lot of debris.

I began climbing out of the wreckage, and when I stood up, I felt something sharp poke the top of my head. I then reached into my pocket and pulled out my cellphone to use as a flashlight. I immediately realized that I had just crawled out from under the bathroom sink and what had poked my head was a tree branch. I then made my way out of the bathroom and saw a tree had smashed through my bedroom. Thankfully, the tree had pushed me out of the way before squashing me like a bug.

Hoping my parents were okay, I began making my way towards their room, which was on the opposite side of the house. As I walked into the living room, I noticed several branches sticking through the roof. The ceiling fan was slowly rotating from the wind seeping in, and raindrops were pooling on the kitchen table. I began to worry even more about my parents, so I rushed to their bedroom. Upon reaching them, I realized they were safe, but they had somehow managed to sleep through the ordeal.

I hesitated to wake them because I didn't want them to go into a panic. I prepared myself and shook my father's shoulder. "Hey, you guys didn't hear that storm that just came through here," I asked. I could tell he knew there was more bad news to follow because I wouldn't have bothered him under normal circumstances. Looking both confused and worried, he sat up and asked, "What? No. Why? What happened?" I hated having to tell him that a tornado had just come through and tossed a tree onto the house, but I did, and he shouted back, "Fuck!" He then jumped out of bed and began putting his clothes on. My mother then woke up, still new to what was going on. I quickly explained the situation to my mother as my father made his way into the living room. And just after I finished telling her a tree had fallen on the house, we could hear my father swearing from the kitchen, "Goddammit! Always fucking something!" My mother then rushed into the kitchen to join him while I walked out of the back door to see what it looked like outside.

When the first stroke of lightning flashed, I saw several trees and other junk scattered about the yard. When the second flash came, I noticed the same tree that had smashed through the house was also sitting on top of my car. Before I had time to react, my parents walked outside and shouted over to me that they were going next door to my aunt's house. I could see that everything appeared fine in her direction, so instead of joining them, I continued standing in the rain, staring at the mangled heap of metal that used to be my car. That was the only thing I had left from the money I had made in the Army, so seeing it squashed like that was devastating.

To make matters worse, I had recently changed my insurance to only liability to try and save some money. My computer, which I had stowed away in the trunk, was also destroyed. So there went my only two means of income. Without my vehicle or computer, I had no idea how I would get out of that dilemma.

After the storm incident, I stuck around my parents' for a couple of weeks, helping to clean all the wreckage and adding new walls onto the house. It took nearly two months to get everything looking close to normal, at which point I finally decided to scrap my car for two hundred dollars. That put my bank account just over seven hundred, but I had no idea how I would start over with only that much. Because I felt as though my next financial move could potentially be my last, I was scared to spend any of it. So if I wasn't outside cutting up the last bit of trees that had fallen, I was just lying on my old bedroom floor, thinking about what I was going to do next.

As more weeks went by, I began to sink into a deep depression, and my motivation grew slimmer. It finally got so bad that I spent about twenty-three hours per day lying on the floor, only getting up to shower and use the restroom. To add to what I was already feeling, my parents were becoming frustrated about me being there, utterly clueless that I was severely depressed. At least I stayed busy in my mind, always trying to think of a way out of my situation. Physically, however, I knew I would have a difficult time forcing myself to do anything.

After months of battling depression, I finally decided to spend a little of my money on a backpack, tent, and sleeping bag. I figured I'd need those things if I would be looking for a new job because I'd have to walk anywhere from fifteen to twenty miles per day if I wanted any luck. Knowing I'd have to walk that far in one direction, camping between towns seemed like my only reasonable option. So, I packed my things once they arrived and began walking between towns, continuing my search for odd jobs and putting in applications anywhere I could find. Although I still wasn't having much luck at finding any work, I enjoyed the long walks and sleeping under the stars.

One day, as I was walking along the train tracks, making my way towards another town, I began to ponder the idea of walking across America. It didn't seem like I would be missing out on much if I were to leave, and the possibilities elsewhere may have much greater potential. I was also getting tired of the same scenery every day, and I felt as though the constant change might help with my depression. Just the idea of hiking across the country, regardless of the reason, seemed to give me something to look forward to when I had nothing else.

I knew walking across America probably wouldn't fix the situation I was in, but it would certainly change it. Since all the walking I had been doing seemed to be helping with my depression and anxiety, I figured that six months of it must help six times as much. I also thought that perhaps at the end of my trip, I could return home, and maybe then I would have a bit more luck with finding a job. There was also a part of me that felt like all of this was happening for a reason. It was as though the universe wanted to take everything away to teach me some sort of lesson. If that were the case, I was no longer going to fight it. Ready to make a change, I turned to step off the tracks and wandered into the forest.

I continued walking through the woods well after dark and didn't stop until I came upon a river. Although I had my tent with me, I decided to build a lean-to shelter and started a small fire. As I sat next to the fire, I finally let myself relax and just enjoyed the sounds of nature around me. Only several hours had passed since I'd decided to walk across America, but I already felt as though I had become a new person. Because of my new and positive outlook, I no longer felt like I had given up but that

I had given in. And at that point, the sense of relief I felt only confirmed that there was no going back on the deal I had made with myself.

After spending a week camping next to the river, I made my way back into Greenfield and walked into the library. I then logged on to one of their computers and searched online for more equipment that I thought I might need. I finally found a website with a ton of outdoor gear, so I began clicking through the pages and quickly filled my cart with various items. After placing my order, I sent a few of my friends a message to let them know about my plans. They all thought that I had lost it when I told them I would be walking across America. Most of them tried convincing me to stay where I was and to keep looking for a job. However, there was nothing anyone could say or do that would have changed my mind, or at least I didn't think so.

After about an hour of telling people my plan, a young man named Matt sent me an email. He was living nearly a thousand miles away in the northeastern state of Maryland, but he had somehow already caught wind of what I was doing. He had decided to reach out to me after a mutual friend told him what I was up to. He mentioned that he was planning to ride a bike across America and wanted to ask if I'd consider riding with him instead of walking. While having some company did sound nice, cycling just wasn't how I wanted to do things, so I made a counteroffer and invited him to walk with me. Unfortunately, there was no persuading him. The idea of walking across America was a little too much for him to handle. Unsure if I wanted to change my plans for someone I'd just met online, I told him to give me a few days to think it over.

A few days had passed when I finally decided that I would cycle the country with Matt. It wasn't exactly how I wanted to do things, but I imagined it would still be a wonderful experience anyway. I was also sure that our company could prove beneficial to one another. However, I was still a bit

14

skeptical about whether he was as serious about crossing the country as I was, so I decided to talk with him about it every day for at least a week before I would start making any purchases.

After a week had passed, and I believed that Matt was firm in his decision to ride a bike across America, I returned all of my unnecessary hiking gear and began searching online for cycling equipment. Since we had planned on starting our ride on September 1st, my time to meet up with him was running short. Without studying too much into it, I quickly ordered a bike, saddlebags, spare tubes, a tire pump, a multi-tool, a couple of water bottles, and all the other things a beginner cyclist might expect to need for a long-distance cycling trip. Then, to top it off, I purchased a train ticket from Memphis, Tennessee, to Washington, D.C. Those were the closest cities between the two of us that had a train station, which was a little over a hundred miles from me and then about sixty-five miles to him.

After I had everything paid for, I had about two hundred dollars left. That may not seem like much, but money didn't seem like it would be an issue anymore. I knew that I could live outside for free, which was where I planned on being for the next few months. I figured I could stretch the amount I had and work odd jobs along the way if needed. I would just have to balance what I spent with whatever work I could find, but not get so caught up in spending that I had to find work all the time. With that mindset, I was confident that I could get by just fine.

My new bike and accessories arrived a few days later, and I had it all put together by the end of that night. The next morning, I headed out for a few days, trying to get a feel of what was in store for me. I had read in several blogs about cycling that you should put at least a hundred miles on a bike before getting ready to tour with it, so that's what I aimed for and corrected any minor problems that came up. After spending some time riding and camping, getting into the swing of things, it seemed as though my setup would be good enough to get the job done. Although I was a bit weary of my bike having a complete breakdown in the middle of our trip, I felt comforted by the idea that I could just walk if that were to happen, since that was my original plan anyway.

My train to D.C. would be departing from Memphis on August 20th, so I had about two weeks before needing to head out. For the remainder of that time, I decided to stay in the woods to acclimate to only being outside. Since I was about to lose all the amenities of being indoors, I wanted to get used to it while I still it as an option. Of course, I had just spent four years as an infantryman, so I knew it wouldn't be hard for me to readjust. Just hanging out in the woods of Tennessee was a lot like basic training at Fort Benning, Georgia, minus all the yelling and other guys to keep me company. To keep myself occupied, I began reading up on all the plants in my area. I was curious to learn what was edible, poisonous, or which ones had medical uses. I was blown away by how much food there was all around me. It wasn't the more obvious things, such as oranges, blackberries, or persimmons, but plants I'd never given much attention. There were the cattails, which I could use to make bread, dandelions for their high content of vitamin A and C, rabbit tobacco to help with pain and coughs, and so on. I grew even more confident with wild edibles as the days went on, not only for where I was but also for anywhere that I may end up. I had done a lot of hunting, trapping, and fishing throughout my life, but I never thought much to learn about foraging until it felt necessary.

August 16th had finally rolled around, and I'd said my goodbyes to everyone. However, my mother and sister, who lived in a completely different city, were still trying to talk me out of leaving. I thought they must have noticed how much happier I'd seemed over the past couple of weeks, though they may have assumed that I'd simply just snapped out of it. However, I wasn't necessarily sure they ever even knew I was depressed. I never talked to them about it, but I assumed everyone could tell. As much as I would have liked to gain their blessings for my trip, their misunderstandings could not sway my new way of thinking. Even if they didn't know what I was truly going through, I knew they would rather me be happy than miserable, which is how I would have felt if I were to stay. Of course, I knew there was the possibility that the reason they didn't want me to go was out of fear that something might happen, but out of everything I had already been through, this was the last thing they needed to be worried about. After all, I had made it back from two tours in Afghanistan, which I'll admit left me feeling somewhat invincible and more than capable of taking care of myself. There was also a side of me that felt a lot of guilt from that, and I secretly hoped this would help me let go of those troubles. I sensed I needed it to regain a piece of myself that I had lost.

To Maryland

After having breakfast with my parents, it was time to start my one-hundred and twenty-mile bike ride to Memphis. The lingering fog made the morning air feel cold, but I could tell that it was going to be a long, sweltering day. I slowly pedaled my way into town and rested my bike against the Greenfield welcome sign. I took a few minutes to reminisce about my childhood in the town where I'd grown up. It was easy to visualize my long-lost friends and me riding our bikes and skateboards along the empty streets and sidewalks. It wasn't like that anymore, though. It was as though we were the last generation of kids to play outside. The streets were now empty and lifeless, a symbol that it was time to move on. I then wondered where all of my old friends had gone and how their lives were going. I hadn't been in contact with any of them since I'd left for the Army, which did leave me feeling somewhat estranged. But I did feel like a child again for that brief moment, and, in a way, I wished everything could go back to the way it was before. A part of me even felt guilty for leaving again, as though I needed to be there to keep the good memories alive. As I hopped back onto my bike and began pedaling away, I could feel myself letting go of the past and embracing the unknown.

As the day progressed, it became increasingly difficult to make it from one shaded resting spot to the next, which seemed to be anywhere from ten to fifteen miles. It was much hotter that day than it had been during my previous rides, with which I'd had no problems. However, this time, I was sweating out my water just as fast as I could drink it. Luckily, each time I needed to fill up again, I would pass by a random house with a water fixture on the side. And as far as I know, no one ever knew I'd made a quick stop at their residence. Although, I was sure that if anyone had noticed me getting a drink, they more than likely would have been okay with it. That was one good thing about the south.

Although I was toting two one-liter water bottles with me, it was apparent that I was going to have to start carrying more. I then stopped at the Wal-Mart in Brownsville before beginning the long, empty stretch into Memphis. As I approached the store, I began to feel nervous about leaving my bike outside. Although I knew the chances were slim, I didn't want to risk someone stealing my things, so I decided to push my bike inside. As soon as I entered the building, a worker told me that I needed to leave my bike outside, but I just kept walking and ignored him. Of course, I did feel a bit rude for behaving this way, but this wasn't a normal circumstance. I couldn't risk trying to explain that to him and for him to not agree with it.

The worker eventually gave up, and I quickly made my way through the aisles to collect two one-gallon sized jugs of water. I then made my way straight to the checkout, where people began giving me strange looks. I knew I would have to get used to judging eyes, so I pretended not to notice them. I then made my way back outside and placed one gallon in the right saddlebag with my tent and the other in the left bag with my clothes and food. Although the water added a bit of extra weight, which I wanted to keep to a minimum, I felt more confident in my ability to make it safely between longer stretches.

As I was riding along, I began to think about how grateful I was that autumn was just around the corner. Although my timing for this trip was a mere coincidence, I had a feeling Matt had chosen to start in September to avoid these scorching temperatures. Although we hadn't discussed what routes we

19

would take yet, I already knew that we'd most likely be heading southwest to follow the seasonal changes. Either way, I'd rather deal with the cold instead of worrying about having a heat stroke, and I was sure Matt had the same mindset.

As hot as the day had been, I had made it more than halfway to Memphis by the end of my first day. I had been keeping my eyes peeled for a secluded place to camp since dusk, but it had been dark for nearly an hour. I supposed I had been too picky with where I slept, but I was still new to sleeping in unfamiliar places. Just as I began to feel a bit of anxiety, I noticed a small light in the distance and began to hurry towards it. As I got closer, I realized the light was coming from a church parking lot, so I rode down the gravel driveway and stood motionless for a few minutes. Once I was sure there no other people around, I made my way behind the small shed that was just across from the church. I then forced myself between the shed's walls and the nearby tree branches to set up my small, one-person tent.

I crawled inside my home for the night and removed my sweat-soaked clothes. Being naked made me feel vulnerable, but it was so uncomfortably hot and humid that I wouldn't have been able to sleep otherwise. Luckily, the rain cover to my tent was removable, so I decided to lie inside just the mesh part, hoping to catch a slight breeze if any should pass through.

After only a few minutes of lying there with my eyes closed, I heard the sound of thunder in the distance. Because of what I had just been through at my parents' house, I was a bit nervous that another tornado might come through, but there was nothing I could do besides hope for the best. I was also a bit frustrated because I knew I would have to put my rain cover on soon, which meant I would be even more uncomfortable than I already was. I decided that I'd let the storm get as close as possible before sealing off the outside world, hoping that I'd get to feel at least a few gusts of wind before turning my tent into a sauna. However, the sound of large raindrops splattering against the shed's tin roof crushed that dream. I then quickly jumped up and connected the rain cover to my tent, just in time before the storm picked up intensity and held me as its hostage for the rest of the night.

The next morning, I packed my things and continued making my way for Memphis. Although the first night of my trip was anything but pleasant, I still had no regrets other than the fact that I was tired from the lack of sleep. I thought that being tired would slow me down, which would have been a good thing since I didn't want to be in Memphis any earlier than I need to. However, once I'd made my way off the highway and found myself on a bike trail, I stopped thinking about time and ended up in Memphis around noon. Since I had made it a whole day early, I figured I would look for a cheap motel. I didn't have the money to do that often, but I thought this would be the last time for a while that I found myself in a similar situation.

Before I had a chance to search for nearby motels on my phone, I noticed a lady walking along the sidewalk in my direction. As she made her way closer, I asked, "You wouldn't happen to know of any cheap motels around here, would you?" When the woman spoke, I quickly realized that she wasn't a woman at all but was, in fact, a gay male prostitute. The man laughed awkwardly and replied, "Oh, yeah! I know a lot of cheap motels around here! How much are you looking to spend?" I didn't know how to respond without sounding rude, so I just stood there being silent. Luckily for me, the man lost patience before I thought of anything to say and continued walking past. I then pulled out my phone and decided to rent a room at a Motel 6, which was only a mile from the train station. I figured that would be a safe place to crash, and it would be easy for me to get to the train station in the morning.

I checked into my room around 4:00 p.m. and tossed my only two pairs of clothes into the bathtub. I couldn't believe how brown the water turned, considering I'd only worn them both for a single day. I then hung my clothes all around the room and hoped they would be dry come morning. Although the day was

21

still early, I went ahead and crawled into bed. As I was lying there, I looked back at all the miles I had just done and felt confident in my ability to cross the country, though I was eager to see what other challenges awaited me.

The next morning, I gathered my things and made it to the train station by 10:00 a.m. As I walked inside and approached the ticket counter, the worker behind the desk walked out and signaled me to follow him outside. Without me having to explain myself to the man, he pointed down at a large cardboard box and said, "Someone just got off a train and left this box here. You can have it for free. We usually charge for them."

Because my train wasn't supposed to leave until midnight, I had plenty of time to take my bike apart, but I went ahead and got to it anyway because it gave me something to do. As I began loosening all the pieces and tossing parts to the side, an older black man walked out of the station and stood next to me to chat. I can't remember what all was said, probably because he rambled a lot, but I already had the feeling this was normal for him. He seemed kind of lonely, and it was likely that the station was where he went to make small talk with all the transients, which I was sure he'd heard a lot of exciting stories that way.

After I'd finished packing my bike, the older man followed me inside and sat next to me as I waited for my train. For nearly eleven hours, he went on and on about random talks of life. He would doze in and out mid-way through sentences and wake back up hours later to continue where he had left off. No sleep for me, though. I was well-rested from spending a night at the motel and wide awake from the excitement of my upcoming journey.

It felt like it took forever for my train to arrive, but once it had come, I wondered where all that time had gone. As I began gathering my things to leave the station, the man that had been sitting with me all day followed me out. For whatever reason, he was excited to see me off and wish me luck on my trip. As the line to board shortened and I was about to climb into the train, the man stuck out his hand for a shake and said, "Marvin. The name's Marvin." He then disappeared into the crowd as I stepped inside to find an empty seat for myself. I quickly plopped down next to a window that faced the station and expected to see Marvin standing there waving, but I didn't see him anywhere. I was a bit baffled that I couldn't see him anywhere, considering he was a slow-moving man and wouldn't have had the time to walk anywhere out of sight. I shrugged it off and tried to get cozy as the train prepared to leave. And as we started down the tracks, leaving the lights and sounds of Memphis, the approaching darkness draped over me like a heavy blanket, and I fell fast asleep.

We were about an hour from Chicago, Illinois, when I woke early the next morning. I looked around at all the other sleeping passengers and decided to make my way down to the kitchen area before it got too crowded. I'd wait to grab something to eat from my bike, but I went ahead and purchased a much-needed cup of coffee. I didn't even mind that it was black, burned, and overpriced. I then took my drink to one of the dinner tables and sat next to the window, watching all the cars outside fight through the heavy traffic on their way to work. I then heard someone standing next to me mention how awful the coffee was. I turned to see it was a young man, who was probably about my age but seemed to be younger at heart. I smiled back and nodded, which he must have thought was an invitation to sit with me. As I turned to gaze back out of the window, he began talking about how he was on his way to visit some family members in Chicago. I probably appeared uninterested, but only because I was busy wondering if I'd have time to make it out of D.C. before it got dark. He then asked, "What about you? Where are you heading?" I paused for a moment because I knew if I told him, he'd be sticking around. I looked at him again and figured his company might not be so bad, so I replied, "I'm headed to Maryland to meet up with some guy I met on the internet. We've made plans to ride our bikes across America together." He seemed excited about it and began asking all sorts of questions. As our train was nearing the station, he asked if we could exchange phone numbers so that I could send him pictures and updates along the way. As he began putting my number into his contacts, I had the idea to create a Facebook Page and title it "Jake and Matt Do America." I felt like I would probably run into many people who were just as curious as this man was, and it would probably be a lot easier to manage a blog than a long list of phone numbers.

A few hours had passed, and I was on my last train to D.C. It was daylight this time, at least for a few more hours, and it was pleasant to see the countryside passing. I knew I would be coming back through here, so I tried not to pay too much attention. I did not want to tarnish my journey by studying the land that I would be migrating through in a couple of weeks. I wanted everything to be new to me. Not knowing what to expect was part of the beauty of it. To pass the time, I tried to rest as much as I could until I finally slipped into a deep sleep. I woke early the next morning as we were making our way through the Appalachian Mountains, and the views were more than welcoming. The thick fog that was sitting in the valley created a sort of eerie setting. The train began to slow, and I was curious as to why. I wouldn't have imagined a scheduled stop out in the middle of nowhere, but I guess I was wrong. As the train came to a complete stop, I looked out the window and saw a small village, which looked like something out of a Tim Burton movie. I had the urge to get out and explore, but we were only there long enough to board new passengers before taking off again.

It was about 3:00 p.m. when we pulled into the D.C. station. That gave me enough time to put my bike together and get out of the city before dark. As I was making my way towards California, Maryland, I passed by a few of the famous monuments in D.C. It was more entertaining to see them in person instead of in books. I was quickly drawn to the Potomac

River, as I had always found water to be alluring. I coveted the idea of going down for a swim, but I wasn't familiar with the area and didn't have the time for any extra stops.

I quickly made my way into the Cedarville State Forest just as it was getting dark. I had no idea where I was going to sleep, but I knew I needed it. I hadn't slept well the past few nights and planned on finishing the next eighty miles to Matt's by the next night. I was slowly moving along, scoping the area for what looked to be a good place to camp. I then saw a white shirt moving quickly through the woods. The person was running along a trail and came out onto the road just up ahead. I made my way to where they'd just come from and got onto the trail. I pushed my bike for about ten minutes and pulled off to camp behind a large tree. I didn't know how busy that trail got, so I made sure that I'd be out of there before sunrise.

I woke the next morning to the sound of people talking as they walked along the trail. I didn't want to make anyone feel uncomfortable, so I waited until the coast was clear before packing up and getting out of there. Soon after I'd left the trail, I saw a small gas station and sat outside of it for about thirty minutes, waiting for them to open. I figured I'd use that time to eat my breakfast, which consisted of a tablespoon of peanut butter and a granola bar. Then, after the store opened, I used the restroom to tame my cowlicks and fill up my water bottles. I sent Matt a text, telling him where I was and that I'd try and make it by that night. I then hopped back onto my bike and made my way through Maryland.

I pulled up to Matt's house around 4:00 p.m. and saw him putting things away from a yard sale. He had not noticed me yet, however, as he seemed to be quite fixated on what he was doing. I assumed that he was trying to gather up a few extra bucks for the trip, as I had done before leaving. I finally decided to shout at him to get his attention, and he ran up to greet me. He was just as surprised as I was that I had made it as early as I did. He then had me follow him to the back of his house to park my bike before going inside. I quickly took him up on his offer to grab a shower and then went back outside to help him put everything away. After we had finished cleaning up, I made my way over to the hammock hanging in the front yard and crawled onto it. I looked over at Matt, "I think I'll just sleep right here if that's okay with you?" That was my sleeping quarters for the rest of the week, which we used to prepare some plans. I didn't mind running around like a chicken with its head cut off, but it seemed like a good idea to have a map for the months ahead.

Matt and I decided that we would start our trek from Crisfield, MD, but that was far away on the other side of the Chesapeake Bay. Luckily, his friend Brady owned a boat and said he wouldn't mind giving us a lift. We loaded up into Brady's truck on September 1st and drove down to the boat ramp at Point Lookout State Park. The water there looked calm, but after we had made it out of the boating area, I was shocked to see how choppy the bay actually was. I was beginning to feel some concern then since the boat was barely large enough for the three of us. With the constant roll of those four-foot waves, Matt and I began clutching onto our bikes, so they wouldn't bounce out into the ocean and put an end to our trip before it even started.

We had made it about halfway across the bay when we came up to an old lighthouse. I had our captain pull up next to the ladder so I could climb to the top. The lower portion of the ladder had been eaten away by the salty seawater, so I had to time it right, waiting for a wave to lift me high enough to reach one of the solid bars. Once I'd worked my way to the top, I had them pull around to the other side so that they could scoop me out of the water. The water wasn't as rough over there because the waves were slamming into the other side. I wasn't going to pass up the opportunity to jump off this thing. I must have been fifty feet above the water, and who knew what was going on beneath the surface. The water was so murky that your hand would disappear if you stuck it in over the side of the boat, but I

26

still felt that I had to do it. I gave Matt and Brady a salute and did a flip off of the statuesque guidepost. I climbed back into the boat and collected a couple of slaps on the back. After taking a few minutes to have some fun, it was time to stop fooling around and get this little craft over to the other side. Time was not only imperative for Matt and me, but Brady would have to endure another trip back on his own, and we wanted him to be able to make it back before dark.

Once we had made it to Crisfield, I quickly realized that Matt wasn't the partner I wanted to have around. It turned out that he had a drinking problem. I was unaware of this before meeting him. I believe any man or woman can do as they wish, within reason, but he couldn't control himself. Hell, I even had a few beers, but he was showing out, being rude, and even had the cops called after yelling at an old lady. I didn't want to be associated with this kind of behavior, so we had to part ways. I'm not sure how the rest of his day turned out because I left once the police got involved. After a few hours of riding along by myself, I took a quick break and switched the Facebook Page name from "Jake and Matt Do America" to "Jake Does America." It just wouldn't make much sense to keep a group name if I was going to be crossing the country by myself.

The Beginning

Since my original plan was to backpack across America, and I had used most of my money towards a bike, I was a little upset about parting ways with Matt. I didn't let it bother me too much, though. I could always switch to walking later if I wanted. So, with a positive outlook, I continued pedaling my way north. The day went by quickly and easily, as my ride through the eastern side of Maryland was mostly flat. After coasting along for several hours, I ended the first night of my cross-country trek in the town of Delmar, which is right on the state line with Delaware. I still hadn't much practice sleeping in new places and had a hard time deciding where to go. I eventually came across a bunch of sheds that were sitting outside of a hardware store. I pushed my bike inside of one of them and tossed my sleeping bag onto the wooden floor. The air inside quickly became warm and stale, and I wished I'd just found a place to sleep outside. I began packing up to leave when I heard several vehicles pull up, all blaring rap music. I decided to wait a bit to see if they'd go away. An hour later, they were still there, so I said, "screw it," and jumped out of the shed. I didn't know what kind of reaction to expect, but I don't think anyone even noticed as I made my way out of there.

Shortly after I'd left the shed, it started to rain, so it didn't take long to regret my decision to leave. It was too late to go back, though. Those people were probably still sitting in the parking lot, and I didn't want them to call the police if they saw me. Since it was dark and raining, and there was no shoulder or sidewalk to ride on, I began pushing my bike through the grass. I was almost out of town when I passed by a motel. A man was standing outside of it and yelled for me to come over. After approaching the man, he asked what I was doing out there, walking my bike in the rain. I told him what I was up to, and he offered to buy me a room for the night. We walked inside, and the clerk seemed dumbfounded by the fact that a stranger was paying for my room.

The next morning, I mounted my bike, ready to take off, when I realized that I had my first flat. I wasn't expecting this to happen so soon, but at least I was prepared for it. I wasn't fast at changing flats yet, but I was sure I would get plenty of practice! It wasn't much longer, and I had claimed my Delaware sign. I took a picture of it and thought it would be fun to collect photographs of all the other state signs as I made my way across the country. It would be something small to keep me motivated, anyway — a simple goal to keep me moving through one state and into the next.

I'd made it through Delaware in only a few hours and was ready to take on Pennsylvania. As soon as I crossed the state line, it was like the earth had tilted to try and slow me down. I must have been going uphill for several hours, which was much more physically demanding than I had anticipated, but the land had a beauty to it that gave the hard work its worth. Once I finally made it to the top of that monstrous hill, there were green fields that rolled on as far as I could see. It was very peaceful, with not much other than the occasional barn or windmill sitting in one of the wide-open meadows.

As I continued my way deeper into the hills of Pennsylvania, I came across several Amish communities. The first group to come up and meet me were a handful of small children, who rode alongside me on their handmade wooden scooters before quickly returning to their houses. Not much further up the road, I passed by a workshop that was only a few feet away from the road. A few Amish men were standing outside of it, who shouted over to ask if I needed any food or water. Although I was still loaded up on everything I needed, it was nice to know I was surrounded by caring people if I had been in any trouble. I then caught a quick glimpse into their shop and noticed they were in the process of building one of those wooden scooters I had seen earlier. I thought about asking if they'd mind showing me how they made them, but I didn't want to make them feel uncomfortable and simply thanked them for their offer to help before continuing on my way.

I had been riding north for a while and decided I would head up to Highway 30, also known as the Lincoln Memorial Highway, and begin heading west once I reached it. I figured it would be easier to follow a straight coast-to-coast highway instead of zigzagging all over the place. However, the sun would be setting soon, so I made sure to look for a place to sleep before it got dark. After riding for a few miles, I saw a church sitting on top of a hill and figured that would probably be a safe bet.

I made my way behind the church, where a large, open field greeted me. It looked like the weather was going to be clear that night, so I pulled out my sleeping bag and tossed it onto the ground next to my bike. I then took a seat on my sleeping bag and removed my shoes to let my feet air out. Then, without warning, a young boy appeared from the side of the church. He just stood there and looked at me for a few seconds before running away. About twenty minutes later, the boy and his mother walked up to me as I was lying on my sleeping bag. The mother then asked, "Excuse me, but what are you doing?" I immediately assumed that she was probably the owner of the church, so I nervously replied, "I'm riding my bike across America and that this just seemed like a safe place to sleep for the night." Nonchalantly, she replied, "Oh. That's fine. My son thought you were some homeless man." I hadn't really thought about it until she said that, but by definition, I was homeless. As the lady and her son walked away, I wondered what the outcome would have been if I had told her their speculations were correct. My thoughts on that lasted until dark, at which point the coyotes came, and their melodic howls helped put me to sleep.

After a couple more days of riding and finding wooded areas to camp in along the highway, I was making my way through the town of Lancaster. I finally decided to stop at a small restaurant while I was there, so I could grab something to eat other than dried noodles and trail mix. When I walked inside, a beautiful Greek waitress greeted me. She had noticed that I came in on a loaded bike, so she introduced herself as Diana and began asking me what I was up to. She was so intrigued by my adventure that she asked to sit with me as I enjoyed my burger and fries. As I was finishing my meal, she offered to pay for it, which she demanded I let her do after I tried refusing the help. I thanked her for her kindness and left the store to get back onto my bike. Just before pedaling away, Diana rushed outside and handed me a large paper bag. "Here," she said, "this is a bit of food to help you on your trip." I thanked her again as I peeked inside to see the bag was full of peanuts.

A few hours after leaving Lancaster, I had found myself in Gettysburg. I rode into the park and studied all the historical monuments. There wasn't a whole lot to look at, but knowing the area's violent history created an eerie feeling. I then began to wonder if all the ghost stories surrounding Gettysburg were true, so I pondered at the idea of staying the night to see for myself. While staying there did seem tempting, there were just too many security guards driving around. While I probably could have snuck away into the forest to set up camp, I decided it might be best to use the remaining daylight to put down more miles.

After leaving Gettysburg, a mountain range that stretched for nearly a hundred and eighty-five miles confronted me. For four days straight, I completed two mountains each day. While two mountains may not seem like much, it took a lot out of me just to get through there. Coming across a black bear helped speed things up, though. As I was making my way up one of the mountains in Buchanan State Forest, I saw the bear standing in the road up ahead. I was half-tempted to turn around and go back into one of the towns. But I was so close to the top, and the bear had shown no interest in me. I then clapped my hands to let the bear know I was there. It immediately darted off into the forest, and I was able to continue without any issues.

After I made it to the top of the mountain where I'd seen the bear, it was getting close to dusk. Since I knew there was a bear in the area, it did raise a few concerns about where I would camp. I picked up the pace, riding down that mountain and almost halfway up the next. I wasn't too worried about the bear, but I felt that putting some distance between the both of us would help me sleep easier at night. As I was making my way up the next mountain, I saw a sign nailed to a tree on one of the side streets that read, "Campground 5 Miles." I then thought that an extra ten miles would be worth knowing I had a place to sleep. However, after riding about seven miles, the only thing I'd come across was a bar. I walked inside and asked the bartender if she knew where a campground was. She and a few of her customers looked at me like I was crazy. They had never heard of any campground in the area. I shrugged my shoulders and thanked them anyway.

I left the bar and had made my way back to the highway just after dark. I flipped on my headlamp and continued riding west until I came across a 4-H camp. As I made my way closer, I realized they had already shut down for the winter. Figuring I should take advantage of it, I pushed my bike past all the empty cabins until I came across a small pond located far away in the back. I then sat my tent up next to the water and ate a pack of crackers before crawling in for the night.

A couple of days later, I had made it into Pittsburgh. Traffic had started to pick up, so I began walking my bike down one of the sidewalks. I later noticed there were bike lanes next to the street, and just before I hopped back onto my bike, five men began to approach me. My loaded bike had caught their attention, and one of them asked where I was heading. I told him that I was making my way across the country, and all the guys got a kick out of it. They thought it was cool enough that they wanted me to get a picture of them in a crazy pose and put it on my Facebook Page, so I did. After taking a couple of minutes to talk with them, I got back onto the road and got out of there as fast as possible. I wasn't going to end up being stuck in any city after dark again.

After making my way through Pittsburgh, I ended up camping somewhere in the Raccoon Creek State Park. They had a campground there, but I stayed far away from it because it was full of campers and they charged a fee for camping there. I suppose I wouldn't have minded pitching in a few bucks for a place to sleep, but I really wasn't in the mood to be around a bunch of people at the time. I felt like peace and quiet was all that I needed after working my way through a busy city.

Wanting to get away from the world and be left to myself, I wandered into the forest. I finally came across a river and decided to do some fishing. After catching my dinner for the evening, I decided I would camp there as well. Preparing to cook my fish, I'd need to prepare my first fire since leaving Tennessee. Besides being used for cooking, the fire's warmth and glow made me feel safe and not so lonely. Nothing could have put me to sleep as well as a full stomach, listening to the coyotes and the sound of a fire crackling.

The next morning, I had traveled only a few miles when I found myself in West Virginia, which was a surprise to me. I hadn't noticed on my map that there was a small section of the mountain state before crossing into Ohio. While claiming another state was a bonus, I wanted to be sure that I hadn't somehow gotten turned around, so I stopped at a gas station to get some reassurance. Most places have a welcome sign, but I hadn't seen one for the small town of Chester. There were a few sites to be seen here, though. There was a large, blue house with a blue mannequin sitting on the front porch, a giant statue of a boy playing the trumpet, and the World's Largest Teapot, which had a stove, couch, and table inside. There was also a sign that read, "From this location, you are exactly 1/4 the way around the world from Greenwich, England." These were all just a handful of neat and random things I would have never known existed otherwise.

After taking a small break in Chester, I crossed the Ohio River, collected a picture of the Ohio state sign, and began making my way for the town of Findlay. It was a bit out of the way, but I had a friend living there who wanted me to swing by for a visit. I began pedaling in her direction and made it halfway there by nightfall. I then set up camp just off the road, hidden within some trees and thick shrubs.

I woke around 3:00 a.m. to the sound of two small engines, which I assumed were four-wheelers. I figured they were probably just hunters on their way out into the woods, but I hoped they wouldn't come riding down the grassy turnoff to where I had set up camp. I didn't notice any fresh tracks when I had gotten there, but that didn't mean anyone would ever come through again. They drove up and down the road just across from me a couple of times but never turned down where I was.

I packed up and started riding around 4:00 a.m. the following morning, hoping to make it to Findlay by lunchtime. During the ride up, I was contemplating on whether I should meet up with Kimberly or not. She had sent a few messages that made me feel like she may be interested in being more than friends, and I didn't want either of us to get caught up in any feelings. I knew she would be a little upset, but I told her that I wasn't going to be able to make it. I passed through Findlay and made my way for Luna Pier, Michigan. It took me another day and a half to reach Luna Pier, but I fell in love with Lake Eerie once I'd made it. I continued pushing my bike around the lake until I hadn't seen anyone for a couple of hours. Even though it was only noon, I went ahead and decided that I would camp there for the night. I spent the rest of the day enjoying the breeze coming off the lake. As the sun began to set, I pulled out all the tabs from the tops of soda cans that I'd been collecting and twisted them into fishing hooks. Luckily, I caught a couple of fish for dinner and thought about how nice it would be to stay here for a couple of days. However, I didn't want to get lazy. I had worked hard to build up my speed and stamina and didn't want to lose it. With my stomach full of fish and crackers, I let the sounds and wind from the lake put me to sleep.

Over the next couple of days, I'd made my way back south into Ohio and ended one of those nights right on Indiana's state line. The weather had finally cooled off, and the land had begun to level out. I figured this would be a good chance to test my endurance. I packed up the following morning and pushed myself as hard as I could, seeing how far I could make it. With plenty of daylight to spare, I'd made it into Terra Haute. I couldn't believe I'd made it through an entire state in one day! Not that Indiana is a vast state, but it still felt like quite the accomplishment. Although, it was a bittersweet feeling because I felt like I'd probably missed out on some great experiences. However, it was nice knowing that I could put down over a hundred and forty miles in a day if I needed to, but I knew I'd have to keep it slow if I wanted to collect any meaningful memories.

I camped in Terra Haute that night and had made my way into Illinois by sunrise the next morning. The heat had returned and slowed me down a bit. Although, I didn't mind slowing down since I had just blown through Indiana. I wasn't riding for long before I found refuge inside of a Pizza Hut. I wasn't hungry, nor did I feel like spending any money, but I went ahead and ordered a pizza and a beer for lunch just to escape the heat. I ended up making my small lunch last about five hours while I waited for the sun to back off. Although I didn't have the patience to wait all the way until dark, I at least wanted to lower my risk of having a heat stroke. I carried on after my long lunch break and made my way into Effingham.

It had been dark for about an hour before I got there. Luckily, I had found a side road to follow into town, so I wouldn't have to worry about being hit by a vehicle on the busy highway. Once I made it into town, I sat outside of a gas station to charge my phone. It was getting late, I was in the middle of a town I'd never been to, and I had no idea where to sleep. I thought about just sitting there on the sidewalk until morning. Around 10:00 p.m., the store manager walked outside and realized that I had been using their power to charge my phone. He yelled at me and said that I was stealing the company's power. I offered to give him a quarter for charging my phone, but he got offended and told me to leave. I probably looked like a jerk, but I knew it would only cost twenty-five cents to charge a phone every day for a year, so I thought a quarter was fair.

After being told to leave the gas station, I walked my bike across the street and tossed my sleeping bag down behind a military monument. While it felt like the appropriate place for a veteran to get some rest, I didn't want to risk being seen and have someone tell me to leave. As I was lying in my sleeping bag, a storm had made its way through. A light rain settled in for the night, and since it wasn't getting any worse, I decided to lie there and get wet. Yes, it sucked, but it could have been worse if I had to leave and were unable to find anywhere else to go.

Before the sun had even peeked over the horizon, I had packed up my soaking wet sleeping bag and made my way back over to the gas station. I was going to need some coffee if I wanted the energy to put some miles down. After all, I had spent the past couple of weeks traveling on very little sleep, on top of barely eating and pushing myself physically throughout the day. And that long, sleepless night in the rain had really taken its toll on me. So, I grabbed some cheap gas station coffee and made my way south to Highway 50, another highway that went all the way across the country.

As I was making my way south, I realized that I was on Highway 45, which led straight to my hometown. I could be there in two days if I wanted. It crossed my mind, but I had no reason to go back. Even if I did, I knew that I would hate the feeling of giving up. It was just that I had been on the road for a couple of weeks, and the loneliness was starting to get to me. Once I made it to Highway 50, I sat at the intersection and stared down Highway 45. I thought about heading home, but I shook my head, let out a sigh, and continued making my way west into St. Louis, Missouri.

I had made it through another state and was feeling stronger, both physically and mentally, but I was a bit concerned about having to go through St. Louis. Wanting to avoid the city, I began looking for some back roads to get around the city instead of going through it. That's when I found out about the Katy Trail, an old railroad path that would take me all the way into Kansas. Not only was I going to be able to bypass the city, but I thought a break away from all the traffic would be nice too.

From beginning to end, the Katy Trail was a calm and leisurely ride. There were several great spots to stop and take it all in. Some of it was pavement, but most of it was dirt, and you never knew what would be around the next corner. I especially enjoyed the sections where it ran along the Missouri River. I was in no hurry to get through this part of my trek, but I did force myself to ride enough miles to reach a good place to camp. After riding all day, I had finally made it to a campground. I pulled up to the check-in counter, but no one was there. I went ahead into the campground and began searching for someone to check me in, but I still didn't see anyone. I then went back to the check-in area and noticed there was a box to leave a payment. I also noticed there was a refrigerator full of snacks and drinks. I said to myself, "Wow! Whoever runs this campground must have a lot of trust in people!" I then grabbed a soda and a small bag of chips before slipping a five-dollar bill into the payment box. I then made my way back to the campground area and was hoping for some company, but no other people ever showed up. It was just me, the coyotes, and a warm fire again.

The next day, I continued riding west along the trail, enjoying the beautiful views and pleasant weather. Eventually, the trail passed by a small town, where the people were having an outdoor festival. I needed to fill up on my water, so I pulled over to see if they had any. I then walked to a large tent and saw several people who had plates of food. I must have looked hungry because a large biker guy asked if I wanted anything to eat. Of course, I did! My eyes grew large as I nodded my head. The man laughed and told me to take a seat at one of the picnic tables. A few minutes later, the man returned with a burger and beer and patted me on the back. I figured I must have been looking pretty rough at that point, considering someone just offered me free food without hearing my story first.

After finishing my free meal, I made my way into town and found a church that had a spigot on its side. I washed all my clothes there and as much of my skin as I could without getting completely undressed. A lot of people were walking by, and I could tell they wanted to stare but forced themselves to look away. By that time, I had completely stopped worrying about what people thought of me. Although I wasn't able to do these things in privacy, they still had to get done. After washing up, I hung my wet clothes all over my bike, filled up my water bottles, and got back on the trail.

I had been on the trail for a couple of days and decided to get off it once I made it to Jefferson City. I'd made it into town after dark and decided to ride until I made it to the outskirts of the opposite side. Once I made it just outside of town, I noticed a group of trees encircled by the interstate exit. I knew I wouldn't be able to have a fire there, but I would be able to sleep in my tent, which was all I really wanted. I was too tired to do much of anything else anyway and figured no one would probably stop on an interstate exit whether they saw me or not.

The next morning, I packed up and began pushing my bike back to the road. As I was walking through the grass, a man yelled at me from the parking lot of a small restaurant and signaled for me to come over. When I reached the man, he asked if that was me who had been camping over by exit. I told him that it was and that I was riding my bike across the country. He then handed me ten dollars and told me to go inside to order myself some breakfast. I shook the man's hand and thanked him before making my way inside. I appreciated the help, as I probably wouldn't have spent my own money on breakfast. I was starting to run low on funds, but a warm meal was just what I needed after a long, cold night.

As I was making my way for Kansas City, a man named Greg contacted me. He was an older man who did some cycling as a hobby and said that I was welcome to crash at his place if I wanted. He had been following my Facebook Page since I started, and I guess I seemed innocent enough. Once I took him up on his offer, he said that he'd come out to pick me up once he got off work. I was still about a hundred miles from Kansas City, though, so I picked up the pace to try and make it as close to him as possible by the end of the day. By the time he had picked me up, I was only about seven miles from the city limit, so I didn't feel like I'd cheated much once I loaded up into his truck.

Once we had made it to Greg's house, he began showing me around so I could get familiar with everything. It was kind of late when we got there, and all I really cared about was getting a shower and some sleep, but he seemed quite persistent in showing me what he kept in the basement. After following him to the underside of the house, I was surprised to see the entire room was done up in legos. It turned out that he had another hobby besides cycling, as it was evident that he'd spent a great deal of time and money on turning his basement into a miniature replica of a large city. He then admitted it all started with his fascination with model trains, which I realized was the main feature after he flicked on the power switch. Once the lights came on, several trains began making their way through the city, complete with smoke and horn noises. Just as I was starting to wake up and feel more intrigued, Greg's wife shouted from the top of the stairs, "Greg! Let the boy get a shower and come help me get dinner ready!" Greg and I both felt like we'd best do as the woman of the house requested, so he ran up to the kitchen, and I made my way into the restroom to get a hot shower. And finally, after eating a nice, homecooked meal, Greg showed me to the spare bedroom. Since it was technically their grandchild's room, in the middle sat a twin-sized bed with toys scattered everywhere. It felt kind of strange sleeping in there, but I was finally able to fall into a deep sleep without having to stay aware of my surroundings.

The next morning, Greg and his wife offered to take me to the zoo. I thought that seemed like a nice way to pass the time and to give my body a break, so I took them up on their offer. And after spending a couple of hours at the zoo, they took me to one of their favorite shops to get a maintenance check done on my bike. While the mechanics were looking over my ride, they discovered a few spokes had busted through both the front and rear rims. It was a complete mystery as to how I'd made it as far as I had, considering I'd heard the strange clanking sound for nearly five hundred miles. While preparing to retire the bike and continue crossing the remainder of the country on foot, Greg told the bike shop to go ahead and charge a new set of rims to his store credit.

By the time we returned to Greg's house, it was beginning to get dark, so he and his wife said I was welcome to stay another night. Returning to their home for one more night sounded like a great idea, so I took them up on their offer and was able to enjoy another hot meal and a cozy bed for sleeping. The next morning, we got up before sunrise and hopped back into Greg's truck. Since the final stretch of the city was interstate, Greg said it would probably be best if he gave me a lift just outside of town, so I could start my ride on a highway and not have to worry about dealing with the city.

After saying goodbye to Greg, I made my way south into Oklahoma until I hit Highway 60 in Ponca City. The land had really begun to change. All the trees had turned to shrubs, and there was very little traffic. The occasional cars that did pass, the drivers would slow down and give me strange looks, probably wondering what a person was doing out there on a bicycle. However, I did love riding through the rolling hills, which went on for as far as I could see. The grass looked like a vibrant, green ocean waving in the wind. It was almost hypnotizing, and being out there alone almost made it seem like I was on another planet.

After riding across the plains for three days with beautiful fall weather, the approaching clouds signified that a large storm was moving in. I checked the weather on my phone and saw there had been several tornado watches issued in my area. I hadn't seen any form of shelter all day, so I began to pedal faster, hoping I would find something before the storm arrived. Thankfully, after a few hours of exerting myself, I came across a rest stop. There was a small building with two restrooms inside and a couple of gazebos beside it. I then walked up to the building and realized it was already closed for the night. I began to feel a little nervous since that was the only solid structure around. However, most of the door was glass, so if it came down to it, I would be able to force myself inside. I then walked around to the west side of the building and placed my tent against the brick wall. I figured the wind would probably come from the east, so I hoped the walls would absorb most of it.

Soon after crawling into my tent, the wind and rain quickly became violent. I laid there quietly, waiting for the sound of things tossing around, which could've meant that it was time for me to go knock out one of the windows. However, as I continued to anticipate the sound of a tornado, I fell asleep and didn't wake again until morning. Although the wind was still blowing wildly and the temperature had dropped significantly, at least the rain had passed. Just after I had finished packing my things, a worker came to unlock the restroom doors. After she had left, I went inside to fill up my water bottles and added some hot water to a packet of oatmeal for breakfast.

After a couple more days of riding and sleeping with the coyotes, I had finally reached Texas. I had been on the road for one full month, and the loneliness was starting to get to me. However, my greatest concern was how underprepared I was for the fast-approaching winter. I hoped that I would have already been over the Rocky Mountains, but I had misjudged myself. I didn't know what to do besides continue riding, so that's what I did. The days were tolerable, though the nights were torturous. Even though I layered up with what little clothes I had and was using my cell phone to produce extra heat in my forty-degree sleeping bag, I would shiver throughout the night.

I had made it into Amarillo after a few days of battling the cold. The sun went fast, and it was another frigid night stuck in the city. I found myself surrounded by homeless drug addicts and gang members who were roaming the streets. I finally made my way to a park and thought I was in the clear. I laid my bike and sleeping bag in the dark shadows of a concession stand and tried to get some sleep. I then woke up around midnight to the sound of people talking next to me. I turned my head and saw a group of people making a drug deal. They were only about ten feet away, but luckily no one ever saw me. I quietly waited until they left, and then I made my way to the McDonald's across the street. The restaurant was closed, but I slept against the wall, trying to make myself look like a pile of garbage. Throughout the rest of the night, I heard crackheads walking around, screaming and acting crazy. I was able to get a little sleep, but only because I was exhausted.

The next morning, I went inside the McDonald's to sit and warm up. I needed to sit for a moment to come up with a way to keep warm at night and to take notes for my upcoming routes. I didn't want to end up in any more cities after dark. As I was sitting there, a man came up and introduced himself as Sam. He offered to have breakfast with me, so I accepted it. We sat and talked for a while before he got up to leave. I decided to stay until my phone and headlamp had finished charging. About thirty minutes had passed, and Sam walked back into the restaurant. He sat across from me and didn't say anything but lifted his hand out from under the table and handed me a wad of cash. I gave him a confused look, wondering why. He then said, "You remind me of my daughter. She was a traveling spirit just like you but ended up taking her life a few years ago. Keep doing what makes you happy. Use it however you want. Good luck." I didn't know how to respond to that, but I didn't think he wanted me to, so I just shook his hand and said, "Thank you."

It felt like it would have been rude to count the cash in front of him, so I waited until he had left. Even after he had left, it still felt kind of rude, but I counted out three hundred dollars! I was almost in tears. The fact that a complete stranger had just given me so much and to do whatever I wanted with just blew my mind. I was very thankful, though, and began to think about what I would do with it. I then went outside to sit on a bench and took a few minutes to weigh my options. I knew I wasn't ready for the winter, but should I get some gear and continue, or should I stop while I was ahead?

I began pushing my bike down the sidewalk and saw a homeless man lying on the ground. I felt bad for thinking I'd had a miserable night when he looked to be in such a worse predicament. I then woke him up and asked, "How would you like a new bike?" Confused and surprised, the man looked at me and asked if I could clarify what I was telling him. I smiled and said, "Look, I've been riding across the country on this bike. There's some food in here, but it ain't much. There's also a pretty good sleeping bag, a tent, and a jacket too. It ain't the best setup, but I felt like maybe you could use it. You can have it all. I'm about to catch the next bus out of here and won't need it where I'm going." The man was speechless, just like I had been with Sam, but I could tell he appreciated it. I then told him to have a nice day and began walking towards the Greyhound bus station.

I entered the Greyhound station and wondered if I had made a mistake, but my options were quite limited at that point. I walked up to the ticket counter and purchased a ticket for Jackson, Tennessee. Since the bus was scheduled to leave in only a few hours, I took a seat and waited. Time had passed, and I was on the bus, watching everything pass me in reverse. At first, I felt like this was for the best, but I slowly began to feel like I had failed. However, I knew this feeling was only temporary because I was heading back to start over and do it again the right way.

Starting Over

After I'd made it back to Tennessee, I went to the town of Martin and began searching for work. It wasn't long before I'd landed a job as a direct support professional, helping to take care of people with disabilities. Although I was still homeless while I was working there, I hid it quite well. I kept my tent in the woods a few blocks from the care center and would clean up in a gas station bathroom every morning before work. It seemed like everything was beginning to fall back into place. Since winter was right around the corner, I used my first three weeks of pay towards renting an apartment. It was about a three-mile walk to and from work, which I actually enjoyed.

By December, I had purchased a computer and a few other things that I would need to pick up where I'd left off with audio engineering. I continued working as a direct support professional until the middle of February. After that, I went on to work from home as a full-time engineer. Within just a couple of weeks, I had completely furnished my apartment and even bought a new car. Things were finally starting to look up for me. I had gotten back all the things I had lost and was making more money than when I owned the studio in Humboldt.

I had spent the past six months sitting in my apartment, racking up money and blowing it on whatever I wanted. I thought that would have made me happy, but for some reason, I was depressed. After weeks of trying to ignore my depression, a psychiatrist admitted me to a hospital for professional treatment.

I was then diagnosed with post-traumatic stress disorder and put on anti-depressants. I had known well before then that I'd had the symptoms of PTSD, but once my life had become stable, it was more obvious. It seemed like it would be the other way around, but that just wasn't the case for me. I couldn't live a normal life because I needed things to be continuously changing, or I would get sucked into all my bad memories.

The doctor recommended that I get back outside and do more hiking and cycling to see if that would help. So, that's what I did, and it didn't take long for me to realize that more time outdoors was exactly what I needed. I had gotten so caught up with making money that I forgot how great simplicity was. Over the next two months, I spent most of my time hiking, camping, and working on my survival skills. I began to feel like my old happy self again but would feel depressed when returning home. I was beginning to hate material things and longed for an escape. I felt like maybe it was time to get back on the move again.

Since I hadn't worked much in the past three months, my funds were slowly diminishing. I decided to sell everything I had and then use that money to get the gear I'd need to ride across America again. I sold most of my things and began to plan out what I would need and where I would go. I still had no idea where I would start my next cross-country trip, but I knew to leave would be better than sitting in that apartment, which was looking almost as blank as the day I moved in. After two weeks of preparing to leave again, only a few small items remained, so I decided to set them outside in some boxes. The next morning, everything was gone. I was down to nothing but a few pairs of clothes.

That same day, I made my way to the library as I had done before and ordered a new bike. Since I had about five thousand dollars to start this time, I could afford a decent ride and much better gear than before. I remembered being underprepared during my last cross-country trek and didn't want that to happen again. Everything I'd ordered arrived a few days later, and I put it all together immediately. I slept on the floor next to my loaded bike that night and wondered where I would go from there. As I was lying there, it hit me that my best friend, Sydney, was living in Foley, Alabama. So, I figured I would head down there to visit her. Then, I would start my cross-country ride from Florida. The next morning, I pulled my bike outside and walked over to my landlord, as she also lived at the apartments and was sitting on her front porch. I handed her the keys to my apartment and said, "Thanks for letting me stay here." She had a confused look on her face, as if she expected an explanation, though I didn't say anything else. I just positioned my bike south and rode away, never to return.

It was August 15th, 2014, when I had left my apartment. It was scorching and humid that day, and I knew it was only going to get worse. Making my way through the south during the hottest month of the year was going to make for a miserable trek, but I thought I was ready for it. Surprisingly, I had made it ninety-three miles to Selmer, Tennessee, by the end of my first day. I thought that wasn't too bad for being out of commission for almost a year. As the sun was beginning to set, I waited until the coast was clear and pushed my bike next to an abandoned building. I then set up my tent between the building and thick bushes. Once I was in my tent, lying on top of my sleeping bag, I could feel the heat radiating from my face. Maybe I wasn't as prepared as I thought, as I had forgotten to pack sunscreen. That was going to be a necessity because there was very little shade along highway 45, and the sun would be beaming down on my face all day. Somehow, I had managed to fall asleep but was awakened a couple of hours later by the sound of something creeping through the bushes. I figured the sound of my zipper would have whatever it was running for its life. Although, whatever it was, couldn't have cared less about me. I popped my head out and saw an armadillo checking out my tent. It wasn't scared of me in the least bit, so I decided to reach into one of my

47

saddlebags to find us something to eat. We sat there and ate a bag of chips together until there was nothing but crumbs, which the armadillo stayed around to lick off the ground. Once the armadillo realized I had nothing else to offer, it hopped away into the dark, and I crawled back into my tent for the night.

I had made it into Corinth, Mississippi, before noon the next day and decided to find somewhere to wash my clothes. Yesterday's sweat had dried and made my clothes feel stiff. I knew if I didn't swap my clothes out regularly, it would take no time for them to start falling apart. That, and I'd end up with a rash that was harder to get rid of than a hungry armadillo.

I later passed by a gas station and noticed a water hose attached to its side. I pulled up next to it and began washing my clothes right there in the parking lot. It was kind of embarrassing, with all the customers looking at me in disgust, but I had to do it. As I was wringing the excess water from my clothes, the store manager walked outside and stared at me with his arms crossed. I kept glancing back at him, with the kind of face that asks, "What? Why are you staring?" Nothing was ever said, though. I did what I had to do and got back to riding, and after another day in the sun, I was ending my ride just south of Tupelo.

I had found myself camping underneath a bridge, as I had done several times before. It seemed like a good spot, far away from the city and any houses, until I woke to the sound of a group of partying teenagers. Thankfully, none of them came up over the hill to where I was. I didn't know them, nor did I want to. I was exhausted and just wanted to get some sleep. It seemed like everywhere I went, there was something or someone that came to visit me during the night.

As I was pedaling along the next day, the temperatures got so high that I was sure I was going to succumb to a heat stroke. I kept getting severe heat cramps, nausea, dizziness and wasn't sweating nearly as much as I had been the previous days. It was also the longest ride without any shade. I kept running out of water way too fast, which was quite scary, though I was able to find a place to fill up just before I killed over. Before I bought a bike, I had flipped a coin to decided if I should take a backpack instead. As I was panting from the intense heat, I was glad I had gotten a bike because I probably would have died if I had chosen to walk through there.

Day five back at it was another scorcher, but it was getting easier as the distance between towns became less. After crossing the Alabama state line, I had been out of water for a few hours. Luckily, I spotted another church with a water spigot on the side of it. I went over to fill up and completely drenched myself. I turned the water on and just laid underneath it for a few minutes. A truck had passed by earlier that day and then drove past me again as I was leaving the church. This time, the truck pulled over, and the man driving asked if I needed a lift. If he had stopped before I noticed the church with running water, I probably would have said yes, but all was well now. I did appreciate his concern, though.

Still soaking wet from the church's water, I pedaled my way into Mobile and pushed through there as quickly as I'd arrived. After making it through the city, I came up to the Jubilee Parkway, a seven-and-a-half-mile long bridge between Mobile and Spanish Fort. After I was halfway across the bridge, a massive rainstorm came out of nowhere. Since I had been burning alive for the past few days, the rain coming down felt amazing. However, the motorists made me feel unsafe because I knew they'd have a hard time seeing me, and no one cared to slow down. I finally made it across the bridge, though, and the rain gave me the boost that I needed to make it down to Foley.

Once I was only a few hours from Foley, I gave Sydney a call to let her know. I had told her that I would be heading down to visit the day that I'd left, but she wasn't aware of how long it would take. She was surprised to know I'd just ridden five hundred miles in five days. She thought it would have taken me at least two weeks. Honestly, if it hadn't been as hot as it was, it probably would have taken me longer, but I wanted to get that ride over with as quickly as possible.

Sydney and I went way back and used to be an inseparable pair of party animals, so we were very excited to see each other. I was beginning to feel drained just before I got there, but my energy levels were back, and I was ready for some fun. We were at Wal-Mart when we met up, and she didn't have a vehicle, so we called a few taxis until we found one that would be able to carry my bike. A short time later, we arrived at her apartment, where I was able to grab a quick shower and leave my things. Then, we made our way to one of Sydney's favorite spots, Orange Beach. We walked along the beach, talking and catching up until we were both ready to head back to her apartment to get some sleep.

The next day, Sydney and I walked to the bar where she was working so I could meet her new friends and co-workers. They all thought it was crazy that I had just ridden a bike down from Tennessee, so a few of them offered me free drinks. Sydney had mentioned that I should stay there with her for a few weeks, and I thought that sounded like a great idea. I would need to wait around for the heat to back off anyway. No way was I going to put myself through that again.

Sydney and I then left the bar and took a few beers to the beach. After walking along the sand and drinking a few beers, Sydney asked if I wanted to go for a swim. We both knew that we shouldn't be in the water after dark since that's when the dangerous marine animals come close to shore, but we decided to go in anyway. It wasn't long before I regretted that. It felt like someone slashed me across the chest with a razor blade, so I got out saw some red welts on my torso. I assumed that I had been stung on my chest by a jellyfish. Now, I'm not sure if it's a myth or not, but Sydney suggested I let her pee on me to neutralize the jellyfish poison. Maybe it was just a good distraction, but it appeared to have helped!

It was about 11:00 p.m. when we decided to make our way back to Sydney's apartment. Before starting our walk across town, she said she wanted to stop by the gas station to pick up some snacks. After we left the gas station, she opened the sandwich she had just bought and begun eating it as we were walking. She then made her way to my left side, where we waited for traffic to clear so we could cross the street. I looked to the right and saw a car up ahead, but the left was clear, so I continued to the median. I kept my eyes on the vehicle, making sure it didn't swerve towards us, and waited for it to be safe to cross. However, when I stopped in the median, Sydney kept walking. Since I had been blocking her view, she had no idea there was a car coming. By the time I could see the accident coming, it was too late. Just before the vehicle struck her, I felt my heart drop.

She had almost made it across the street, which was something we both would have joked about, but she got hit. The car was only going about twenty-five miles per hour when it struck her, which was fast enough to send her flying into a nearby driveway. Certain that she was dead, I ran up to her lifeless body and began screaming her name. The lady who hit her got out of her car and called 911, so I focused on Sydney. Thankfully, she wasn't dead, but she was severely injured. Her mouth was open, and there was some white stuff hanging out. I thought she had suffered some severe head trauma, but it was only the sandwich, which she continued trying to chew once she regained consciousness. I realized then that she still had no idea what had happened, but her awareness soon came, and agonizing screams quickly followed that brief moment of peace.

The medics arrived at the scene within a few minutes and took us to the hospital in Pensacola, Florida. She was going to be okay but had several broken bones in her legs and pelvis. I decided to stay with her in the hospital until her parents got there a few days later. They then took her back to Tennessee, where she would have to undergo several months of therapy. I didn't know what I would do for the remainder of my time there, but at least Sydney was okay.

After Sydney was gone, I needed to find a way to keep myself occupied while I waited for the weather to cool off. Over the next few days, I continued riding along the beaches into Florida, sleeping on the sand, and basically being a beach bum. One night, as I was lying on the beach, I finally decided to post on my blog about what had happened to Sydney. My uncle, Johnny, was following my journey and said I could stay with him. I knew he was living in Florida, but I didn't know where exactly. It turned out that I was only a couple of hours' drive from his house, so he said he could pick me up and that I could stay with him for a while in Fort Walton Beach.

While I was staying with my uncle, waiting for the weather to cool off, I spent most of my time at the beach. However, one day my uncle took his family and me to float a river with paddleboards. I can't remember exactly where we went, but people were living alongside it in huts. There was also this one spot where the water was crystal clear, and I could see thousands of tadpoles swimming around underneath me. I was so excited that I rolled off my paddleboard and dove down to swim with them. It was amazing how clear the water was and how many tadpoles there were. It was like swimming around in one of the large aquariums that I'd seen on TV, though I'd never been to one in person. After being submerged for a few minutes, I began to make my way to the surface when a giant tadpole swam right into my hand. It was the largest I'd ever seen, so I brought it up to show everyone. This thing was massive! I had to use both hands just to keep it from falling out. When I let it go, I was curious about what it would look like once it became a toad. I later did some research and discovered these are known as cane toads, which are a nonnative species that came from Central America.

I attempted to leave Florida on September 1st. I had ridden about fifty miles inland when I realized that I was sweating more than I could drink. I don't think I had ever sweat so much in my life. I had to head back down and wait another two weeks before I could get out of there. That was enough time for me to give my journey some meaning. I figured if I was going to be riding my bike from Florida to Alaska, I might as well use all those miles towards a charity. I would be helping others, and it would be something to keep me motivated. I looked around for a few different charities and decided to go with Shot at Life. They were raising money to help give children vaccinations in developing countries. They also had an app for my phone, where all I had to do was turn it on while I was riding, and sponsors would donate so much per mile.

The South

The days were still too hot out in the mid-western states, and, at the rate I traveled, it would still be that way by the time I got there. I figured it would be best to find a way to kill some time until it cooled off. I then left Florida and began heading north. Thankfully, it didn't take long for fall to come as I continued my way through the eastern side of Alabama. It was comfortable again, and I could get nearly two hundred miles down if I wanted to. I tried to take in more of my surroundings this time, although I put down a lot of miles some days. I'd pick a spot on my map that looked interesting and make it there as soon as possible, so I could take some time to enjoy it. After about a week of waking up every morning to find my food bag covered in ants, I had made it just south of Columbus, Georgia.

I didn't plan on going to Columbus, but I wanted my Georgia sign. I needed to stock up on food and water first, though. Luckily, I came across a Dollar General Store on the outskirts of town. The manager there talked with me for a few minutes and offered to purchase my food for me. He let me use the microwave in the back so I could heat a frozen pizza, and before I left, he handed me a twenty-dollar bill. I took that amount from my checking account and donated it to the charity. I didn't tell him that, but that's what I chose to do with it. As long as I was getting by, I didn't feel the need for any extra money.

I headed back into Alabama after leaving the store in Georgia and made my way towards Lake Martin. There was a campground nearby, so I decided to stop and stay for two days before moving on. It was too cold for a swim, but I got in for a quick wash. The cold water helped to soothe my sore muscles. From there, I made my way to the Talladega National Forest. I didn't go too far into the forest, but I found a great spot on top of a hill, which offered a relaxing view of the sunset. A storm came through later that night, though, which meant that a cold front was moving in. After spending a lot of time outside, you can pretty much tell what the weather is going to do. It's just something that you get used to, like a basic instinct that returns after some time.

After I had awakened in the Talladega National Forest, I stuck my head out of my tent to feel the cold breeze. I looked down and noticed a large dry spot on the ground in front of my tent. The rain had stopped about an hour before I woke, and it started as soon as I laid down the night before. The spot was oddly shaped and about the size of my tent. I thought this was strange because I never heard anything, and I am a very light sleeper. I was curious, but whatever had caused it was gone. There were no branches overhead and no tracks of any sort. I shrugged it off and made myself a cup of cold, instant coffee and oatmeal before heading out.

On my way into Huntsville, another set of mountains confronted me. And while I had no issue with the hills, there was a tornadic storm headed my way from the valley. If I could make it to the top in time, I would be able to coast down the other side, out of the storm's path. With no time to spare, I got a flat tire about halfway up the mountain. I could see the storm approaching from behind, and it was picking up strength. It took about ten minutes to fix the flat, but before I could get moving again, the rain had begun to fall. I was hoping I could still beat the worst of the storm to the top, so I pedaled as hard as I could. My energy, however, was wasted. As soon as I made it to the top, the storm was directly over me. The rain was heavy, and the wind was strong, but the lightning was my greatest fear. After getting caught in this situation, there wasn't much I could do except curse myself for trying to beat a storm up a mountain. I knew it wasn't wise to get close to trees during a storm, but I crouched down next to a large oak anyway. I then pulled out my phone to look at the weather and noticed the tornado was headed straight in my direction. I proceeded to get up and jump across the guardrail and into the ditch on the other side. As soon as I took a step towards the railing, lightning hit it, so I decided to sit back down and take my chances with the tree. Lightning began striking everything, and the trees were snapping all around me. After about thirty minutes of waiting out the storm, it was finally over, and I was back on the move again.

I had made it into Middle Tennessee by the next morning and began making my way for Murfreesboro. As I headed towards the city, I came across a bike trail and decided to follow it into town. However, after turning onto it, I noticed the flooding had caused the city to close it down. I wasn't sure if the waters had receded into the river yet, so I cautiously made my way onto the paved path. I then saw a cyclist heading in my direction from up the trail and figured it must have been safe. Then, the man on the approaching bicycle stopped beside me and asked, "Jake?" I gave him a confused look and asked if I knew him. He said that he had seen one of my gear reviews online and was following my Facebook Page. We both thought it was crazy that he had found me, especially on a closed trail. He said his name was Mark and asked if I'd be interested in staying the night with him, so I said yes. We then rode to the parking lot to where his car was and loaded up for the short drive to his house. Once we made it to his house, we sat around and talked mostly about cycling gear while waiting for his wife to get home. He then called and told his friend, Adam, to come over to get in on the conversation, too. The two of them were planning a cycling trip in another country and wanted to get some pointers.

After Adam arrived, the three of us went to the garage to look over my setup. I pulled out all my gear and scattered it on the floor so they could see everything I carried. Mark had noticed my bear spray and asked how effective it was. I told them about a time I had to use it on a large dog that wouldn't back off and how some of it came back at me with the wind. I did not doubt that it would deter a bear or anything else for that matter. Mark then asked me to give it a quick tap into the air, so they could see how strong it was. I gave them what they wanted, and it sent all of us running back into the house, coughing and agreeing that it was quite powerful. Mark's wife arrived home about an hour later and complained about the garage smelling like peppers. We all had a good laugh about that.

The next morning, we watched the weather, and it looked like another storm would be there in the afternoon. Mark asked if I'd like to stay another day, but I told him I could probably make it to Nashville before the worst of it came. So, I headed out after breakfast and made my way into Nashville just before dark. I didn't want to get caught up in the storm outside of the city, so I hung out at a park in the downtown area. I wasn't there long before a news van arrived to broadcast the approaching weather. I knew it was going to be a long night as the darkened sky began rolling over the city. Luckily, there was a hotel nearby that I could use to take cover. I hid my bike in the corner of the lobby and took a seat. The storm finally hit several minutes later, and people began running in off the streets. The hotel manager then came and told everyone they had to leave because the hotel was for guests. I was shocked that they would make people vacate during a storm. Luckily, I had gone in before the weather got bad, so he probably assumed that I was a guest. I wanted to look like I was supposed to be there, so I casually walked up to the coffee area and poured myself a cup.

After sitting there for about thirty minutes, this older man comes over and begins talking to me. His features reminded me of Obi-Wan Kenobi of Star Wars, though his actions were entirely different. He began comparing me to his boyfriend, saying how he would rather have me than him. He stood up and said he needed to go up to his room and would be back in a few minutes. I took that time to get out of there. I'd rather wager my chances with the storm, which was a lot worse than I had thought. A few tornadoes had touched down in the surrounding area, and, according to the weather map, it looked likely to happen again. I decided to find a cheap motel for the night and ended up staying in the one where the movie "The Thing Called Love" was filmed. My tent had proved itself time and time again, but I felt safer behind some solid walls and a roof over my head.

The next morning, I decided to head east because I had been covering more distance than I had intended. I wanted to give the seasons a bit more time to change before heading west. As I was making my way into the Catoosa Wildlife Area mountains, a professional photographer approached me. He had been taking pictures of the scenery when I accidentally rode in front of his shot. As I was riding past, he asked what I was up to. I told him that I was riding from Florida to Alaska, which he thought was funny because I headed in the wrong direction. He then asked if it was okay to take my picture, but I wasn't sure why he wanted it. After parting ways with him, I began to think he probably wanted it as evidence in case I came up as a missing person.

A few hours later, I had made my way into Rockwood. There was a couple there who said I could crash at their place on my way through. When I got there, Bee and her husband, Andrew, greeted me into their home. They had just finished making chili for dinner and offered me a bowl. After eating, I got a shower and then had a few beers with them afterward. We sat around and talked for a few hours before they went to bed and let me take over the couch for the rest of the night.

The next morning, I thanked Bee and Andrew for letting me stay and continued making my way towards Knoxville. As I was riding through the mountains, I found a pair of three hundred-dollar women's sunglasses and figured I would try to sell them. I posted them on my blog, but no one seemed interested, so I tried to pawn them. However, after a few pawn shops looked at me like I had stolen them, I gave up trying to sell them and tossed them into one of my saddlebags.

As I was making my way into Knoxville, a girl named Rachael said she'd like to meet up with me. She was busy with work and school when I got there, so I decided to find somewhere to camp. I made my way to the outskirts of the city, where I spotted a church that looked like it would be a good place to sleep. The church's side door was open, so I knocked on it, hoping to ask for permission to camp in the back. I waited a moment and had no response, so I made my way inside. Just as I entered the building, an older lady came out of a room, and she looked terrified. She immediately asked, "How did you get in here?" Her tone of voice sounded as if she was accusing me of breaking in, so I tried to diffuse the situation. I then told her the door was unlocked and that I was cycling across America for a charity. After finding out she owned the church, I asked if it would be okay for me to camp in the back, and she said that it was. I made my way behind the church and put up my tent. A few minutes later, two police officers pulled up in their patrol cars and parked in the lot across from where I was sitting. They were sitting there for about a minute before they walked up, and one of them said, "You can't camp back here, but there's a homeless shelter downtown." I replied to the officer, "I'm not going to any homeless shelter. I'm riding a bike across America for a charity called Shot at Life, and the owner of this church said I could camp back here." I didn't have any problems with them after that, and I felt even better about my decision to stay there because they said they would keep an eye on the area for me throughout the night.

The next morning, I went to meet up with Rachael. She was a beautiful nurse with dark brown eyes, long, dark red hair that heavily contrasted with her fair, white skin, a dizzying smile, and some vibrant tattoo work on her arms. I was a little nervous about meeting her because of how pretty she was, but that's also the reason why I made sure to meet up with her. Not that I expected anything to come of it, but who doesn't love to be in the presence of beautiful women? She recommended that we meet up for breakfast at a Mcdonald's, so I made my way over. I arrived there before she did, so I went to the restroom to get a little cleaned up first. As I was walking my toiletry bag back out to my bike, she pulled up. I saw the sunglasses sitting in my saddlebag and figured she would probably like them, so I pulled them out. She was already walking up to me, so I turned and said, "Hey! Gotcha something!" She loved them and was intrigued by the fact that I had found them on the side of the road. We went in to have breakfast when she mentioned that she had wanted to invite me over the night before but didn't want her daughter to be confused. I understood where she was coming from, but I didn't mind sleeping outside. For some reason, that always seemed to make people feel a little guilty, but I enjoyed it unless I was stuck in a city or some dangerous weather. Before we parted ways, she kissed me and said it was for the sunglasses. I thought that was a fair trade!

After leaving Knoxville, I began making my way north for Kentucky. As I rode through the mountainous backroads, I noticed the leaves had finally changed to their fall colors. I had found myself riding alongside a slow-moving river for most of the day, which added to the serenity. The hot days were well behind me, but that also meant the days were getting noticeably shorter. As the sun was beginning to set, I pulled off to camp behind another church about ten miles from the state line. I made my way to the back and had dinner at one of the picnic tables before setting up my tent and turning in for the night.

Not long after going to bed, I woke to the sound of something knocking over one of the steel garbage bins. I peeked my head out and saw a bear digging around for scraps, probably interested in the leftovers from my prepackaged tuna. I screamed at the bear to get out of there, but it didn't run off as I had hoped. Instead, it stood upright and began sniffing at me. I already had my bear spray in my hand but didn't want to use it unless it was necessary. I then remembered seeing a brick on top of the air conditioner beside my tent, so I reached out for it and smacked it against the unit's metal frame. Luckily, that got the bear out of there, and I knew to be a bit more cautious with my food as I made my way through the Daniel Boone National Forest.

The next day couldn't have been more pleasant. All was going well until I came up to a field full of little orange balls. I couldn't tell what they were from the road, so I parked my bike and began walking into the dirt-covered field. I picked up one of the little orange balls and discovered they were baby pumpkins. I felt a little silly for not knowing what they were and began making my way back to my bike. Just as I lifted my bike from the ground, I heard a loud bang that sounded like a gunshot. It sounded like it came from the house across the street, but I didn't pay it much mind. I then hopped back onto my bike, ready to ride, when I noticed a pungent chemical odor and smoke coming from behind the house. I thought it might be someone cooking meth, so I began pedaling and heard a second bang. However, this time, I also heard shotgun pellets scattering on the road around me. Man, I got out of there! I would have called the cops, but there was no cellular service due to all the mountains.

I had made it to the outskirts of Burnside when a white van pulled over. I'd become accustomed to people stopping to ask if I needed anything, so I figured this was just another considerate civilian. I approached the van to see a large, heavyset white man. He appeared to have just gotten off work, with his paint-covered hands and overalls. I assumed this must be his work van, and it probably was, but things were about to get weird. At first, he asked if I needed a ride, which I declined since I was doing this for charity. He then asked how I made money while traveling. I told him that I had some money in my bank account, but I'd do odd jobs on the side if needed. The man then asked if I was looking to have some fun. I had my guard half-choked because, who knew, maybe he just wanted to go fishing or something. So, I replied, "Maybe. What kind of fun are we talking about?" He then went on to say that we could get a motel room and have a few drinks. I'd had people offer to rent me motel rooms before, but this man had something different in mind. When I declined his offer, he asked if I carried a gun. I began to feel a bit edgy when he asked that, so I told him I did. He replied, "Oh, okay. I do too. You wouldn't want to be out here without one." Of course, I wasn't carrying a gun, but I wished I was at the time. I tried ending our conversation by telling him I'd best be on my way because I needed to get to the next town before dark. He continued talking, trying to persuade me to get into his van. I then backed away and pointed my phone at him, so he would think I was taking a video of him. He then covered his face and sped off in the opposite direction. I got out of there just as fast as he did.

Early the next day, I had made my way into Bowling Green. It was a cold Sunday morning, and even though I had my phone, I only knew it was Sunday because I saw that church was in session. I had stopped worrying about what day it was a long time ago but decided to stop at one of the churches to fill up my water. I pulled into the parking lot and made my way to the front door, where I saw two homeless people sitting on the steps. It was a young man and an older woman, both dressed in all black. The man, who went by the name Raven, looked up at me and said, "They don't serve lunch until 11:30, man." I wasn't there looking for food, but I went along with him anyway and walked over to join them in conversation. He then went on to say they were sitting on the steps because someone in the church had asked them to wait outside. When I asked why, he replied, "Because we're wearing all black, they seem to think we're devil worshippers or something." The woman who was with him never said anything. However, she had a constant cough, so I asked if she was okay. Raven replied for her, "She has lung cancer." We were then interrupted by someone honking their car horn. When we looked up, we noticed it was someone leaving the church. Someone was in their way, so they were laying down the horn and giving them the middle finger. Raven laughed, shook his head, and said, "We can't go inside because of the way we're dressed, but they'll let people like that in there." I began laughing because I understood where he was coming from. I then told them to have a nice day and walked inside to fill up on my water before getting back on the move.

From Bowling Green, I began making my way back into Tennessee. I hopped onto Highway 79 and came out at Land Between the Lakes. I used to do a lot of fishing and camping there when I was a kid, so it was nice to be back in familiar territory. I hadn't been to this lake in about seven years, so I was surprised to see that everything was pretty much the same. I decided to set up camp and do some fishing for old times' sake. As I was lying in my tent that night, I figured I should head back to visit my parents since I was only a full day's ride away. I needed to see a doctor anyway because I had lost feeling in one of my hands and had signs of muscular dystrophy.

I pulled up to my parents' house the next night, and they were surprised to see me. They had no idea I had been traveling this second time, so I had to get them up to date. I was a little shocked that neither of them seemed to care. At the very least, I expected my mother to scold me for selling all my belongings to travel, but she thought it was cool that I had been raising money for Shot at Life. However, they were both a bit concerned about my endeavors to make it all the way to Alaska, which I felt I did a pretty good job of giving them some assurance.

I made an appointment with my doctor the next day, who referred me to a neurologist. However, I had to wait two weeks for the next appointment, so I spent that time camping in the woods behind my parents' house. They thought that was kind of strange, but I had become accustomed to sleeping outside and didn't want to grow soft. On the plus side, it was fall, so it felt amazing outside anyway. The temperatures had dropped to freezing a couple of times, so I was able to get some practice with snaring and hunting. It was very nostalgic hunting with the same atlatl and darts I'd made when I was thirteen. I hadn't done much trapping or hunting in the past few years, so I was a little rusty but picked it back up rather quickly.

Two weeks had gone by, and I was finally visiting with the neurologist. It turned out that I had a crushed ulnar nerve from poor bike fitting. Since I was leaning too far forward, I had too much weight on my wrists, and the nerve to my right hand was getting pinched. Sitting in that same position for nearly two months had really done a number on me. The neurologist recommended that I stay off the bike for two weeks, make some adjustments to take some weight off my wrists while riding, and do some hand exercises to get my strength back up. I was okay with taking two weeks off since Thanksgiving was right around the corner, which meant I'd be able to spend it with my family.

Heading West

Before leaving Greenfield and getting back on the road, I decided I would try to help raise funds for the Wounded Warriors Project. After reaching out to them, they asked if I could wear one of their hats. I figured that would be much easier than having to deal with an app. I guess their idea was that it might encourage people to donate to them. The hat arrived in the mail before Thanksgiving, which I was able to enjoy with my family. The very next day, I was back on the move, making my way to Memphis on the same route as before. As I was pedaling along, I noticed how much easier it was for me than the first time. I was cruising right along and made it all the way to Memphis in one day instead of two. As I was nearing the city limits, I found out Sydney had moved to a nearby town, so I turned and made my way towards her. I arrived at her new place that night, and it was great seeing her again. She had recovered significantly but still had a bit of a limp and some gnarly scars. She commented on how much I had changed, too. Not only had I lost weight, but I was a lot happier, though a lot dirtier. I ended up staying with her for two nights before getting back on the move.

It was about 4:00 p.m. when I left Sydney's house, and I had made it into Memphis just as it was beginning to get dark. I didn't want to get stuck in the city, so I pushed through even after the sun had gone down. After about an hour of riding through the night, I had made my way over the Mississippi

River and crossed into Arkansas. As soon as I could get off the highway, I began looking for a place to sleep. I noticed an old auto repair shop just off the road and thought it looked safe enough. I pushed my bike behind it and found myself ankle-deep in mud. It was too late to do anything about it, so I continued pushing my way through the muck until I'd reached a large mound of dirt. The ground behind it was solid, and no one would be able to see me, so I tossed my new zero-degree sleeping bag onto the ground and crawled in for the night. I slept cozy but woke the next morning to see everything covered in ice. That made me feel confident in my new sleeping bag, but nearly two inches of mud had frozen over my tires and boots. It took almost an hour of chiseling away at the mud with my knife before I was able to get back on the move.

It was probably around noon when I reached the large, green welcome sign for Palestine. I decided to pull over next to it and grab a bite to eat. I laid my loaded bike over on its side and began rummaging through my saddlebags. I grabbed hold of what felt to be a can of soup, but it felt solid. My face scrunched in confusion as I pulled it up to see what it was. I immediately realized that it was a frozen can of Campbell's soup. I had been exerting myself all day and didn't realize how cold it had gotten. A large truck then passed by on the two-lane highway, which was only about two feet away from where I was sitting. The wind that followed the passing truck chilled every drop of sweat on my body. As if eating a beef-flavored slushy wasn't bad enough, each bite was only adding to the misery of feeling cold. I finished it as fast as I could and hopped back onto my bike. While I didn't feel like I'd had the rest that I needed, riding my bike meant that I'd be warm again.

After I'd made it through the small town of Palestine, I found myself crossing a long stretch of wetlands. There was nothing but brown, murky water and dying Cyprus trees on either side of the highway. Now and then, I would pass by a truck that had backed off the highway to launch their hunting boats. One of those times, I saw two men who were leaned up against the side of their truck, having a couple of beers. I knew they were there well before they had noticed me. As I got closer, I let out a sigh and thought to myself, "Here we go. I'm about to get an earful of redneck gibberish." I picked up the pace so I wouldn't have to deal with the social awkwardness. As I zoomed by, I noticed they had stopped talking, and I assumed it was because I'd come into their line of sight. I then faintly heard one of them yell in the distance, "What the hell? Was that person on a bike?" As I had no map, I had no way of knowing how far it would be until I reached dry land. I didn't want to waste my time trying to explain myself to a couple of drunks.

With maybe an hour left of daylight, the water began to turn back into dry land. Shortly after that, I arrived in the small town of Biscoe. The first sign of civilization was a little old convenience store on my left. There was a drink machine sitting out in the front, so I made my way over to it. It was strange to me, craving sodas. I never used to like them, but they were hard to resist since I'd been traveling. I reached into my pocket, digging through the change I'd been picking up alongside the road. I found a few quarters that were still usable and crammed them into the machine, clicking wildly at the button to give me an orange soda. I finished it with a few gulps and felt the needed sugar coursing through my veins.

I tossed the empty can into the trash and turned my attention to the sky. It looked like it was about to start raining at any minute. I then noticed an old baseball field just on the other side of the street. The grass within the field was all grown up and looked like it had gone unused for several years. I figured that would be a good place to camp for the night, so I pushed my bike over and made my way straight to one of the dugouts. I propped my bike up against the fence and began walking around to scope out the area.

I saw a shed nearby and decided to investigate. I looked around a bit and found an old baseball trophy with the same date as my birthday. I wanted to keep it, but I knew I'd eventually just end up tossing it in the trash somewhere down the road. I didn't have the space for anything extra, let alone useless junk. I looked around a bit more and noticed that people had been using the shed as a place to skin their deer. There was a fresh pile of guts thrown to the side, along with several bones and hides. I walked back to the dugout to collect my things. I didn't want to be too close to that rotting meat in case something decided to chow down on it during the night, so I pushed my bike along the fence and followed it to the other side.

As I was walking along the fence, I realized that I must have been visible from the road. Not that I thought a passerby would be looking in my direction, but I didn't want someone to come over and investigate if they did see me. I then looked around and noticed a group of trees that would be perfect for camouflage, as well as keeping off some of the rain. Just as I was setting up my tent, the sun had completely disappeared, and the rain came as expected. I rushed to get everything ready for bed, trying to beat the downpour. As soon as I crawled into my sleeping bag, prepared for a long, cold night, the large raindrops began crashing down and the sound of them pelting my tent soothed me to sleep.

It was another cold and wet morning as I made my way to and through the town of De Valls Bluff. Shortly after passing through the city, a white truck pulled up beside me. I noticed two men and a dog inside, and I figured they were probably going to offer me a ride since that had happened several times. They didn't offer me a ride, though. They were just curious as to what I was doing. When I told them that I was making my way to Alaska, they both said that I was living their dreams and wanted to get a picture with me. I can't remember the passenger's name, but the man driving told me his name was Anthony. He handed me a twenty-dollar bill, shook my hand, and wished me well. They then continued making their way to work, and so did I. My job was just a little bit different. At that point, all I wanted was to keep peoples' dreams alive. The money was always helpful, but a few encouraging words did way more to keep me motivated.

I continued riding along the highway, which eventually turned into an interstate. There was no warning or anything, and I'd found myself surrounded by a ton of traffic. There were walls on each side of me, so my only option was to keep riding and hope I didn't get stopped by the police, or worse. It was starting to get dark, and I was still stuck on the interstate, crossing narrow bridges and weaving in and out of traffic to make room for myself. I had finally found an exit and made my way into downtown. I was both physically and mentally exhausted and had a pounding headache, but I still had to deal with the city. I was finally able to get outside of the metropolitan area and found myself in an affluent neighborhood. I then found what I thought was a backroad and made my way down it to see if it would make for a safe place to camp. There was a line of bushes and trees between the road and a cemetery, so I decided to toss my sleeping bag on the ground within them.

I fell asleep for about thirty minutes before waking to the sound of a vehicle pulling up. Then, I heard what sounded like someone unlatching and opening a metal gate. I peeked around the tree that was blocking my view and realized that I was in someone's driveway. The sound that I'd heard was them locking the gate to their house before leaving. They hadn't noticed me, so I figured it would be safe to go back to sleep. I turned back over and then heard another car pull up. I thought maybe they'd forgotten something, so I didn't care to look again. I was just lying there, listening. About five minutes had passed, and I could still hear the car running but never heard the gate or anyone getting out of the vehicle. I finally decided to turn my head to see what they were doing and realized it was a security guard. I hoped he wouldn't see me and think I was trying to rob them or something.

The security guard then stepped out of his vehicle and began walking around, patrolling the area. At one point, he stood about ten feet away from me, and I thought he'd seen me. Thankfully, he was distracted by his cellphone and began walking back to his car. I then decided to take my chances of getting out of there unnoticed. I slowly stuffed my sleeping bag back into the saddlebag and gently lowered all my gear over the fence and into the cemetery. I then jumped over the fence and quietly pushed my bike back out to the street.

I was exhausted and didn't feel like riding with the heavy traffic after dark, but I was desperate to find somewhere to sleep. I made my way back to highway 70 and rode for about a mile outside of town before a car's tire threw a rock at my face, barely missing my eye. I decided that was a sign for me to stop where I was. I then pushed my bike across a field that was just on the other side of the street and put my tent up amongst the trees. I wish I had known about that spot before because I had already wasted a couple of hours that could have been used to get rest.

The next day, I'd made it about halfway to Hot Springs when my mother called. I pulled over on the side of the road and sat on the grass while we talked. For whatever reason, I decided to stand back up and push my bike somewhere else. I walked about twenty feet from where I had been and stood there to finish up my phone call. As soon as I hung up, a car came speeding around the curve up ahead. The car ended up sliding off the road right where I had been sitting when I first answered the phone. If I hadn't moved, I would've been hit. The driver and his vehicle were fine, though, and so was I. Although, I was a bit shaken up by how close to death I'd just come.

I finally made it into Hot Springs and thought it seemed like a nice town, especially compared to Little Rock. There were fewer people anyway, and that meant less stress for me. There were also a lot of Christmas decorations out and made the town feel even more welcoming. I then noticed a large, white tower on one of the mountains and decided to check it out. I spent almost an hour making my way to the top and discovered it was the Hot Springs Mountain Tower. There was an elevator that you could take to the top of it for a fee, but I decided to just take in the view from where I was. As I was sitting there, looking out at the fall colored hills, an Asian couple came up from behind and asked if I could take their picture. I then noticed a large van of tourists making their way over, so I decided to get out of there.

From Hot Springs, I began heading south towards Highway 70. I had a spare tire shipped to the post office in De Queen, and it looked like I was going to arrive just in time to pick it up. As I was riding along, I passed by a medical office in Glenwood and decided to stop by. I'd been having some trouble sleeping and needed something more potent than some pills you can just get over the counter. However, the clinic had already closed before I made it, so I decided to camp in the back and would talk to them in the morning. Thankfully, the doctor there was able to prescribe me something to help me get some sleep. Only getting an hour or two of rest every night was beginning to take a toll on me.

After leaving Glenwood, I made it halfway to Daisy by that night and was finally able to get the sleep I needed. The next morning, as I was continuing into Daisy, I stopped at a church to have breakfast. There was a basketball goal and volleyball net set up in the cemetery, which I thought was kind of strange, but they had a picnic table sitting in the front. I figured that seemed like the perfect place to take a quick break. As I was eating, I noticed a truck had passed by a few times, and the driver kept eyeballing me. Not long after the truck had driven away, a police officer arrived and began questioning what I was doing. Feeling a bit annoyed by his tone, I replied, "What does it look like I'm doing? I'm sitting here eating my breakfast." He acted as though he'd never seen a traveler before, so I vividly explained what I was doing, but he still insisted that I leave. Not wanting to argue anymore, I made my way up the street and came across a lake at Crawford Park. I decided to finish up my break there and preferred it over the church anyway. The water had recently receded, so after I finished eating, I walked around the extended shoreline and helped to rid the area of invasive zebra mussels.

Once I'd made it into Dierks, I saw a gas station and decided to stop by. I hadn't had anything to drink other than water for a few days and was beginning to crave something else. As I was standing outside, filling one of my canteens with a sports drink, an older man walked up to me. He began questioning where I was heading and was surprised when I told him I was making my way for Alaska. With a big smile on his face and placing one hand on my shoulder, the old man said, "You just may be the wisest, bravest young man I'd ever met. You're living the dream. If I weren't ninety years old, I would have to join you." It sure was refreshing to hear that because there had been occasions where I felt almost selfish for taking the time to enjoy myself. Everywhere I looked, I saw people who were miserable and hating life. Those same people would often snap at me for not being miserable with them, saying things like, "Get a job," "Stop running from your problems," and "Grow up." It wasn't like I didn't think of all those things myself. The whole reason I was out there on a bike was to see if it would help my PTSD, but getting some reassurance from a ninety-year-old man helped to curve any negative thinking. He'd been around a while and probably knew it was more important to enjoy life than spend it stressed out and worrying about what other people thought.

I continued riding into the night and made it about a mile from De Queen before realizing I had dropped one of my gloves. It was near freezing outside, so I thought it would be worth backtracking to look for it. I was hoping to find it sitting on the road somewhere but gave up after about ten miles. I turned back around and made it to De Queen by 10:00 p.m. It seemed like a

72

nice, quiet town, so I wasn't too worried about finding a place to sleep. I found my way behind a four-wheeler shop and set up my tent. The next morning, I made my way to the post office to pick up the extra tire I'd ordered. I didn't want to be in anyone's way, so I took my package to the sidewalk and sat at a bench while I figured out how I wanted to strap the new tire to my bike. As I was sitting there adjusting my things, a man named Randell walked up and began with the usual questions about my travels. After we finished talking, he reached into his pocket and gave me a handful of hard candies and a packet of cocoa mix. I didn't want to be cliché and not take candy from strangers, so I stuck one in my mouth and put the rest into my pocket. Just as I was getting ready to leave, Randell came back over and said he felt bad for just giving me candy. He then reached out and handed me seventy dollars! I was very appreciative but thought it was kind of ironic since I'd just spent that much on those spare tires. I thanked him for his help and continued making my way west.

Just before nightfall, I'd crossed over into Oklahoma and entered the outskirts of a town called Broken Bow. I noticed a bar just off the highway and saw the woods behind it were very dense. I made my way behind the bar and pushed my bike into the forest. I saw a few beer cans and whiskey bottles strewn about in the woods, so I continued walking until I stopped seeing them. I didn't want someone to end up tossing one back there and hitting me with it. Right before it had gotten pitch dark, I'd found the perfect spot to put up my tent and crawled in for the night. After getting only a couple of hours of sleep, I was awakened by some strange noises. It sounded like a boar was snorting and digging away at the earth. The sounds began getting closer, so I clenched my machete and prepared for the worst. Just as I was about to climb out of my tent to try and scare the boar away, a group of people showed up at the bar and began making a lot of noise in the parking lot. Luckily, that was enough to scare the boar out of there, so I didn't have to deal with it.

The next morning, I made my way into the heart of Broken Bow and stopped at a Mcdonald's. I purchased a small cup of coffee and made my way over to one of the power outlets to charge my phone. There wasn't any cell service in the area, but I at least wanted enough charge to use their wi-fi to check my map and decide which direction I wanted to go. After sitting there for about ten minutes, the manager walked up and told me I needed to leave. When I asked why she replied, "The customers are looking at you instead of where they are walking, so you're a tripping hazard." I asked if she was serious, to which she replied, "Yes. You are going to have to leave. If you don't, I am going to call the police. You are making it unsafe here for the other customers." I couldn't believe what I was hearing, but I did as I was asked and left the building.

I posted on my Facebook Page about what had happened, and a man by the name of Scott replied to it. He said he lived there and would like to apologize for how his town's people had treated me. He said he was at work at the time but would send out a friend to meet me. I wasn't sure when or why he wanted to send one of his friends to meet me because my phone died after he said that. I shrugged my shoulders and made my way into a nearby Wal-Mart. After grabbing some lube for my bike chain, a pair of brake pads, and a new pair of gloves, I made my way out of the store. I hopped on my bike to take off when I heard a man's voice, "Jake?" I turned and looked at the man with a confused look on my face. The man continued, "I'm Scott's friend, Terry. I've been looking all over for you, man!" I was just as glad as he was that he found me because Scott had sent him out to give me forty dollars. I thanked him and made my way back into Wal-Mart to do a bit of grocery shopping. I was able to refill my nearly empty food bag and even picked up a new machete since the one I had was old and dull.

As I was leaving Broken Bow, I realized it was Christmas Eve. I wanted to make sure I found a place to camp where I could have a fire, so I turned down an old dirt road about ten miles from Hugo. I wandered down the dirt road for about half a mile and pushed my bike into a densely wooded area. It seemed like the perfect spot because there were no people around, and pine trees surrounded me. I then put my tent up in an open area and noticed a baby pine tree right across from me. I then decided to decorate it with my green chain lock and red carabiners. Then, underneath my Christmas tree, I laid the two beers I'd picked up at the last gas station I'd passed, the hot chocolate powder Randell had given me, and the new machete I'd picked up in town. The sun was beginning to set, so I began collecting sticks to have a fire. Once I had some flames going, I decided to heat a can of chicken soup. It was much better than eating it frozen, and it paired nicely with my two beers. Clouds of condensation soon began slipping from my breath, reminding me that the fire was about to die and that it was time to turn in. It was the end of a perfect night as I crawled into my warm sleeping bag and fell asleep to the sound of the coyotes howling at the full moon.

I woke to a lovely, frigid Christmas morning and decided to build another fire. On most days, I would have just packed up and headed out immediately upon awakening, but this was my favorite holiday, and I wanted my hot cocoa! I took my time to enjoy it and slowly began making my way for Hugo once I'd finished. I had a present from one of my Facebook followers, Lori, waiting for me at the post office there, but I wouldn't be able to pick it up until the next day. As I was making my way through town, I received a few other gifts from kind strangers. There was a man who stopped to give me a banana, the HiWay Inn Express hotel let me take a shower, one lady gave me a box of sausage, cheese, and crackers, and another lady gave me twenty dollars! After having a good run-in with some friendly town people, I decided to head to the town park. I assumed the park was empty because it was Christmas, so I took advantage of it and stayed the night there.

The next day, as I was making my way to the post office, I decided to toss my anti-depressants into the trash. I felt like they had probably helped up until then, but I also felt as though they were no longer needed. They made me feel kind of strange, and I wanted to feel normal again, even if that meant feeling sad. However, I had faith in the thought that I was happy because I was spending so much time outdoors and getting a ton of exercise. I also felt that I could then be an advocate to help people who were dealing with depression to get outside more. I posted on my Facebook Page that I had ditched my medication, and a lot of people were worried about it. However, the people who were on anti-depressants were very supportive, and those were the people I was trying to reach anyway.

After ditching my medication, I made my way to the post office and waited outside for them to open. While I was sitting there, I wondered what kind of things Lori may have sent. I was a little nervous that she may have sent more than I needed, but I figured I could find someone else to share it with if it came to that. They finally opened the doors and said, "I bet you're the guy who got that general delivery package." I replied, "Yeah. Probably. I'm riding my bike across the country, and that's the only way I can get mail." The clerk smiled and handed me my package, and I opened it in front of her. She seemed almost as excited about my first care package as I was. I reached in and pulled out some granola bars, trail mix, a pack of double-A batteries, cookies, a toothbrush, and toothpaste, which I thought was funny because I was always posting pictures of myself brushing my teeth, and a handwritten letter of encouragement.

I left the post office and crossed into Texas. After riding in the rain for several hours, I'd finally made it into the town of Paris. Although I was wearing a rain jacket and waterproof pants that had kept my clothes dry, the freezing rain was making my face sting. Luckily, I came across an old, run-down motel with an awning that I was able to use as shelter. I sat there for a few hours, waiting for the worst of the storm to pass, and continued riding once it had. Just a few hours outside of Paris, I was between towns and decided to just push my bike into one of the empty fields that ran alongside the highway. I walked around in the field for a bit and finally decided to just set my tent up in the middle of it. Although there was probably an hour or two left of daylight, I went ahead and crawled inside my sleeping bag since it was raining.

That night, as I was camping between the small towns of Paris and Honeygrove, a cold front came through and brought with it gale-force winds. Those winds had taken me by surprise, so I hadn't thought to use the guy lines on my tent. I hoped my tent would be able to handle it, but it finally came crashing down on top of me after a couple of hours of fighting back. A part of me wanted to try and fix it, but I knew it would probably be pointless and tried to ignore it the best I could. However, I didn't get much sleep that night because my tent's violent flapping was so loud and annoying.

After the sun came up, I crawled out of my wind-flattened tent and noticed about a hundred snails had attached themselves to the walls. Between all the snails and fierce winds that had yet to back off, I had a hard time trying to pack everything away. I finally got back on the move, though, and began making my way for Dallas. My old friend, Rob, from Tennessee, was living there and thought I would swing by to meet up with him. It would only take me several hours to get there, and I hadn't seen him in years. I finally arrived at Rob's house around 3:00 p.m., and it felt like old times. Although there isn't much to talk about, he was living in an apartment with his mother and sister, who were also excited to see me. At least, during the two nights I stayed with them, I was able to eat a couple of homecooked meals, wash my clothes, and get a hot shower.

I felt rejuvenated after leaving Rob's house and made my way for Throckmorton. As I was getting close to town, I saw an old white Oldsmobile heading in my direction. Just after they'd passed, I could hear the tires pulling off onto the gravel shoulder. I stopped riding and turned my head to see what they were doing. The car's reverse lights came on, and it slowly began backing towards me. The car finally stopped about ten feet away, and a scrawny older man in a black suit stepped out. It looked like he was having a hard time walking, so I walked up to him so he wouldn't have to. When I got up to him, he asked, "What's your favorite pie?" I was taken completely off guard by that question. I laughed and asked him if he could clarify. He asked me again, "What is your favorite kind of pie, young man?" I thought for a moment and replied, "Hmm. Pecan, I guess. Why?" The older man then lifted his finger in the air and turned back to his car. He then popped the trunk open and pointed inside. I walked a little closer to get a better view and saw a pecan pie sitting there! He then reached in and handed it to me, "Jesus told me you were going to say that. You enjoy it and enjoy the rest of your trip, young man." He then got back in his car and drove away. Although I was an atheist at the time, I was starting to question my beliefs. Holding the pie, I looked at it and wondered what would have happened if I had said any other pie. I also wondered if the pie was safe to eat because that was a bizarre situation, but of course, I couldn't say no because it was my favorite!

After the mysterious older man had driven away, I continued riding and made it into Throckmorton just as it was getting dark. I put my tent up behind a church and posted a picture of it on my Facebook Page. It turned out that one of my followers, Mary, lived there and recognized the church. She sent me a message and asked if I'd let her get me a motel for the night, to which I accepted. I packed up my things and waited for her to get there. A few minutes later, a truck pulled up, and Mary stepped out. She had a very carrying, motherly presence about her, which made sense when I saw she had brought her son and daughter with her. I tossed my bike and saddlebags into the back of the flatbed, and we made our way across town to the motel. She'd already had the room paid for and handed me the key, so all I had to do was walk right in. I pushed my bike inside my room and walked back out to thank them. When I opened the door, Mary was standing there with a large plate of food. She then asked if it would be okay to get a picture of me with her kids, to which I agreed. She then hugged me goodbye and wished me luck for the rest of my journey.

The next morning, I left the motel and made my way to the post office to pick up my new bivy. It was supposedly waterproof and had a much smaller profile than my tent, which was why I wanted to give it a try. Later that night, as I was camping between Throckmorton and Haskell, a storm came through. I had a lot of hope for my bivy, but it did a terrible job of keeping me dry. By the next morning, my sleeping bag and the clothes I'd slept in were all soaking wet. I had an extra pair of clothes, but I was nervous about my sleeping bag because the temperatures were supposed to drop into the teens that night. I strapped my sleeping bag to the outside of my bike and hoped that it would dry throughout the day. I arrived in Haskell just after dark and realized my sleeping bag was still soaking wet. I knew I was probably in trouble, but I didn't know what else to do besides hunker down and hope I didn't succumb to hypothermia during the night. I was inside of the sleeping bag for about an hour before my clothes were wet. Another hour had passed, and I was already beginning to shiver. The temperature was supposed to drop twenty more degrees by morning, so I knew I had to do something.

I remembered seeing a motel on my way through town, so I decided to make my way back to it and ask if they had a dryer I could use. As I was pushing my bike through the parking lot, I saw a lady tossing blankets into a dryer and felt a huge relief. "Excuse me, ma'am, do you work here," I asked. The lady turned back and snapped, "Yes. I do. Why? What do you want?" She looked terrified of me, which made me feel awkward, but I continued, "Would it be okay if I used the dryer for my sleeping bag? It got wet the other day. If I can't get it dry by tonight, well, either I won't be able to sleep, or I'll freeze to death." She snapped again, "No! I don't think so! I'll go get my husband!" The lady stormed into the front office, and I stood patiently, hoping her husband might be more reasonable. About a minute later, her husband came stomping over. "Can I help you with something?" He sounded very annoyed, but I kept my composure and replied, "I'm riding my bike across America for the Wounded Warriors Project. My sleeping bag got wet last night. May I please use your dryer?" The man gave me a stern look and asked, "Wounded Warriors? Are you a vet?" I felt some relief when he asked that because I was, and his change in tone sounded like he was going to let me use the dryer. When I told him that I was a veteran, he laughed and said, "Angie didn't say you were a vet! She told me you were some crazy homeless person. Of course, you can use the dryer! Hell, you can have a room if you want." Feeling like I'd just dodged a bullet, I replied, "Sure! That sounds great!" The man then walked back to the motel to get the key for my room. When he returned with the key, he handed it to me and said, "My name is Ed. If you need anything, let me know. The dryer is right there. You can help yourself. Also, we eat breakfast every morning at 7:30. If you want, you're welcome to join us." Just before going into my room, I shook Ed's hand and thanked him for his help. As soon as I walked into my room, I stripped down to nothing but my last pair of clean underwear and carried everything outside to the laundry room next door. I tried doing everything as fast as possible since I was in my underwear and didn't want them second-guessing if I was crazy after all.

The next morning, I was all packed up, looking and feeling fresh with my clean clothes and sleeping bag. I made my way over to the motel office and knocked on the door. I was greeted inside by Angie, and she had me follow her to their housing area behind the desk. As we entered the living room area, she said,

"Ed's in the kitchen, cooking breakfast. You can have a seat on the couch if you'd like." I took a seat on the couch and noticed they were watching the weather. I knew it was cold outside but was surprised that it had dropped to fourteen degrees. I felt even more thankful that Ed had decided to give me a room for the night. I then heard the back door open, and the sounds of dogs barking soon followed. From around the corner, two chihuahuas came running up and jumped right into my lap. They acted like they had known me forever, which made me feel more at home.

A few minutes later, Ed walked into the room and handed me a plate with two biscuits and gravy and a side of scrambled eggs. Angie came in behind him and gave me a cup of coffee. They didn't seem to be the hard, stern people I had met the night before. As we were all sitting there, eating our breakfast, they both apologized for the way they had reacted. As it turned out, they'd recently let a small group of traveling homeless people stay in one of the rooms, and they made a mess of it. They had littered the room with dirty needles and even stole a few things. It was then obvious why they'd treated me the way they did at first, but I was glad we were all able to get past that. I then began sharing stories with them about my experiences from living on the road so far, and they shared some about how they were grandparents, bragging about their grandchildren. After about an hour of getting to know the real Ed and Angie, it was time for me to get back on the road. I thanked them for their hospitality and for giving me the chance to show them I wasn't some disrespectful hooligan. I walked into the front office, where my bike was waiting for me, and layered up with my winter clothing. I then pushed my bike out to the parking lot, where Ed and Angie saw me off as I jumped back onto my bike and prepared to continue my way west.

New Mexico

After leaving Throckmorton, I crossed into New Mexico and made my way into Roswell. As I was making my way into town, a small car pulled over. An eccentric older man stepped out and introduced himself as a newspaper reporter. He thought I looked as though I might have had an interesting story and decided to stop. Well, I guess I did, because after explaining myself, he invited me to his house. I needed to take a few days off to see a dermatologist while I was there, so the reporter said I could camp in his back yard while we worked on something for the paper. I thought that seemed like a fair trade, so he gave me his address, and I rode my bike over to his house.

I arrived at the reporter's house about an hour later, and he greeted me with a snifter of whiskey neat. I followed him into his home office, and we began the interview. A few hours later, we were interrupted by his wife. We had gotten so caught up in the report that time had slipped away, and it was time for dinner. The reporter didn't want to lose his momentum, so we carried our food back into his office and continued to work. After about eight hours of writing up his story, he thought he had all the information he needed. It had been a very long day for me, so I was happy to know I had a safe place to sleep.

The next morning, I made my way to make an appointment with a dermatologist. I had a spot on my nose and back that had both been there since a bad sunburn I'd gotten in Florida, so I was beginning to feel concerned. I walked into the medical office, and the receptionist was such a jaw-droppingly beautiful Latina that I almost forgot why I was there. After cutting to the chase, I would be able to be seen the next day since it was kind of an emergency. I left the office and began making my way downtown. The reporter had told me the night before that I could pick up a free lunch from Carmine's Italian restaurant, so I began making my way there.

As I was sitting there enjoying my free lunch, I noticed I had a call coming from an unknown number. I thought it would be one of those scam callers, so I answered it, ready to mess with them like I usually did. "This is the dermatology office of Roswell. May I speak with Jake?" the voice on the other line asked. I recognized the voice. It was Myrna, the sexy receptionist. I replied, "This is Jake." There were a few seconds of silence, and then, somewhat nervously, she asked if I'd like to stay the night at her place. Surely, I thought, she was out of my league, but I wasn't about to pass up any chances. I told her I'd be around and to give me a call when she was ready for me to head over.

After getting off the phone with Myrna, I finished my meal at Carmine's and made my way back to the reporter's house. He had called and said he wanted me to swing by, so I could look over his report before sending it to the newspaper. Everything looked good to me except for the title, which read, "Veteran Cycles America for PTSD." That was partly true, but I didn't want to use the fact that I was a veteran as leverage, similar to what had happened with Ed and Angie. I just wanted to be treated like an average guy who happened to be a veteran. Not the other way around. I asked the reporter if he could figure out a way to reword the heading, and he said it wouldn't be a problem. We had mentioned everything in the article. I just didn't feel comfortable with the title. To me, it was kind of like those signs that you see homeless people holding on the side of streets, "Homeless veteran. Anything helps." Perhaps I was a bit embarrassed by the fact that I had PTSD and the stigma that came along with it. While being mentioned in the article was fine, it just felt kind of invasive, having that title slapped across the front page.

After fixing some issues with the reporter's article, Myrna called and said I could head over to her place. I arrived at her house about an hour later, and it was like we'd known each other for years. We were both really comfortable with each other's company. Not long after I'd been there, we put on some music and began working on dinner. While we were cooking, she drank wine, and I was drinking beer, so we quickly loosened up and started acting silly. I hadn't felt that way with anyone in a long time, so it was very refreshing and exciting. After dinner had finished cooking, we took our plates to the living room, where we could eat and watch a movie. About halfway through the movie, I accidentally spilled some beer on myself, so I threw those clothes into the washer and got a quick shower. After I got out of the shower, I was wearing the shorts that I usually only slept in, and Myrna had changed into her pajamas. We went back to the couch and continued watching our movie. At some point, she leaned in to get a picture with me, but even after she got what she wanted, she didn't move away. I hadn't felt the warmth of a woman in about a year, so I was really enjoying her body being against mine. It was almost like I needed to pinch myself. Since I'd been sleeping outside and alone for so long, it was hard to believe being with her was real. I guess neither of us could take it anymore because it wasn't long until our hormones had gotten the best of us.

The next morning, Myrna left for work, and I made my way into town. I decided to stop by a gas station when I noticed I was on the front page of the newspaper. I went in to buy a coffee and asked if I could get a couple of quarters back. I walked outside and purchased a copy so that I could send it back home to my mother. I knew she would get a kick out of it. And although I was a bit upset because the reporter never did change the title like he said he would, I knew it was just to increase their sales, but there was nothing I could do about it. As I was sitting there on the curb, enjoying my coffee, people began looking at me in a way they never had before, pointing and whispering to each other. It felt a bit strange, knowing most of the town knew who I was, while I knew nothing about any of them. After finishing my coffee, it was time for me to go and see the dermatologist.

It was kind of strange seeing Myrna again. We tried to keep it professional, but it was fun knowing we had a secret. The doctor finally called me to the back about thirty minutes later and began examining my sores. She immediately said the spots were called basal cell carcinomas, and I probably got them from not wearing any sunscreen. They were benign tumors and nothing to worry about, but I needed to have them removed because they could become malignant.

The doctor left the room for a few minutes and returned with some numbing shots and a special laser tool. She released one numbing shot into my back and the other one into my nose, which made my entire face feel tingly. After I couldn't feel anything, she began burning the tumors off, starting with the one on my back. I could hear my skin sizzling from the heat of the laser, and it smelled like someone was cooking bacon. The unusual sensation amplified once she began working on my nose, though it didn't take long before she had finished the procedure. I walked back to the office entrance to sign out, and Myrna handed me a sticky note just before I left. When I walked outside, several nurses were waiting for me beside my bike. They had seen me in the newspaper and pitched in to get me a card and a little cash. I thought that was very nice and got a picture taken with them. Then, after I left the building, I opened the little pink note from Myrna. It read, "Come by later," and had a smiley face drawn on it. So I wouldn't forget, I stuck the note in my pocket.

I had a lot of time left before Myrna would be off work, so I made my way to the outskirts of town. I eventually wandered down an old dirt road, which ended at a small creek. It was very peaceful and beautiful out there, so I decided that's where I would stay until making my way back to Myrna's house. After a long day of relaxing, the sun was finally setting, so I dusted myself off and rode over to her house. It was pretty much a replay of the night before, except everything moved along faster. I truly enjoyed my time with her, but by the next morning, we both knew I was about to ride out and would probably never see her again. But by that time, she was already following my Facebook Page, so I told her to keep in contact.

After leaving Myrna's house the next morning, I was making my way out of the city when I received a call from the local radio station. They asked if I'd be interested in being a guest on their show the following day. I said I would, so they got me a room at the Holiday Inn. It was still early, so I made my way back into town and dropped my things off at my hotel room. I then decided to walk downtown to check out all the cool alien stuff that Roswell was well-known for. I made my way into one of their museums, where the manager recognized me from the newspaper article and gave me a free pass. They had all kinds of fake alien paraphernalia but had actual newspaper clippings from the UFO crash of 1947. I probably spent an hour walking around the museum before making my way back to Carmine's restaurant. They had really hooked me with that free lunch they offered a couple of days prior.

I made my way back to my hotel room after lunch and soaked in a hot bath, getting my muscles ready to put down some serious miles. I turned in early and enjoyed the warm, cozy bed. I figured it would probably be a while before I got to enjoy that feeling again. The next morning, I made my way to the outskirts of town and pulled up to the radio station. I'd gotten there a little earlier than everyone else, so I got a free cup of coffee and waited for them to set everything up. A few minutes later, one of the radio hosts called me into her office, and it was showtime. I'd had plenty of practice talking to everyone about my journey so far, so I already knew most of what I wanted to say. I was on the first show for about fifteen minutes, and then I was passed on to two other shows, also fifteen minutes each. After I'd finished talking with the disc jockeys, I was ready to get back on the move. I made my way outside, and there was a group of about ten people standing in the parking lot. Four of those people were also veterans who had PTSD, so they kind of understood where I was coming from. Everyone out there said I was doing a great thing and wished me luck for the rest of my trip.

After leaving Roswell, I began riding west on highway 380. It wasn't long after I'd left that I'd found myself ascending into the Rocky Mountains. I knew it was about to get challenging, but it had been flat for so long, and I was ready for some change. By the time I had reached Hondo Valley, I had received several winter storm advisories. Shortly after that, it had begun to snow. I was a little nervous about how bad it could get, but I felt as though I could make it through if things didn't get too serious.

As the day went on, the snow had begun to pile up faster than I had anticipated, but I'd made it into San Patricio in one piece. It looked as though the town had been deserted. Everyone had probably retracted into their homes to get out of the storm. Since the road had completely disappeared beneath the snow, I pulled over to strap some zip ties onto my tires for added traction. As I was getting ready to get back on my bike, I noticed I'd been standing beneath a sign that read, "State cop ahead with a bad attitude, PMS, and a gun." I got a good laugh out of that, which helped me get into a better mood as I ventured deeper into the storm. As I pedaled along, I passed by several old forts used by the Lincoln Army settlement during the 1850s. I thought about how they'd probably spent several winters out there and what that must have been like. It was beginning to get dark, but I still had a lot of energy left, so I decided to push on.

As I'd been distracted by all beauty around me, I had neglected to dawn my balaclava. The high altitude, mixed with the frigid air, had set me up for a sore throat and a frost-covered beard. I stopped to put my mask on and noticed a small light in the far distance. As I got nearer, I discovered it was the town of Capitan. I began pushing my bike once I made it into town and walked over to a convenience store, happy to see it was still open. As I was leaning my bike against the wall, a lady approached me and introduced herself as Trish. She probably thought I looked miserable and offered to buy me a warm meal. I really appreciated that since I'd been in the snow for most of the day. As I was standing underneath the awning, eating my dinner, I looked across the street and noticed an RV park. I wondered if they would mind me setting up my tent, so I finished eating and made my way over.

The park owner lived in a small house in front of the entrance. I walked up to the porch and didn't see or hear anyone- just the howling wind and the snow smacking the metal siding. I hesitated before knocking because I didn't want to disturb anyone. That, and I could only imagine how crazy I'd look if I asked to put up a tent in this weather. I prepared myself for the worst, which would be them telling me I couldn't stay, and knocked on the door. An old lady answered, and I asked, "Hi. I'm currently riding a bike across America and was wondering if it would be okay if I put my tent up out here?" Just as I suspected, she looked at me like I was crazy and asked, "Out there? In the snow?" I laughed and replied, "I know it sounds crazy, but I'd really appreciate it." She poked her head out from the door and looked towards the RV park, "I guess you can put your tent up over there, next to my shed." I thanked her for allowing me to camp there before making my way to my spot for the night. I sat my tent up, right there on the snow, and crawled in. I thought lying on the snow was much more comfortable than being on solid ground, though I did have a sleeping pad between my sleeping bag and the tent floor. I closed my eyes and focused on the sound of the wind and snow brushing against the tent fabric.

I woke the next morning and noticed the weight of the snow had squished in the ceiling and walls of my tent. I wondered what it looked like from the outside, so I got dressed and unzipped the main flap. The condensation from the inside of my tent had caused the snow to melt and refreeze, so I had to knock away the ice covering the entrance. Once I was able to, I poked my head out and saw that it had snowed an additional eight inches throughout the night. I knew it was going to be difficult to get very many miles down, but the views were breathtaking, and the cold air felt energizing. After pulling all my gear from the snow, I made my way back over to the convenience store. I walked inside and discovered they had free coffee, so I grabbed a cup and took it outside. As I was standing there, a large man with long gray hair and a huge beard walked out of the store. He looked at me for a few seconds and asked where I was heading. After I'd told him I was making my way for Alaska, he went on about how he'd moved to Capitan from Fairbanks a few years back. He said he used to do a lot of hunting, trapping, and fishing up in Alaska, so we exchanged a few outdoor stories. After chatting with the mountain man for several minutes, he said, "Keep doing what you're doing and stay away from the booze. The reason I'm here, I used to drink too much and ended up getting cancer because of it. Well, they think that's why anyway. So, I came down here to enjoy the rest of my time with the family, but I sure do miss Alaska." I looked at the case of beer he was holding and looked back to his face. He looked away, and as he began walking back to his truck, he said, "No sense in stopping now."

As the mountain man drove away, I took the last sip of coffee from my cup and tossed it into the trash. I let out a sigh and began walking my bike further into the mountains. I must have walked about ten miles through the snow before I was able to ride again, though even then, it was still rather difficult. I'd finally reached the top of the mountain, and the snow was beginning to turn to ice. I had been walking my bike nearly all day, so I decided to be risky and coasted down the other side and into the valley below. As I began my descent, I was picking up a lot of speed and had to dodge all the random patches of snow and ice. It was quite the rush because my bike probably weighed nearly two hundred pounds, so stopping under those conditions would've been a challenge of its own. However, I made it down safely and stopped in front of the Rainbow Inn motel to take a short break. As I was sitting there, eating my trail mix, the motel manager, Scott, walked up and asked what I was up to. After I told him everything, he offered me a free night at the motel. Since it was beginning to get late and I planned on stopping soon, I took him up on his offer. I'd had no cellular service since I'd left Roswell, so I made sure to use the motel's wi-fi to let everyone know I'd made it through the mountains.

I left the Rainbow Inn the next morning and began making my way for Kiritimati. The scenery was pretty much the same as it had been since Capitan, with the snow, rocks, and ice. Although, the snow and ice had finally started to disappear as I lowered in elevation. Since the road was clearing up, I was able to put down some pretty good distance. I continued riding into the dark again and finally stopped once I'd made it to Valley of the Fire. I pulled off the highway and began pushing my bike into the field of massive stones. I then laid my bike behind one of them and began walking around. I noticed one of the stones had been carved away, resembling a small cave, so I tossed my sleeping bag inside and climbed in.

The next morning, I left Valley of the Fire and began my ascent into another set of mountains. As I was making my way up, I turned to look at how much ground I had covered. Far away in the distance, I could see the mountains I'd passed through the day before. There were deep, dark clouds sitting right on top of them. I knew I'd made it through there just in the nick of time. The view was astonishing, though. To the east, there were snow-covered mountains and hills as far as I could see. To the south, a light blanket of snow covered the entire valley. I probably stood there for about fifteen minutes, just taking it all in. I then turned my focus on making it to the top and picked up my pace. Once I'd made it down into the next valley, I finally had service on my phone. I noticed that I had received a message from a young lady named Barbie. The message stated that she and a few of her friends would like to have me over once I made it into Socorro. I still had a hundred miles before I got there but told them I'd be there by that night.

Averaging close to twenty miles per hour for the rest of the day, I made I'd into Socorro around 4:00 p.m. and gave Barbie a call. She wanted me to meet them at one of their favorite restaurants in two hours, so I used my extra time to find a restroom where I could wash away some of my sweat and change into clean clothes. I then made my way over to the restaurant where Barbie was waiting for me with her friends Kris, Marty, and Jonah. We made our way to the back, where they had reserved a table for us. Each of Barbie's friends had also invited a couple of friends, so it turned out to be a large gathering. It was kind of strange being the center of attention in front of so many people, but they'd all come to hear my stories of the road. As the night went on, I'd lost count of how many drinks they'd given me. Everyone wanted to get on my level, so they suggested we all go back to Barbie's house to keep the party going. I loaded my bike into Marty's truck, and we started on our way.

Once we arrived at their house, I learned Marty was a bartender and had a large supply of alcoholic beverages. He made me a few of his most recommended mixed drinks as the house began to fill with more and more people. The next thing I knew, I was playing beer pong with some of the most down-to-earth people Socorro had to offer.

I woke up the next morning on the living room couch and had no idea where I was. I was used to waking up either outside or in my tent. But strange people were sleeping all over the floor, and I was still a bit drunk. I pulled out my phone and looked over the pictures from the night before. Everything slowly started coming back to me, and I hoped I hadn't done anything too embarrassing. However, by the looks of it, no one would probably remember anyway. Marty then walked in through the front door with a big smile on his face and asked how I felt. "Never better, man," I replied. Soon after that, I grabbed a quick shower and then helped clean up around the house before getting back on the move again.

After leaving the party house, another couple, Amy and Marcus, wanted me to swing by while I was in town. They lived on Socorro's outskirts, along Highway 60, which was where I was heading anyway. When I got there, I was greeted inside by Amy and took a seat on the couch while she went to the kitchen to prepare us both lunch. Amy was on the phone with Marcus, who was on his way over to meet me. Her two young children were running around the house and screaming their heads off, stopping every couple of minutes to give me weird looks. Amy finally walked into the living room and handed me a BLT, which I decided to put into my saddlebag for later. We then sat there for about twenty minutes, carrying some casual conversation while waiting for Marcus to arrive.

We walked outside when Marcus got there, and he seemed rather excited to see me. He asked which way I would be riding out of there, and I pointed towards the mountains to the west. He nodded and said, "Just keep your eye out for mountain lions. I go hiking back there every weekend, and I always see them. Never had any problems, but you wouldn't want one to sneak up on you." I thought it would be cool to see one, so I was happy to hear he'd seen them often. After being there for an hour, I told them it was time for me to get back on the road. I hopped on my bike to leave when Marcus shouted from the front porch, "Oh! I meant to give you this!" He ran up to me with something in his hand, so I stuck mine out to take whatever it was. Marcus smiled and said, "This is some strong stuff, man. Use it sparingly." I opened my hand and saw he'd given me a fat blunt packed with some quality bud. I laughed and said, "Thanks, man! I'll hang onto this for emergencies!"

As I was riding through the mountains between towns, a small car sped past and slammed on its brakes. I immediately stopped riding and waited to see what the person was doing. I saw the man look at me through the rear glass and then reached for something from the passenger seat. The car then switched into reverse and slowly began backing towards me. I didn't know what to expect from people at that point, but I was beginning to feel a bit uneasy. The car then came to a stop, and the driver's door swung open. I looked around to think about what I was going to do if this guy pulled a gun on me, but the only protection I had was my bike. The man then stepped out onto the road, and I noticed he had a camera in his hand. I looked up to the sky in relief and eased up the grip I had on my handlebars. "Are you Jake?" the man asked with a big smile on his face. It turned out, he was a reporter for Socorro and wanted to do a story on me. He went ahead and took my picture but had to run back to his house to grab his recorder for the interview. I told him I was going to continue riding, but he could catch up if he wanted.

By the time the reporter had caught back up with me, I was taking a break in front of the fire station in Magdalena. Even though I'd been waiting for him for a while, he thought it was unbelievable that I'd rode twenty miles in under an hour, through mountainous terrain and at such a high altitude. Around that time, I'd also noticed some obvious improvement to my endurance and realized that I rarely felt tired anymore, and I certainly didn't feel sore. The reporter then pulled out his tape recorder and began asking all the usual questions. I probably sounded like I had no interest in talking with him, but only because I felt like I was on repeat with everyone. It was just the same conversation over and over again, but I tried to make it seem fresh to people when I talked to them. Once we felt like he had enough for his report, he said he would let me know when it would be in the paper, and then we parted ways.

I still had about an hour of daylight left, so I stopped by a local store to fill up on water before continuing. As I was riding along, the sun had set, but I decided to keep going until midnight. The moon was high, there was zero traffic, and the sky was clear with the stars in full show. I thought the view couldn't get any better, but then I reached the top of a mountain, and it was like someone had painted the universe. I was so amazed that I decided to look for a place to camp on top of the mountain. It wasn't hard to find a spot. I walked about fifty feet from the road and went over a small hill, where I found a soft patch of grass that offered the perfect viewpoint. I set my tent up and got everything ready for bed. Then I took the blunt and sandwich Amy and Marcus had given me and took a seat on a rock to enjoy them. My mind drifted away into the galaxy. Some time had passed, and I was ready to turn in for the night. I stood up to walk back to my tent, but I had a hard time walking. Marcus wasn't kidding when he said he'd given me a potent strain. I got a case of the giggles when I had to crawl on my hands and knees back to my tent, which was only a few feet away.

The next morning, I packed up and continued heading west as usual. After a few hours of riding, I came across a bunch of satellites that were scattered across the desert. I wondered what they were until I finally saw the Very Large Array sign. I knew I'd seen this place in books and movies before but had no idea it was between Datil and Socorro. The road back to the visitor center looked to be about five miles long, which was a bit out of the way, but I figured it would be worth checking out. I had to cross a cattle guard to follow the road up to the visitor center and saw several cows in the field around it. I continued my way down the dirt road, hoping I wouldn't have to deal with any bulls. I finally reached the gate without any problems, though. However, when I made it up to the gate, I realized the visitor center was closed. I had hoped to get a tour, but I still thought it was cool to get some pictures from the outside.

After I had made my way back onto the highway, I ran into a couple from Germany. They were also on bikes and were riding from Las Vegas, NV to Dallas, TX. They were hoping to check out the VLA as well, but I saved them the extra miles. They were curious as to why I was heading west instead of east. Supposedly, most cyclists prefer to ride from west to east to avoid the headwinds. That made sense to me because some days were so windy that I would be forced to walk my bike or even pedal when going downhill. It was never fun having to walk my bike down a mountain after I'd finished struggling to make it to the top. They thought I was crazy for riding west, so it blew their mind when I told them I was heading for Alaska.

I made it into Datil around 4:00 p.m. and decided to stop by the gas station. There was a sign outside promoting fresh barbeque, so I made my way in to see what they offered. I walked in and didn't see anyone, so I made my way over to the section where the grill was. I then noticed a sign sitting on the counter that read, "Closed until Spring." Reading that made my stomach turn in knots. I looked around to see if they had any deli sandwiches for sale, but there was nothing but junk food. As I was making my way out the door, I heard a man's voice ask, "Can I help you?" The cashier had been in the back but came to the front just in time. I replied, "I was just looking to buy some food, but I've already noticed your kitchen is closed for the winter. How far to the next restaurant?" The man laughed and replied, "You're not going to find anything for quite a while. All the restaurants around here have closed for the winter. You might have some luck in Pie Town, but I wouldn't hold my breath." Although the man hadn't been of much help, I thanked him anyway and got back on the road.

I made it about ten miles from Pie Town when I decided I'd best start looking for a place to sleep. I noticed a small gravel pull-off on the side of the road and a large tree just on the other side of that. I made my way around the tree and saw something had recently crushed the grass. There were two rectangular patches imprinted on the ground, so I bet that those two German cyclists had camped there the night before. I figured if it was good enough for them, then it was good enough for me. I only had about fifteen minutes of daylight left, so I immediately set up my tent and crawled inside. A few hours later, I had fallen into a deep sleep, but it wouldn't last until morning.

I was awakened around 3:00 a.m. by how cold it had gotten. I was a warm sleeper, but I wasn't expecting it to drop down to five degrees that night. I then sat up and began searching through my things, looking for my extra base layers. As I was digging around, I realized how bright everything was even though I wasn't wearing my headlamp. Almost bright as day. I said to myself, "I don't remember there being a streetlamp out here? No way." I finished putting on my warmer clothes and popped my head out to see where the light was coming from. I looked up and saw the moon, the brightest I think I'd ever seen it. I supposed that would explain why the animals were so noisy that night. I probably heard at least one of every animal that was native to New Mexico. I then climbed out of my tent and began doing a round of exercises to get warmed up. Just before I was about to break into a sweat, I dove back into my sleeping bag and sealed in enough body heat to last until morning.

At the crack of dawn, I was back on the move. After about ten miles, I'd finally crossed the Continental Divide Trail at an elevation of 7,796 feet. I knew I wasn't far from Pie Town because I'd heard stories from CDT hikers, saying they'd stop in Pie Town and grab a slice of pie. As I made my way into what looked like another ghost town, I noticed a couple of people walking in and out of a convenience store. I made my way inside, hoping to get a slice of pie and a cup of coffee. I was a little disappointed to find out they only made pies during the summer, but they did have coffee and hot food. After finishing my breakfast, I made my way outside and crossed the street to use the outhouse. As I was walking my bike back to the road, I looked down at the frozen mud and saw a line of bear tracks. It looked like a mother bear and her two cubs had recently passed through there. However, I didn't think they were still anywhere nearby.

As the sun was going down the next day, I'd reached the top of my last mountain in New Mexico. I watched the sun land on Arizona and was excited to know I'd almost finished another state. I wanted to get as close as I could, so I would have an early start in a new state, so I continued riding into the night. I probably put down an extra fifteen miles before pulling over on the side of the road. The land had flattened out quite a bit, so when I noticed a hill that I could hide behind, I made my way over it. I then saw a sleeping pad and sleeping bag lying on the ground. They looked almost brand new, but I knew whoever had been there was nowhere around. I could see for miles in any direction, and I would've noticed a person. I thought it was kind of strange that anyone would dessert these things. Perhaps something had happened to them. However, that was the best sleeping spot around, which was probably why the other person had slept there, so I wasn't going anywhere. I tossed my gear down next to it and crawled into my sleeping bag, waking every hour or so to make sure no one had returned for their things.

I woke the next morning and began making my way for that Arizona sign. By lunchtime, I was about five miles from the state line and came across a small rest stop with a few parking spots, a couple of trash cans, and a few picnic tables. I was out of food, so I began looking through the trash, hoping to find something that looked edible. The only thing I found was some french fries, but they looked like they'd been there for about a week, and I wasn't that desperate. When I threw the french fries back into the trash, a large van pulled over. It was a large family that looked like they were probably on vacation. The woman in the passenger seat rolled down her window and called me over. I walked up to her as she held out a can of ravioli and a box of crackers. They must have seen me digging through the trash and thought they would stop to help. I pulled two one-dollar bills from my wallet and offered to pay them for the food, but they refused to take it. I thanked them for the help and took my donated food back to the picnic table. I must have been hungrier than I thought because, by the time I'd finished, there was not even a crumb left. I was feeling good, though. My energy levels shot back up, and I was ready to take on Arizona.

Arizona

After several hours of pedaling through the canyons, I'd finally made it to Arizona! As I approached the state sign to get my picture, I noticed two state troopers parked beside it. They then stepped out of their vehicle and made their way over to me. "Where you headed," one of them asked. I could tell by his voice that he wished he could be out traveling himself, so I perked up and elaborated on my plans of making it to Alaska. Both officers seemed to be interested in hearing more, but my attention quickly returned to the fact that I was starving. "How far to the nearest restaurant," I asked with my hand pushing into my growling stomach. The second officer then pointed west and said, "Springerville will be your best bet. It's not too far." So, I thanked them both and picked up my pace to continue my search for food.

I made it into town about three hours later and went into the first restaurant I saw. I took a seat and began looking over the menu. Once I saw the display picture of one of their hamburgers, my mouth began to water, so I reached into my wallet to see if I had enough to cover it. My stomach knotted up when I realized I didn't, so I got the idea to ask the manager if he'd mind me washing dishes to pay for my meal. Thankfully, he accepted my offer and even had the cook put two beef patties on my sandwich instead of one. They also loaded my plate with more fries than I could stomach, but I appreciated it! I was also able to finish washing the dishes in about twenty minutes, so when the manager offered me more work, I figured I had plenty of time to spare. I then followed him outside, and he pointed over to a pile of logs, "I'll give you a hundred dollars to split and stack my firewood." Of course, I agreed to it, and it only took about an hour to finish. I then felt as though I'd made enough money to stretch for a while and got back on the move.

It wasn't long after I'd left Springerville when I found myself in the next small town of Eagar. As I was pedaling through, it almost reminded me of my hometown, so I decided to take some backroads and ride through the neighborhoods. I eventually came across a firehouse and remembered reading somewhere that a hiker had gone into one once and could get a shower, so I thought I'd try it. When I walked inside, I saw a lady who was mopping the floor. I asked her if they had a shower I could use. She asked, "Are you one of those hiker guys?" I told her she had made a pretty good guess and then explained what I was doing exactly. She then showed me to the washhouse, which looked as though it had gone unused for about a year. There were spider webs everywhere, dried dirt on the shower floor, and a bar of soap that had dried out and split apart from sitting there for ages. I didn't mind any of that, though. As long as I had a little privacy and some running water, I wouldn't complain. About halfway through my shower, I reached out to pull my clothes in with me. I didn't know the next time I'd be able to do my laundry, so I made sure to take advantage of it.

With my clothes hanging all over my bike to dry, it was time to find a place to camp. I quickly noticed a water tower on top of a hill and decided to see if it looked like a good place to set up my tent. Once I'd made it to the top, I realized the water tower's location was inside of a cemetery, and I had just wasted a lot of time getting to it because I could have taken a paved road. Anyway, following the rugged dirt-trail helped to make things interesting. I then stopped to think it was kind of strange to put a water tower in a cemetery, but I figured it would probably be a safe place to camp because I didn't see any other people.

Satisfied with using the cemetery to camp in, I sat up my tent against the metal fence that surrounded the water tower and crawled inside. After about thirty minutes of lying in my sleeping bag, I heard what sounded like people laughing. I stuck my head out of my tent and saw a teenage couple walking around in the graveyard, flirting with one another. They noticed me about the same time I noticed them, and they decided to get leave. I was nothing for them to worry about, but it was probably unusual for them to see someone camping up there. I had a bit of a laugh at what they were probably thinking and turned back over to try and get some sleep.

I woke early the next morning to the sound of idling trucks and the voices of men talking to one another. I crawled out of my tent and saw several construction workers had gathered up there for breakfast. I felt a bit awkward as I began packing up my things, but who were they to judge? Who camps in a cemetery? Who eats breakfast in one? I guess we all had a reason to feel out of place, but this was probably a regular meet-up spot for them. I then finished getting my things together and began making my way for the next town of St. Johns.

As I was riding between towns, I decided to take a break in the Lyman Lake State Park. I'd been riding along a creek for a while, so I decided to stop and explore it. I began following the slow-moving water and kept my eyes peeled for animal tracks. I saw a few coyote footprints and then felt a change in the air pressure. The sky was clear, but I knew that feeling meant rain was on the way. I was still a few hours from St. Johns, so I hopped on my bike and tried to beat the storm. Luckily, the rain held off just until I was making it into town. My first impression of St. Johns was that it looked deserted. I saw a few houses, but I wasn't seeing any people, and there was junk scattered all over the place.

As I continued making my way farther into town, I realized it wasn't as empty as I had thought. The town actually had a population of about three thousand people, but the outskirts looked unpromising. Since a storm was moving in and it was going to be dark soon, I began searching for a place to sleep. I continued through town and began heading west on Highway 180 for a couple of miles before I came across a church with a large parking lot. It looked like I might be able to hide from everyone there, so I made my way to the back of the building. I then noticed a hidden corridor that led to the church's back door, so I pushed my bike inside to take refuge from the upcoming storm. Strong winds came whipping through just after lying my bike down. The trees around the church began to sway wildly. I sat there for a while, watching the storm intensify and feeling lucky that I'd found a safe place to keep dry. As the storm began to weaken, I pulled out my sleeping bag and slid inside to get some sleep.

Although the storm had passed, it was still pouring rain when I woke the next morning. Since I didn't care to ride in it, I decided to charge my electronics from one of the church's power outlets while waiting for the weather to clear up. By the time my batteries had enough juice to last me a while, the rain had backed off, so I began making my way for the Petrified Forest. That was only about a forty-five-mile ride, which I could have traveled in no time, but I had decided to slow down and enjoy my loneliness.

By the time I'd reached the Petrified Forest welcome center, it was just beginning to get dark. I made my way inside of the welcome center to use the restroom and to ask about camping somewhere on their property. The lady working at the cash register said I could stay inside one of the tepees located near the side of the building. I went outside and pushed my bike over to one of the tepees, which was about twenty feet tall and made of plywood that had traditional paintings all over it. There were benches along the inside walls, but the floor was just dirt. I figured that should work well for the night, so I tossed my sleeping pad and sleeping bag down on the ground and settled in for the night. I was awakened a few hours later by the loud sound of a thunder's roll. The rain had begun to flood the floor, and the wind was causing the tepee to shake and creak. A few loose boards were sitting on the ground, so I took them and laid them across two of the benches, making myself a raised platform where I could sleep without getting wet.

The next morning, even though I was cold, wet, and covered in mud, I was excited to go through the Petrified Forest. As I made my way to the entrance gate, the chain on my bike broke. I didn't have any extra links and was about twenty miles from the nearest town that might have some. I wasn't going to let that stop me from enjoying my day, so I decided to walk my bike through the park. I pushed my bike up to the gate and realized there was an entrance fee. I already knew I would have to buy another bike chain and needed to watch what I spent, so I turned back around and went to use the restroom at the welcome center. When I walked inside, a different lady was working at the cash register from the night before. I walked past her and towards the restroom when she stopped me and said, "I'm sorry, but I can't let you use the restroom." When I asked her why, she replied, "I know how all of you traveling types are. You're going to go in there and get all cleaned up and make a big mess." My face scrunched as I thought of how I wanted to reply to that. "Ma'am, I just need to pee. I'm not going to make a mess. I used the restroom here last night, and I didn't do anything, did I?" She gave me a dirty look and said, "I don't care what you did last night. I wasn't the one working. I'm going to have to ask you to leave." I couldn't believe she had talked to me like that. Just because I was a traveler, she assumed I had no common decency or self-respect. I walked outside and said to myself, "Okay. If you want to treat me like an animal, then I'm going to act like one." I then proceeded to relieve myself on the side of their building.

I then made my way back to the road and began pushing my bike towards the town of Holbrook. I'd only made it halfway before dark and slept behind an old billboard. I continued walking before sunrise and was on the outskirts of town by noon. A large white truck pulled up next to me, and the old cowboy in the driver seat, Elliot, leaned past his wife and asked if I needed a ride. I told him that I thought I had everything under control but wondered if he knew where I might be able to find a chain for my bike. Elliot and his wife began talking amongst themselves. He then looked back at me again and said, "You might have some luck at Walt's Hardware. We can give you a ride there and get you a bite to eat if you're interested." He seemed persistent at trying to do me a favor, so I took them up on their offer. I tossed my bike into the back, and we made our way to the hardware store. They only had one bike chain to choose from, and it was the wrong size. The man working at the hardware store said I could have it for free since it had been there forever, and he didn't think anyone would ever buy it. That sounded fair to me because missing a cog every few turns would still be faster than walking. I walked outside and began preparing my bike to install the new chain. While I was doing that, Elliot and his wife left to pick up our lunch. They said there was a park up the road with picnic tables where I could meet up with them in about thirty minutes. I figured that would be enough time to finish working on my bike and get over there. I limped my bike through town and slowly made my way to the park. Not long after I'd made it, the couple arrived and brought with them fried chicken, mashed potatoes, corn on the cob, and cornbread. I must have looked like I was starving because Elliot's wife handed me a plate large enough for two people, which I finished. It was nice taking a break to eat and have some casual conversation with the friendly couple.

The next thirty miles into Winslow weren't too bad. The new chain had worked well enough to keep me going downhill, but I decided it would be best to walk it the rest of the time. I finally reached a Love's truck stop just after dark. I waited near the entrance, watching the trucks' headlights shine in various directions. Once I noticed a spot that never got hit by any lights, I made my way into the shadow and set up camp for the night. The next morning, I crawled out of my tent to see a dense fog. I didn't think it would be very wise to take my bike down the interstate with such poor visibility, so I went inside the gas station and enjoyed a cup of coffee while I waited for better conditions.

After the fog had lifted, I continued west and made my way into Meteor City just before dark. I noticed a large dream catcher just off the highway, so I made my way over to it. It looked as though someone had put it together out of a trampoline's frame and some ropes. When I stood inside it and looked through the center hole, I noticed a tunnel running underneath the highway. I then made my way over to the tunnel and decided I'd sleep there for the night. The loud echo was almost deafening when vehicles passed over, but there weren't very many places to go unseen out there.

It wasn't long after I'd left Meteor City that I could see Mt. Humphrey's Peak in Flagstaff. It was nice to have a landmark to lead me in, but judging by the mountain's size, I probably still had about forty miles to go. I ended up walking through the night and made it into Flagstaff by morning. As soon as I got off the interstate and took the exit into town, a police officer pulled me over. He'd seen me come in off the interstate and was curious about what I was doing. However, he didn't seem to believe me until after he'd ran my driver's license and saw that I didn't have any warrants. I then continued into town and was enveloped by what appeared to be a friendly community. I entered the first bike shop I came across and had them slap on a new chain. After I had my bike fixed up, it was time for lunch, and I was in the mood for some Mexican food. As I was eating my taco and sipping on a Corona, I decided to contact the company that made my sleeping bag. The zipper had busted off the one I was using, and it was still under warranty. It would take a few days for the new one to arrive, but I felt like Flagstaff would be a good place to wait.

I'd posted on my Facebook Page that I would be in Flagstaff for a couple of days. One of my followers, Skip, was in the area and said he'd like to get me a motel for the night. I rode across town to meet up with him at a Motel 6. He didn't stick around for long but seemed happy to help. I probably looked tired and dirty, and he likely just wanted to give me all the time I needed to get myself together. I really appreciated the help, though. I knew a warm shower would help soothe my muscles, and having clean clothes would help me fit in a little better during my time in the town.

After I got all cleaned up, I crawled into bed and turned on the television. I began flipping through the channels, and nothing I landed on could compare to the excitement of life on the road, so it didn't take long for me to start feeling bored. As I was just sitting there with nothing to distract my mind, I began to feel lonely. The shower I'd just taken had also rejuvenated all my energy, so I began to crave something exciting. That's when I had the idea to create a profile on a dating site. I didn't really think I'd have any luck, but I felt like I would enjoy the company if I did. Surprisingly, within the next hour, a beautiful Latina woman sent me a message. I was very blunt about what I was looking for, which I thought would probably only hurt my chances, but she didn't seem to mind how open I was and agreed to meet up. It was a bit awkward when she first got there because I'd never been the type of guy to just hook up with a woman, but I'd never been alone for that long either.

The next morning, I was riding around downtown Flagstaff when I ran into a guy named Gabriel. He was kind of like me, in the fact that he was a traveler on a bike. He said he had been living in Flagstaff for a few months with a few other cyclists, though they traveled all over the country. After talking with him for a bit, he asked where I was staying while in town. When I told him that I hadn't had the time to scope out the area yet, he offered to show me some spots he'd recommend. I thought that sounded like a good idea, so he took off, and I followed him. We began making our way northwest until we were on the outskirts of the city, riding along a dirt-trail near the Lowell Observatory. As we began riding deeper into the forest, I started to fall in love with the area. It was hard to believe such a beautiful and dense forest was only a few miles outside the city limits. It was reassuring to know I had a quick escape from the city, should it become too much for me. Gabriel decided to head back to town after riding for an hour, but I chose to stay in the forest for a while longer.

As the sun was beginning to set, I decided it was time to make my way out of the forest and back down into the city. A man named Jody was driving up from Phoenix to hang out with me for his birthday. He had been following my journey ever since I'd first started in Maryland. It felt as though we'd become friends since then, as we were always joking around in the comments of my posts and would occasionally message one another. Once I made it into town, Jody sent me a message and asked if I'd like to meet up at Pizza Hut. I told him that sounded great and made it there thirty minutes before he did. As I sat there waiting for him to arrive, I decided to go ahead and grab a beer to help pass the time. There was no mistaking him when he walked through the door. He was a large biker guy with long, wild hair and a matching beard. He had a huge, welcoming grin on his face too, so I knew I was in good company. He'd also brought along his wife, Lisa, and twin grandchildren, Jake and Makayla. They all thought it was cool to meet me because I was kind of like a celebrity to them. I'm sure hearing Jody talk about me all the time is what made them feel that way.

While Lisa and her grandchildren focused on eating their pizza, Jody and I continued drinking beer and talked about everything I had been through up to that point. Typically, I tried to avoid conversations about my travels, but I was excited to tell

Jody about everything, including the things I hadn't told anyone else yet. As I was carrying on, Jody said he'd always wanted to do something like what I was doing and admired me for taking the initiative. I was both sad and happy to hear him say that. I wished he'd been able to do it himself, but I was happy that I'd been able to allow other people to travel vicariously through me. I knew watching me was the closest some people would ever get to being able to do it themselves. It was bittersweet as we were getting ready to part ways. Jody and his family had been great company, but they had to get back home, and I had my journey to continue. We left the restaurant and walked out to the parking lot for a group photo. Then, just before leaving, Jody walked over to his truck and pulled out a large bag of food. There was way too much for me to carry, so I figured I would share some with Gabriel. I knew he was around there somewhere, probably dumpster diving. I then wished Jody a happy birthday and told them to have a safe trip back to Phoenix.

I didn't have much energy after I parted ways with Jody, so I pushed my bike down the street until I found a large bush I could hide behind. I tossed my sleeping gear on the ground, and that was the end of my night. The next morning, I made my way to the UPS store so that I could pick up my new sleeping bag. Ironically, I ran into Gabriel while I was there and gave him a few handfuls of food from the bag Jody had given me. He then asked if I'd like to come over and have dinner with his "family" later in the afternoon. I said that I would love to, but he told me they were a bit skeptical of strangers. He would have to check with them first but was sure it would okay. I gave him my number and told him to give me a call when he found out. In the meantime, I took off to spend my time in the woods, relaxing and enjoying the tranquility.

Gabriel finally called and asked if I could meet up with him back at the UPS store, and then I could follow him to his house. So, I hurried back into town, and there he was. Before we started for his house, he warned me that the people he lived with were a little strange. As we were riding along, I wondered what he could have meant by that. I thought everyone was strange, including myself, and probably myself more so than others.

We finally made it to his house, and I realized what he meant. They were indeed different in the fact that they were an Amish-like group of people. I would describe them as being between Amish, hippies, and nomads. I didn't think they were strange, but I did find them to be unique and exciting. I wasn't entirely sure what their motive was, but they seemed to be nice and modest. As far as I could tell, about fifteen of them lived together, and they had all come from different walks of life. Adults and children alike, the women wore plain white dresses, and the men wore canvas aprons.

As I sat there wondering what they all did for work, it didn't take long for me to figure it out without asking. It was apparent they were running an underground bike shop from their home, but the town was trying to shut them down. I wasn't sure why they couldn't go about running their shop legally, but I felt it would be too invasive for me to ask. However, I did ask where they would go if they lost their house, and Gabriel replied, "Wherever the road takes us. That's how we wound up here. We've been traveling and doing this bike shop gig for about ten years now." Everyone there only traveled by bicycle, including the children. They cycled all over the country with the adults and were home-schooled. I was curious about how well that had been working for the kids, but I would soon see for myself. One of the younger boys, who was around six years old, took me outside to show me his hydrogen generator, which he created to help power his bike. Whenever I told him I was impressed with his work, he said he was envious of my trek to Alaska. He had always wanted to run away to Alaska and live off the land. I'd say he was even a bit obsessed with the idea. He had all kinds of 3D maps and places marked that would work best in his favor.

Dinner was ready to be served, but they had strict rules regarding how they went about their meals. I didn't want to be disrespectful or interrupt how they normally did things, so Gabriel told me to follow along. First, we let the women and children get their food. Then the men could get whatever was left, starting from oldest to youngest. Once we were all ready to eat, the men had to face away from the women. That was the only thing that I thought was strange, but I enjoyed experiencing something different. After we'd finished dinner, the men brought out a couple of guitars and bongo drums. The younger ones began singing and dancing, while the women began tidying up the house before getting ready for bed. Gabriel then came up to me and said I was welcome to camp in their back yard, so I accepted his offer and made my way outside to set up my tent.

The next morning, the oldest man, who was probably in his mid-60s, came outside to see if I was awake. It was still dark out, which was normal for me, but I was a little surprised that he came to wake me up so early. I left my tent and followed the older man back into the house. Even more surprisingly, everyone else had already left except for the older man and one of the younger women. Before leaving the room, the older man told me to have a seat at the kitchen table, and the woman began making me breakfast. I didn't notice any other dishes and wondered if everyone else had already eaten. It felt a little awkward to assume she was making breakfast just for me, but if that was the case, then I figured I should accept their kindness. However, I felt a bit unsure of being left alone with her, as they seemed to be very particular about how the men acted around the women, although I had no intentions other than being a good guest.

The woman handed me a plate with four sausage links, a bagel cut in half, two fried eggs, and a spoonful of almond butter, which I'd never had before. I told the woman I had seen almond butter in grocery stores, but I never cared to try it because it was so expensive. She laughed and replied, "That's why we make our own! It's delicious, isn't it?" I thought it was incredible, so she handed me a small jar to take with me on the road. After breakfast, I thanked the woman for her generosity and told her to relay that to everyone else. Then, I made my way outside to gather my things and decided to head off into the forest.

I began riding along the trails that I had taken the last time I had been out there, but after I'd gone about five miles from town, I decided to get off my bike and go for a walk. I reached into my saddlebag and pulled out my collapsible backpack, carrying only some essentials. I then hid my bike inside some bushes not too far from the trail and began hiking into the forest. The air was cold, with gray skies, and the wind was just heavy enough to make the tops of the trees bend slightly. Light snow began to fall and added just a pinch of surrealness. As I continued walking, I had noticed a multitude of wildlife. I saw several birds and squirrels, a fox, a badger, a couple of rabbits, a skunk, a coyote, and even a small herd of antelope. I had not seen another human since leaving the city and felt at one with the animals. It was a very peaceful feeling and one that I thought I needed. As darkness settled, I found a perfect spot for my tent and crawled inside, cherishing my discovered sense of freedom. However, the reality was that danger could be lurking about, so, just in case, I slept with my bear spray and bowie knife lying within reach.

I made my way back into town the next morning and stopped by a coffee shop. It wasn't just about the coffee this time, though. For some odd reason, I wanted to be surrounded by people. I supposed that it should be a normal feeling, but it was often a problem for me because of my PTSD. I made my way inside the coffee shop and felt it had a relaxing atmosphere, so I bought a drink and took a seat to enjoy the presence of other people. As I was sitting there, I noticed a man sitting across from me was acting very strange. He had wild, frizzy hair with an anxious look in his eye and appeared to be arguing with himself. I was about to ask if he was okay when a woman sat in the seat next to him. He completely changed his attitude and began awkwardly flirting with the woman. She was quickly put off by his behavior and left. After the lady left, the man then went back to acting crazy again, so I decided just to let him be.

After finishing my cup, I made a quick run to the restroom before going back outside to get on my bike. I then saw a note that someone had stuck to my seat. The note read, "You remind me of my son." And underneath the note was a twenty-dollar bill. I looked around to see who could have left it, but I didn't see anyone I thought would have. Before getting on my bike to leave, I stuck the money in my wallet and thanked whoever had left it.

I left the coffee shop and began making my way towards Mt. Humphrey's Peak. I'd been thinking about hiking it for the past few days and couldn't wait any longer. The closer I got, the bigger the mountain seemed to get. Although the size wasn't a problem, I began to feel a little intimidated because of how much snow and ice there was on the top. I finally made it to the base of the mountain and began pedaling up the road towards the ski area. I thought I was in excellent shape, but the steep climb and low oxygen levels had me stopping every few minutes to catch my breath. I'd finally made it about halfway, and the snow had begun to pile up in the forest, though the road had been kept mostly clear. About a mile later, I made my way around a large curve and noticed there had been an accident. I immediately recognized it was a silver Nissan Altima, just like the one I used to have. It looked as though the car had slid off the road and smacked into the guard rail. The driver was fine, but the front of the car was smashed in pretty bad. As I walked past the accident, I had a strange feeling come over me, as if this was the reason why something had happened to my car.

I'd finally made it to the ski lodge and walked inside. I asked the manager if there was anywhere to keep my bike while I left to hike up the mountain. He looked at me for a moment and asked, "You're hiking up? Do you have a permit?" I replied, "A permit? Why would I need a permit for that?" He went on to say that I could purchase a backcountry permit online, but it might take a few days for the application to go through. At that point, I knew I wasn't going to be getting any permit and would just have to risk getting a citation. I understood rules were in place for a reason, but I didn't have the time or money to waste on something so fruitless.

I made my way back outside and noticed the park rangers building on the other side of the parking lot. I walked over to the building and knocked on the front door. No one answered. I stood there for a moment, trying to think of where I could hide my bike. I looked up and got the idea to climb a tree and strap my bike to the top. Then, I heard a man ask, "Can I help you?" The park ranger had just gotten back from a patrol, and I asked if I could keep my bike behind his building while I hiked up the mountain. The ranger thought he had a better idea and said I could keep it inside of his building. He then asked, "How long are you planning to be gone for?" I figured I would be back down by the next day, but I told him three days in case I decided to stay longer. "Do you have crampons," the ranger asked, "There's a lot of ice at the top." I didn't have any crampons with me, but I didn't want that to deter him from helping me out, so I said I did. He looked at me for a moment, probably trying to remember my face should I not return, and told me to have fun.

After grabbing my backpack and a few items, I proceeded to the trailhead. As I approached the forest, I saw a sign that read, "backcountry permit required beyond this point." I looked around and didn't see anyone, so I shrugged my shoulders and continued onto the path. The snow was knee-deep, and I didn't have any snowshoes, so it was more physically demanding than I had expected. I also hadn't been able to make out where the trail was for quite a while, but I didn't need any trail to tell me which way was up. As I was sure I was creating my own path through the forest, it felt as though I was making pretty good time, but there would be no way to know for sure until I made it above the tree line. It got dark before I could make it out of the forest, so I decided to camp. I had opted for my tarp instead of my tent because I wanted to shed weight. Since there was so much snow, I decided to dig a hole and use it as insulation. After I'd carved out a makeshift den, I tossed my sleeping bag inside and dug a trench around it to act as a cold sink. Then, I tossed my tarp over the hole and kept it in place with heavy branches. Ready to enter my cramped icebox for the night, I crawled in through the small opening at the foot of the tarp.

I woke a few hours later to the sound of heavy footsteps crushing through the snow nearby. I thought it might be a person until I heard branches snapping, which did not sound human. I knew that I had wandered into black bear territory, and I had a feeling that's what I was hearing. I stayed as quiet and still as possible. I figured if it were a bear, it would probably pass right by and make its way to the small bag of snacks I had hung in a tree about thirty yards away. As the steps sounded to get closer, I began to worry that whatever was heading in my direction might accidentally step onto my tarp and come crashing down on top of me. Whatever it was, it stepped on the branches that were holding down my tarp, and then it stopped. I grabbed my twelve-inch hunting knife in one hand and bear spray in the other, preparing to fight for my life. Then, the footsteps continued deeper into the forest, and I felt like I could breathe again. My adrenaline wore off about thirty minutes later, and I was able to go back to sleep.

I woke the next morning and immediately checked to see what had come through. Sure enough, there were black bear tracks all around. I packed up and made my way over to my food cache. The tracks were leading me straight to it. I had a feeling my food would be gone, but then I could see the bag was still hanging. The bear had come around to check it out, but everything was still there. The footprints went back and forth from the tree and the bag several times. Luckily, I had tied the anchor to a different tree, which probably confused the bear because it looked like it knew what it was looking for. I then took my food down, shoved it into my pack, and began making my way for the peak.

After hiking for about an hour, I spotted the bear that had come around the night before. It hadn't noticed me yet, so I yelled at it, hoping it would bolt the other way. The bear heard me and took off. However, it ended up running in the same direction that I was heading. As I followed the bear with my eyes, I noticed it had come out to a clearing and continued running into the forest on the other side. Curiously, I walked to the edge of the forest and looked up and down the long, empty path. I guessed that there had been an avalanche, but it didn't look to have happened recently. I then looked up towards the mountain, and it didn't appear as though another avalanche was likely, so I began following the clearing towards the top.

As I made it closer to the peak of the mountain, I noticed a large piece of metal. I wondered what it was and why it was there, but I saw another piece before I had time to come up with an idea. I then passed by several more pieces and realized I was looking at the wing of an airplane. I noticed that I had service on my phone, so I decided to do some research. I discovered that a B-24 had crashed on Mt. Humphrey's Peak back in 1944, and the accident took the lives of all eight crewmen. I also read that a lot of people would go looking for the site, but most of them had a hard time finding it. I just so happened to stumble across it by accident. I felt privileged, but at the same time, I felt sadness for them and their families. I then said a few words for the lost and continued hiking my way to the top.

It wasn't long after the wreckage that I had reached an elevation of about 11,500 feet. Not only was there less oxygen, but the terrain became much more difficult. The snow was deeper, the slope is steeper, and there were huge ice-covered boulders that I had to maneuver around. I needed to stop and catch my breath, so I decided to take a seat on one of the large rocks. As I sat facing down the mountain, I realized that if I fell, then I'd be done for. If I did fall, I knew I would be in for a long ride, slamming into rocks and trees on my way down. I turned to look back at the top of the mountain, and it didn't look like I had much further to go, so I gathered myself and continued to climb.

As I made my way up and around the icy boulders, I heard something that sounded like a snake hissing. However, I knew I was too high up, and it was too cold for any snakes. Perhaps it was just the wind hitting my ear at a weird angle, I thought. I then continued to step over another boulder and heard the hissing sound again. However, that time, something had hit me in the face. Whatever it was, it was wet and had a red tinge to it. I then had the immediate sensation that my face was on fire. I stumbled back, nearly falling to my death. I couldn't open my eyes, so I felt around for a boulder and sat in the snow behind it so that I wouldn't tumble down the mountain. When I went to sit, I felt something poke my side and heard the hissing sound again. I reached over to see what it was and realized I'd lost the safety switch for my bear spray. I took the bear spray out of my holster and began shoving handfuls of snow into my face, trying to regain my breath and my vision. It took about ten minutes to get my senses back, but I continued making my way to the top with my face still burning.

I'd finally made it to the ridgeline, and it was solid ice. The wind was blowing about fifty miles per hour, strong enough that I began sliding all over the place. Luckily, there were a few rocks and patches of snow that kept me from blowing right off the top. The side that I had come up from was steep and had lots of boulders, and the other side was about a two-hundred-foot drop. However, I hadn't reached the peak yet. I thought I had, but then I noticed small wooden trail markers pointing along the ridge. I followed the signs with my eyes and realized I still had about forty yards to go. I managed to get within fifteen feet of the peak, but I just couldn't reach the top. It was just too steep and too slick. I even tried to cut steps into the ice with my knife, but the ice was rock solid. I'd made it as far as possible, so I was satisfied and stood there to enjoy the view. In either direction, I could see as far as the earth would allow. The sight was beyond beautiful, and I wished I could have camped up there. However, the wind was very intense, and I started to feel the effects of altitude sickness. I sat on top of the mountain for about thirty minutes before heading back down, which initially seemed more treacherous than going up. After I'd reached approximately one-third of the way down, I decided to slide whenever it looked safe.

It took nearly ten hours to reach the top, but I'd made it back down to the ski lodge in only two. I felt hungry after burning all those calories, so I went inside and grabbed myself a slice of pizza and a beer. After finishing my lunch, I went over to the ranger's station to pick up my things. Since the ranger wasn't there, I left a note saying that I had made it back and thanked him for watching over my things. I put everything back into my saddlebags and coasted down the mountain. After about ten minutes, I reached the bottom of the mountain and decided to spend one more night in Flagstaff.

I got into town around noon and decided to stop in and see how much it would be to rent a room at The Canyon Inn. I walked in, and the owner immediately began asking about my bike. After discovering what I was doing, he offered to let me stay a night for free and said I could even come back and join him for dinner later. I thanked him and began walking my bike over to my room. I looked up and saw a young woman sitting in a plastic chair beside the door to my room. As I got closer, the woman said, "Hey, you look like you could use a beer." She pointed towards her room, "You want one?" It was like she could read my mind. I replied, "Sure! Just give me a minute to put this stuff away, and I'll be right back out."

After dropping off my things, I went back outside, and the woman, who had introduced herself as Sarah, handed me a beer. She was short and petite with short curly brown hair and had a southern accent. I thought she might have been from Tennessee, so I asked where she was from. "Texas," she replied, "What about you?" I told her I was from Tennessee, which she had a hard time believing because I didn't have a southern accent. She then wondered why I was in Flagstaff on a bicycle if I was from Tennessee, so I gave her the whole story. When I asked about her, she said she was a fiddle player for a touring band. They had just finished up a show the night before and would be leaving early in the morning to perform at another. I asked if she thought she would do that forever, and she replied, "Nope. Just doing it until I can get a yak farm." That was the first I'd ever heard of anyone dreaming of a yak farm, but she seemed very passionate about it. After talking with her for a bit more, she began gathering her things to make a trip to the grocery store. Before driving away, she popped her head out of her van window and asked if I wanted anything. I jokingly replied, "Get me something exotic." She laughed and gave me a thumbs-up before pulling out of the driveway.

After Sarah left, the owner of the motel came over and told me dinner was ready. I followed him over to the lobby and had a seat. He went to the back for about a minute and came back with two large bowls of soup and some cornbread. We didn't talk much because he had turned on the television to watch a football game. I wasn't too interested in the game, but I did appreciate the food and company anyway. After dinner, I was walking back to my motel room when Sarah pulled up. She hopped out of her van with her hand behind her back and said, "Hey, you told me you wanted something exotic, right?" I nodded, and she threw a can of sour cream and onion flavored chips at me. I looked at the chips and asked, "This is your idea of exotic?" We both had a good laugh about that. Her sense of humor reminded me of my own, which made me feel like I was in good company. We then sat in front of our rooms, where we shared those chips and continued drinking beer, talking the night away.

Feeling rested, I woke the next morning and began making my way for the Grand Canyon. It was perfect weather and only an eighty-mile ride, so I took my time to enjoy it. Since I was going at a leisurely pace, I still had twenty miles to go by dusk. I was riding through tight canyons and debated on whether I should climb up to find a place to camp. Finally, the canyons began to flatten out on the right side, so I slowed down to keep an eye out for a good place to sleep. Just when I thought I'd found a great area to pitch my tent, I turned to look at the canyons on the left side of the road and saw a mountain lion staring down at me. I decided to ride a bit more to put some distance between us. I probably rode another ten miles before finding another opening in the canyons, which I took advantage of and found a place to set up camp.

I woke the next morning at the crack of dawn and continued my ride into the Grand Canyon. As I was getting close to the entrance, I noticed a small store and decided to stop and grab a cup of coffee. I guess the cashier had seen that I came in on a bike and told me I could have the drink for free. I hadn't kept up with what day it was in quite a while, but as I was walking away, she said, "Happy Valentine's Day." I then took my coffee outside and sat on the curb to enjoy it.

After I'd had my coffee, I continued into the Grand Canyon. Traffic had already begun to back up near the entrance, but since I was on a bike, I got to go in for free and zoomed past everyone. I then made my way to the visitor center, where I had my first full view of the Grand Canyon. It was a lot larger than I thought it would be, but I was unmoved by it for some reason. I could see a river at the bottom and wanted to explore it, but I couldn't understand why all the tourists around me were so excited. I went to check the map to see what trails I could take to the bottom. I finally found one on the eastern side and began riding over towards the trailhead. When I got there, I noticed it was seven miles to the bottom. Not wanting to be away from my stuff for too long, I chained my bike to a picnic table and began running down the trail. I made it down in about an hour and wandered around for about four hours before deciding to head back up. I wished I could have stayed down there for a few days, but I was worried someone might steal my bike. I figured the chances in that were slim, but it still had all my gear on it. Even taking the time to run down seemed a bit risky.

Running back to the top sure was a rush, but after I'd reached about a third of the way up, I began to feel the onset of altitude sickness. Once I made it back to my bike, I felt unusually drained. Then, I noticed a sign that read, "Do not attempt to descend and ascend the entire canyon in one day as it can cause health problems." It was a little too late for me, though. Thankfully, I was in excellent shape, so I was able to shake it off within about ten minutes. Once I started to feel better, I decided to go ahead and eat dinner, which was a packet of tuna and a granola bar. After I had finished my meal, I began following the road east to get out of there. It was starting to get late, and I thought about doing some night riding into Cameron, but I noticed a sign that said to watch for mountain lions for the next ten miles, so I decided to wait until morning to continue my ride out of there.

There was still enough daylight left for me to find a comfortable spot to set up camp. I wandered off about a hundred yards from the road and began searching for a good place to sleep. As I walked around in the forest, I found some fresh signs of bear, elk, and mountain lion. I wasn't so sure if I was in the best place to be trying to camp, but it was completely dark by then, and I didn't think it would be any safer trying to find a different spot. For a little added security, I placed my tent to where the back of it was against a large tree. Then I made a barrier around myself, using logs and sticks. I didn't build the wall to keep anything out, but at least I would hear it falling if something got curious enough. Although I did hear a lot of noises throughout the night, nothing ever came around my tent.

Another night had passed, and I was on the move again. As I was riding along, the road brought me close to the Grand Canyon several times. One of those times, I came across a pillar supporting a large rock formation that looked like a duck. The natural structure had been adequately nicknamed "Duck on a Rock," though the power of erosion would likely transform it into something else within the next century. The next thing to grab my attention was a seventy-foot tall cylindrical structure made of stone. I followed along the path leading up to it and discovered it was built in 1932 as a rest stop and observation point. I felt tricked into thinking it may have had more importance, but at least the designer, Mary Colter, did a good job of making it fit into the setting. As I was leaving the Desert View Watchtower, I rode around a curve and saw two large bull elks standing only twenty feet away. They seemed to be content with grazing, but they were in the path of my exit. Although they didn't seem to mind the cars driving right by them, I was skeptical about how they would react to me. I slowly approached them, trying to stay as far to the opposite side of the road as possible, though they were only about ten feet away from the road on the other side. I'd made it halfway between them and the curve when they stopped eating and stared at me. I knew they could be aggressive, but I hoped they wouldn't see me as a threat. About a minute later, they went back to eating, and I was able to pass by them without any problem.

I had made it about twenty miles from the Grand Canyon before dark. As the day was coming to an end, I watched a beautiful sunset, spreading out orange and purple hues over the desert. I continued riding through the night until I made it into the small town of Cameron. It was probably around 11:00 p.m. when I got there, and I was exhausted. I noticed there was a gas station, and to the left of it was a small unoccupied area of land. I figured it would be okay to sleep there, so long as I woke early enough to beat the everyday commuters. Initially, I decided just to throw my sleeping bag onto the ground to keep a low profile. However, after lying there for about an hour, I began feeling a slight tickling sensation on my stomach. I unzipped my sleeping bag and shined my headlamp down towards my torso. I then saw a spider sitting on my chest, so I casually brushed it away and tried to go back to sleep. I continued feeling the tickling sensation, so I looked again, and, to my surprise, I saw hundreds of them all over the inside of my sleeping bag. I jumped up and began brushing myself off, watching the spiders scatter as they landed back onto the ground. After reassuring myself they were all gone, I decided to put my tent up and take a chance with someone telling me to leave. Luckily, no one ever said anything, and I was able to get about four hours of sleep.

The next morning, as I was riding out of town, I approached a bridge that crossed over a dried riverbed. I saw several small caves and crevices, so I made my way down to explore. After checking out nearly twenty caves, I found one that was quite large. I went inside and noticed there was a hole towards the top. I pulled myself into the hole and noticed soot on the walls, indicating there had been several fires inside. Then, I found several spearheads and pieces of petrified wood. I thought about taking one of each of them, but I decided to leave everything as it was because I probably would have lost it anyway. Feeling pleased with my discovery, I made my way back to my bike and continued riding north.

I was beginning to run low on water, so I decided to take a small detour into Tuba City. The road to Tuba City was open desert, unlike the highway I had been riding on, which had hills and canyons. I was about halfway to town when the wind began picking up out of nowhere. Grains of sand began whipping through the air, so I put on my sunglasses and wrapped my face with a bandanna. About two minutes later, and with nowhere to hide, a massive sandstorm came barreling across the desert. It seemed like, within seconds, everything had turned orange, and I couldn't even see ten feet in front of me. I got off my bike and sat on the ground with my back facing the wind, and my only shelter was myself. The sandstorm lasted about fifteen minutes and disappeared as quickly as it had come. I then proceeded into town, where I was able to find a gas station and fill up on my water.

As I was heading back to the highway from Tuba City, my stomach began growling fiercely. I had already gone through the snacks Jody had given me, as well as the small jar of almond butter. As long as I had water, I knew I'd be okay for a while, but I was burning a ton of calories and could feel my body begging for fuel. As I continued to ride, I began craving meat so badly that I thought the shrubs blowing in the wind were either deer or rabbits. After making it back to the main highway, I made it another ten miles before I had about an hour of daylight left. I pulled off the road and made my way to some canyons about a hundred yards away. I set up my tent in what looked to be a good spot and pulled out a few strands of steel wire from my saddlebags. I then curved and twisted the wires to make snares and took them into the desert, placing them along rabbit trails. I ended up setting three rabbit traps, but I was doubtful about catching one since I hadn't seen any out there. I returned to my tent and began gathering old dried sticks and plants. There wasn't a whole lot to collect, but I felt I had enough to cook dinner should I get lucky enough. As darkness fell, I crawled into my tent and nestled in for the night.

It was around 3:00 a.m. when I heard the unmistakable sound of a rabbit that had found its way into a snare. I waited a few minutes for the sound to stop and then made my way over to see my catch. I scoped out the rabbit, and it looked healthy from the outside, so I carried it with me as I collected the other snares. I then walked about a hundred feet from my campsite to dress and inspect the rabbit. Its eyes were bright and crisp, with no sign of fleas or spots on the liver. I left the entrails to the coyotes and brought the meat back to my camp. I then ran one of the steel wires through the rabbit's core and sat it on a bed of sage while I prepared the fire. Once my fire was ready, I tied one end of the wire to a stick, which I'd shoved into the sand, and took the other end with my hand to lead the meat into the fire. Without any seasoning, that rabbit wasn't the best meal, but I appreciated it as I felt my body soaking up the protein. Since the sun would be rising in a couple of hours, I decided to use the rest of that time to get some sleep.

The next day, I continued my ride into Page and got there around midnight. I posted on my blog that I had arrived, and I received a message from one of my followers, Kanani. She said her friend owned a motel in Page and could stay the night there if I wanted. She had already called her friend earlier in the day, so he was waiting for me. I then made my way into the Sleep Ezze motel, where Kanani's friend, Matt, greeted me. He immediately showed me to my room, and I was quite surprised. The outside looked very basic, but the inside seemed nice, complete with a kitchen and living room. I fell asleep shortly after I arrived, so Matt said I could stay one more night to get some laundry done. Around lunchtime, my second day there, he even came by to give me a frozen pizza and a six-pack of beer. After staying there for two nights, I was all cleaned up, rested, and ready to get back on the move.

Shortly after leaving the motel, I came up to a bridge that crossed the Colorado River. I decided to make my way down to the water and walked along the bank. The water was crystal clear, and I wanted to jump in for a swim, but it was still too cold for that. After walking around for about an hour, I decided to see what it was like on the other side of the bridge. I made my way back to the road and noticed a sign that read "Horseshoe Bend ahead." I wondered if the sign referred to the same famous bend that I had seen so many pictures of. It was a bit out of my way, but I decided to go check it out anyway.

I finally reached a small parking area and followed one of the trails towards the river. I eventually made it to the edge of a cliff and looked down to see the amazing Horseshoe Bend! I thought it was queer to stumble across it on accident. It hadn't even occurred to me that its location was in Page, Arizona. I sat and admired the natural beauty, which, of course, was simply a deep U-shape curve within the canyons of the river, but I was impressed by its immense size.

After leaving Horseshoe Bend, I made my way back to the bridge and crossed to the other side. On the right-hand side of the road, I looked up towards the cliffs and saw a cave. It looked as though reaching it would be simple enough, so I decided to park my bike and climb up to check it out. Once I reached the cave, I immediately noticed a lot of graffiti. I'll never understand why people like to ruin these precious parts of our past with their toxic gang signs and vulgarity. Besides the fact that idiots had ruined the cave, it was still a pretty cool find. I could tell it had been well used because there was a lot of soot inside. Looking around, I imagined that living freely along the Colorado River would have been difficult back in the day, but the views alone would be worth it if you could survive.

Utah

It was beginning to get late, but there was still enough light out that I could see the large, blue Utah sign up ahead. Once I'd reached it, I pulled off the side of the road to get my usual picture. As I was getting back onto my bike, I noticed a strange man walking towards me. I'm not sure how I didn't see him sooner, but he looked completely out of place. We were about ten miles from Page, and he didn't have any gear with him. He had no backpack and no water. He only had the clothes on his back, which looked very city-like with his football jersey, long jean shorts, and a flat bill hat that he wore cocked to the side. He was probably within three feet of me and asked, "Sup, dawg? You know where I can get some meth?" I gave him a confused look, wondering if I should take his question seriously. I then replied, "No. I don't have any drugs. Sorry." Before continuing his walk towards Page, the man smacked his lips and said disappointedly, "Awe, you don't? Alright then. You crazy to be out here on a bike." I wondered if he realized how crazy he had looked to me, but I also wondered if I looked like the type of person that would have meth. I surely hoped not.

I continued riding for about five miles until I came across some buttes about a hundred yards from the road. I pushed my bike into the rock formations and climbed to the top of one to set up camp. Nothing but beauty surrounded me in every direction. There were no lights or noises from any city, and I hadn't seen a single vehicle in hours. The sky was clear and full

126

of vibrant stars, and the weather was perfect for my liking, although most people would probably say it was too cold. I would have slept right under the stars, but I was still a bit shaken from being covered with those spiders back in Cameron. I decided to set up my tent without the rainfly, so I could admire the beauty around me but still be safe from the insects.

I woke the next morning and continued riding until about noon. I decided to take a break as I was passing by a large collection of rock formations. I just couldn't help but park my bike and explore the area. There were buttes, caves, and cliffs everywhere, a rock climber's dream. I wished I could sit out there all day but needed to stay on the move to keep up with my water supply. However, I did get to walk around and enjoy myself for a few hours before getting back on the road.

I continued riding until I came across what looked to be some sort of ranch with guest housing. There were two rentable cabins to the side, another small one in the back, which I assumed was the owner's, and a small area for loading and unloading horses. There was also a picnic table underneath a small pavilion, which was what caught my eye. I walked around for a bit, hoping to find someone I could ask for permission to camp, but there was no sign of anyone. I went back to the picnic table and sat there until it got dark, waiting to see if anyone would show up. No one ever did, so I went ahead and set my up tent next to the pavilion. As soon as I had finished setting up camp, I heard what sounded like a small engine. I stood up and saw a guy coming over on a four-wheeler. "What are you doing?" the man asked angrily, with his eyes switching back and forth between me and my tent. I replied, "I didn't feel like riding through the dark to Kanab, and this seemed like a pretty good place to camp. I've been waiting for someone for almost two hours, but I haven't seen anyone until now."

After explaining myself to the man, he didn't mind if I camped next to the pavilion but said he would have to charge me five dollars. I'd been collecting all the change that I saw while I was riding, so I reached into the bag where I'd been storing my coins and counted out five dollars' worth. Because I paid him in coins, he must've assumed I was low on cash. He then asked if I'd like to help move some old junk from one of the cabins onto a trailer. He said he would pay me forty dollars for my help, so I accepted it. After I finished helping him move everything, he handed me the money and said I was welcome to use the shower in one of the guest cabins.

I figured I would wait until morning to get a shower, but I decided to take a look around inside of the cabin anyway. The inside looked like something straight out of an old western movie. There was an old pool table, a lot of antique things, a wood stove, and a lot of black and white pictures of people from the old west. I began to get an eerie feeling from the cabin, so I walked back outside and saw two people standing on the porch. They had pulled up while I was inside. They turned out to be a middle-aged couple who were traveling the country for their first anniversary. They had rented one of the cabins there but had been gone most of the day. We began talking, and they invited me into their room, where we continued our conversation and shared a few beers.

After visiting with the travelers for about an hour, I walked back outside to my tent and quickly fell asleep. I woke the next morning and noticed the light coming in from my tent was brighter than usual. As I reached up to unzip the vestibule, a layer of snow slid down the side. I wasn't expecting any snow, so I stuck my head out to see how much had fallen. About three inches had accumulated on the ground, and it was still coming down. After packing everything up, I locked my bike to one of the pavilion poles and made my way into the cabin to take a shower. I had looked at the shower the night before but never checked to see if there was any hot water. Thankfully, there was, so I was able to get my muscles relaxed before another long ride through the snow.

Feeling restored from the hot shower, I hopped onto my bike and began riding for the town of Kanab. It was about fifty miles away, and I'd have a package from Jody waiting for me at the post office the next day. I figured, in that weather, my timing should be about right. Surprisingly, even through all the snow, I had made it into town by lunch. I didn't know what to do with my time, so I decided to see about getting a room at the Aikens Lodge. The owner there said he would rent me a room for twenty dollars, which seemed like a fair deal, so I took it. It was nothing fancy, but a good place to wait for my package to arrive. After checking in to my room, I made my way into town and began searching for a place to eat. I figured something cheap would do, so I stopped by a McDonald's and grabbed something off the dollar menu. As I was leaving, I noticed the couple I'd met back at the cabin had just pulled up, so I made my way over to say my goodbyes to them one more time.

After staying a night at the Aikens Lodge, I woke the next morning and made my way to the post office. I walked up to the woman who was behind the desk and said, "I'm here to pick up a general delivery package." The lady gave me a dirty look and replied, "Sorry, but we don't do general delivery here." I could see my package sitting on the table behind her, so I pointed at it and said, "Oh. That's it right there." She scoffed and said, "Well, I have to charge you the shipping cost to pick it up." I'd never had to do that before and was pretty sure it was illegal for her to hold my package hostage, but I didn't want to argue with her. She scanned the package and said, "That'll be thirty dollars." I had to bite my tongue, but I paid for it because I knew Jody had put more than thirty dollars' worth of items in the package. I took the box outside to open it, and there was about ten pounds worth of food and two twenty-dollar bills.

After leaving the post office, I made my way back to the motel to collect the rest of my things. When I got there, the owner was shoveling snow from the parking lot. We started talking again, and I told him about what had happened at the post office. He didn't like that I'd been screwed over and said if I shoveled the rest of the parking lot, he would pay me forty dollars and let me stay another night. I wasn't on a schedule for anything, so I thought that sounded like a fair trade. I took my package inside and went back out to shovel the snow.

After cleaning up the parking lot, I walked into the lobby to collect my pay. The man handed me the payment as he had promised and asked if I'd like a bowl of soup. Of course, I couldn't say no to hot soup on a cold day, so I took it back to my room and began watching the news, trying to get caught up on what was going on in the world. As always, everything seemed to be one big mess. It didn't take long for me to feel annoyed by it, so I turned the television off and went to soak in a hot bath instead.

I went outside the next morning and noticed most of the snow had melted from the concrete, though the grass was still covered. I then began making my way out of town and passed by a music store. I decided to stop by so I could strum on a guitar for a few minutes. I first started playing guitar when I was three years old and played every day until I joined the army at eighteen. I always felt like it was a great escape from whatever problems I was dealing with. I tried picking it up after I got out of the service, but it just wasn't the same. I grabbed one from the shelf and began playing to see if it felt like it did when I was younger. As I began playing and the feeling returned, the owner came up and said he would take twenty dollars for it. The sales sticker was about six times that much, so I couldn't pass up the deal. However, I had no intention of keeping it. As I was riding through town a few minutes earlier, I had passed by a young woman and her son who looked like they were down on their luck. I made my way back into town and saw they were still sitting on the same bench as before. I pulled up to the boy and his mother. I then looked at the boy and said, "I've been traveling with this guitar but don't feel like carrying it anymore. I thought I'd see if you wanted it before I tossed it in the trash."

130

His eyes nearly popped out of his head as I handed it over to him. I didn't know if he'd actually stick to trying to learn it or not, but I felt good for giving him the opportunity anyway. I then turned back to the highway and began making my way for Mount Carmel Junction.

It was a short but serene ride as I made my way for my next pit stop. There was a slow-moving river running through the canyons beside me for most of the ride, which was very relaxing. I also passed by a couple of old barns and even saw a herd of deer making their way into the mountains. With everything still covered in snow and almost no traffic to share the road with, I felt isolated, but in a good way. However, my beautiful solitude came to an end as I made my way around a curve and saw a large sign of a woman holding a pie. The flashing lights surrounded the letters that read, "Home of the Ho-Made Pie." Connected to a restaurant, I assumed they probably made pies. I pulled into the gravel parking lot and went in to check and see what they had to offer. I noticed they made fresh coffee every morning, so I decided to camp nearby so I could grab a cup after a good night's rest. I went back outside and noticed my rear tire was getting low. There was a large patch of grass in front of the restaurant, so I took my bike over to it and began patching the hole in the tire. As I was putting the tire back on, a school bus pulled up next to me. "Hey, man," a woman's voice shouted from the bus's window, "You need a ride?" I quickly skimmed over the van and noticed about eight other people inside, all of whom appeared to be happy and living life. While part of me wanted to say yes because they looked fun, I had to turn them down because I was on a mission.

After the bus full of hippies drove away, I walked my bike behind the restaurant and noticed an entrance to Zion National Park. It had long been on my bucket list to visit Zion, but I didn't feel like paying the fee to go in. Instead, I hid my bike behind some boulders and went for a walk. Technically, I was inside of Zion, but I didn't go through the gate. I probably only walked half a mile back before returning to my bike, but I enjoyed my time out there anyway. It was beginning to get dark by the time I made it back to my bike, so I decided to go ahead and set up my tent.

The next morning, I went down to the restaurant to grab a cup of coffee. As I was filling my cup, I heard a man's voice ask, "Are you the person who was camped back behind here last night?" I finished pouring my coffee and took a sip, "Yep. That would've been me. I do a lot of camping." The man replied with a surprised look on his face, "Wow. You must have some pretty good gear, huh?" I wondered why the man said that and replied with a confused look on my face, "Yeah, I guess so." The man must have noticed my expression, so, to clarify, he added, "It got down to zero degrees last night. You weren't cold?" I was shocked to hear him say that because it never felt unbearably cold. Typically, if it got below freezing, I would wake up in the middle of the night to do some exercises. I laughed and replied, "I knew it was cold, but I didn't think it was that cold.." Knowing I'd had no problems at zero degrees boosted the confidence I had in my sleeping bag.

I finished drinking my coffee and continued riding until I reached the town of Panguitch. When I got into town, I made my over to the Days Inn motel and walked into the lobby. An older lady with curly gray hair and large round reading glasses was sitting at the front desk. She looked up at me, and the magnification from her thick glasses almost made her eyes look cartoonish. I smiled because of her appearance and said, "Hi! I'm riding a bike across America. You wouldn't happen to have any work I could do in exchange for a room, would you?" She looked at me as if she was wondering if there was anything I could do. She then told me to excuse her for a moment while she went to check on something. Feeling hopeful, I took a seat in the lobby and waited to hear back from her. A few minutes later, the bells hanging from the front door rattled and dinged as it swung open. The old lady stuck her head inside and told me to follow her. I hopped out of the chair and walked outside to the sidewalk where the old lady was standing with two other people. After introducing all of us, the lady looked at me and said, "We bought some new furniture for a couple of the rooms. I asked them if they wanted any help, and they said they could use you. Would you be interested?" Without any hesitation, I accepted the offer. It took us about four hours to finish setting up two rooms. The old lady, who I assumed was the manager, seemed satisfied with our work. She then paid the other two and handed me the key to a room. About an hour later, I heard someone knocking at my door. When I answered it, the manager was standing there with a cardboard box. Reaching out for me to take it, she said, "I thought you might be hungry." I told her I was and thanked her for thinking of me. I took the box back inside and opened it to see half a pepperoni pizza and a few slices of cheesy bread. I still had plenty of food left from Jody's care package, but those were mostly just snacks.

I left Panguitch the next morning and began making my way for Junction. I was between towns when I came across a back road that led into the mountains. The mountains looked to be about twelve miles away, so I figured I had time to explore and still be able to make it to Junction by that night. The road, which was a mix of sand and clay, was slightly damp from the recently melted snow but still frozen enough that I wouldn't sink all the way into it. All around me were open fields of sagebrush that were still lightly covered in snow and the white-capped mountains in the distance. After I was about halfway to the mountains, I looked down and saw some old tire tracks, so I lined up my bike inside of one and began following it along. After being distracted by the tire tracks for about thirty minutes, a heavy gust of wind came out of nowhere and knocked my hat off. I walked back to retrieve it and turned back to see a massive black cloud that had come from over the mountain. The sky continued to grow darker, and the wind was picking up speed. I turned back to look at how far I had gone from the road and realized there was no way I could make it back before things got bad, but I knew I had to try.

The wind was blowing too hard to ride out, so I had to continue pushing my bike. I knew walking out of there would take at least twice as long as it would take to ride, and I didn't have much time to waste. I kept my eyes toward the road as I was walking, hoping I would be able to see it before the storm hit. Peering through the gaps in the sage, I caught a glimpse of a vehicle making its way along the highway and guessed it was about two and a half miles away. Snow began to fall lightly around me, and the wind began picking up speed. The chilled air made my eyes feel uncomfortably dry and cold, so I squeezed them tightly shut and placed my hand over my face to warm them. When I lowered my hand and opened my eyes, it was like someone had covered me with a white blanket. The wind and snow began coming from every direction, which was very disorienting. I couldn't see more than ten feet in front of me, and the road beneath my feet slowly began to disappear. I had about half a mile left to the highway, and nearly six inches of snow had already fallen. The only way I could tell that I was on the road was by the large gap between the sagebrush. By the time I had made it to the highway, the storm was nearly over. I was shocked by how fast nearly a foot of snow had fallen, but I was happy to be back on the highway. I continued pushing my bike through the snow along the highway for about five miles before it was shallow enough to ride again. Then, after about five more miles, I'd made it into the small town of Circleville. There were only a few houses there, so I continued pushing my way for Junction. When I got there, I realized there wasn't much in Junction, either. Although, I did find an awning to stand under while I took a short break.

It wasn't long after leaving Junction that the snow had finally disappeared from the road, and I was riding full speed ahead through deep canyons. There were steep mountain walls on both sides of the highway, so there was no way to escape if I needed to. That made me feel a bit claustrophobic, so I picked up my pace and tried to get through there as quickly as possible. As I was riding through the canyon, a car passed me from behind. That was the first car I'd seen all day, and I wondered where it had come from. There was no way that car could have driven through the blizzard, so I assumed it must have come from Junction. After making my way around several curves, I saw the same car that had just passed. However, this time, it was facing me and had stopped in the middle of the road. I didn't feel like riding any closer, so I stopped and waited for the driver to make the next move. A man then stepped out of the car and began pointing something towards me. To this day, I don't know what it was, but I pulled out my phone and pretended I was taking videos of him. He then jumped back into his car and sped past me while covering his face. I shook my head and asked myself, "What the hell was wrong with that person?" I didn't know if he had bad intentions or not, but I thought it seemed very strange for him to stop in front of me when we were fifteen miles between any towns and surrounded by canyons.

After the strange man had driven away, I continued making my way north. The snow had begun to fall heavily again, but I was able to make it into the small town of Marysvale before it got too bad. I saw a building up ahead, and the sign over it read "Hoover's Restaurant." I decided to go inside and wait out the worst of the passing snowstorm. I hadn't planned on getting anything to eat, but I felt kind of obligated after the waitress asked, "just one?" I followed her to a table and ordered some fries, which I hoped to make last longer than the storm. As I was sitting there nibbling on my fries, the waitress walked up to me and handed me a burger. Before I could say anything, the waitress smiled and said, "Don't worry about it." After I'd finished eating, I thanked the waitress for the meal and made my way back out into the cold.

The snow had finally stopped, so I continued riding until it was close to dark. I was between towns and didn't have many options for picking a place to camp. As long as that strange man from earlier couldn't see me from the road, I figured I would be fine. I then hopped off my bike and began pushing it into the hills. After crossing over two of them, I decided to camp just on the other side of the second one. I could oversee everything, and there were mountains in every direction. The sun's light slowly faded behind the mountains and was replenished by the rising moon, and the snow-covered earth began to glow in its reflection.

The next morning, I packed up and made my way for the town of Joseph. It was about thirty miles away, but the snow disappeared after I'd rode ten miles, and I was able to ride at my normal speed again. Although the snow was gone, the air began to feel much colder. As I continued to ride, the wind made its way through the tiny holes in my boots, and my feet began to sting. After making it into town, I came across a small gas station, which only had one pump. I made my way inside, and straight across from me were two older ladies sitting in front of a woodstove. They both turned to look at me. One of them then patted the milk crate sitting beside her and said, "You look cold. Come have a seat." I felt almost relieved to see that fireplace and replied, "You bet! But, before I sit, do you guys have coffee?" The woman who had offered me a place to sit stood up and said, "Take a seat. I'll grab a cup for you."

I pulled the crate back a bit and sat with my legs crossed and stretched out, my boots as close to the stove as they could be without melting. The other woman was still sitting beside me and began asking questions about where I was from and where I was heading. After I told her, she leaned behind the counter towards the woman who was getting my coffee and shouted, "Janet! He's riding a bike from Florida to Alaska!" "What!" Janet screamed from behind the counter, "That's crazy!" She then ran back over and handed me my drink. A couple of other customers then walked in and ordered breakfast, so the two women had to leave me and get back to work. I continued sitting there, drinking my coffee and warming my feet while enjoying everyone else's conversations. Even though most of what they talked about sounded like problems, I still enjoyed listening to them. Their issues were all prevalent within normal society, and hearing them reminded me the real world was still there. As I was swallowing my final drop of coffee, I felt my mind put up a sort of shield so that I could walk away and not remember the comforts of everyday misery. As I got up to leave, I thanked the cashier for allowing me to enjoy my coffee in front of their fire.

After leaving the store, I made my way towards the highway and suddenly lost the motivation to ride. I felt like I needed a break from it, so I made my way behind an old truck stop that looked like it hadn't been used in at least twenty years. I put my tent together next to the building wall and tossed my sleeping bag inside. I crawled inside and began to think about trading in my bike for a backpack. I was just growing tired of dealing with a bike and felt that it was limiting me to where I could go. The only good thing I saw about a bike was that it could get me between places quickly and that it was carrying all the weight for me. After spending the entire day thinking about it, I put my bike up for sale. If no one bought it, then I would continue to ride, but if someone did, then I would switch to a backpack. I put my fate into the hands of the universe and fell asleep.

The next morning was March 1, 2015, and when I woke up, I checked my phone and saw someone had wired me five hundred dollars for the bike. I took a deep breath and began searching online for a new backpack. It didn't take long for me to decide on which one I wanted. It was a green internal frame pack with seventy liters of space, large enough to carry all my gear. I noticed that it would take two days for it to be shipped to the post office in Delta, which was about ninety miles from Joseph. I figured I could slow down and make it there by the second night and pick the pack up on the third morning. That seemed like a good idea to me, so I continued heading north for Highway 50.

I made it to Highway 50 in the town of Salina around 2:00 p.m. and pulled into a McDonald's. After feeling up on water, I took a seat next to the window, where I could charge my things and keep an eye on my bike. After sitting there for a few minutes, a Greyhound Bus pulled into the parking lot, and everyone got out to take a break. A group of three guys walked over to my bike and began looking it over, which I could understand because it was fully loaded and looked like something out of a Mad Max movie. I kept my hunting knife strapped to the front of my bike, just below the handlebars, and saw one of the guys point at it and say something to the guy next to him. He then took the end of his sleeve and wrapped it around his hand. He then reached down and pulled my knife out of its sheath. He looked at the blade a few times, nodded his head, and put it back into the sheath. I was ready to run out there if he had tried to steal it, but that wasn't the case. Still, I felt it was foolish and disrespectful for him to touch my knife without asking.

After charging my things and filling up on water, I got onto Highway 50 and began to make my way west. I made it about twenty miles from Salina when I came across Scipio Lake. It was still early, but I thought it would be a good place to stop since there was an interstate coming up. I found a spot that looked like a good place to camp and parked my bike. Then I wandered off on foot until it got dark. I knew the next couple of days would likely be uneventful, but I needed to get used to slowing down anyway.

The next day, I continued making my west and came across a sign that read, "28 Miles to Delta". It felt impossible to go any slower than I had been, so I figured I would go ahead and get into town a day early. As I was finishing the last few miles of nothingness, I noticed a large black horse running alongside me in the distance. I decided to stop and see if it was actually running with me or if it just appeared that it was. As I hopped off my bike, the horse turned and made its way towards me at full speed. It came to an abrupt stop once it made it to the fence line, and a large cloud of dust shot out over the highway. I lowered my bike onto the gravel shoulder and walked over to the fence. As I approached the horse, it began to nicker and stuck its head over the wire. I reached out to pet her on the head, and she had the most gracious look in her eyes. I looked up to see if there were any other horses, but it appeared she was as lonely as I was. She had no branding or tags and didn't seem to be brushed, at least not recently. Her hooves didn't appear to have been trimmed by any farrier either, though they looked naturally worn and complimented her appearance. I started to think she may be a wild horse, which made it even more bizarre that she had run up to me. I scratched her ears for about thirty minutes before kissing her on the nose and making my way back to my bike. As I was walking back to gather my things, she began neighing and running in circles. I felt like she wanted me to stay with her longer, but I had to be on my way. I began riding down the highway, and she started following me again. I got up to about thirty miles per hour, and she had no problem keeping up with me for almost two miles before being forced to stop by another fence. As I continued to ride further away, I looked back and waved goodbye to one of the most majestic horses I'd ever seen.

I was about five miles from Delta when a blue van passed by from behind and pulled over just up ahead. As I rode next to the rolled-down passenger window, I stopped to see what they wanted. There was an older lady inside, and she began asking what I was up to. After I gave her a short rundown, she offered to pay for me a motel room. I told her I would appreciate that and could meet her in town in a few minutes. However, since it was raining, she insisted that I let her give me a ride. I didn't mind the rain and knew I could probably get there faster than the time it would take to disassemble my bike, but I could tell she really wanted to help. I removed my saddlebags and front tire, then tossed everything into the back of her van. I then hopped into the front passenger seat and shook the lady's hand, "Nice to meet you. I'm Jake." "Karen," the lady replied. As we began driving along, she continued, "I would invite you to my house, but I'm Mormon, and my family would disapprove of you being there. Not unless you're Mormon. You're not Mormon, are you?" Not only was I not Mormon, but I didn't practice or believe in any religion. Although, I refrained from telling her that. Instead, I smiled and said, "Nope. I'm not Mormon. I'm not much of anything." I could tell my answer kind of bothered her because she didn't say anything else until we got to the motel. As I was pushing my bike into my room, Karen stood at the doorway and asked, "Would it be okay if I brought my family in the morning so we could talk with you about Mormonism?" I already knew about Mormonism and didn't care to hear more about it, but I figured since she had helped me, I told her that would be okay. She then told me to enjoy the rest of my night, and I thanked her one last time before closing the door.

I woke the next morning feeling excited about my new backpack. I looked at the clock, and it was 6:00 a.m., so I had two hours before the post office opened. I went to the motel lobby and poured myself a cup of their complimentary coffee. I then took a seat near the window and sipped on my drink while waiting for Karen and her family to arrive. Nearly two hours had passed, and I still hadn't seen her, so I figured they weren't coming. I began making my way for the post office and could feel myself become anxious. At that point, I knew there was no going back and hoped I wasn't making a mistake. I pulled up to the post office with sweaty palms and parked my bike outside next to the front door. I walked into the empty lobby, and the clerk asked, "You must be Jake?" She was curious to figure out who had sent the "general delivery" package, but it was probably obvious when she saw me. I took the package back outside and began to feel like a spoiled child on Christmas morning. A crazed smile grew across my face as I lifted the backpack, a three-liter water bladder, and two trekking poles from the box, "Oh, Bessy! Bessy, the back-breaking backpack! About time you showed up!" I immediately knew it was the right backpack for me, so I began loosening all the straps and removing the tags. I then emptied all four of my saddlebags and began sorting out everything I needed to keep. First, I emptied my water jugs into my new water bladder and shoved it into its own compartment. Next, I pushed my sleeping bag into the bottom. Then, I rolled up my tent and put it inside. On top of my tent, I placed my clothes, toiletries, and survival bag. Then, I took the two tent poles and placed them vertically into each corner. My food bag then slid perfectly into the top compartment. Then, my two water canteens went into each side pocket, along with my machete in one and a hunting knife in the other. Lastly, I attached my sleeping pad to the bottom straps and let my solar panel hang over it from the top straps. Just like that, my setup was complete, and I was ready to start walking.

Once I felt satisfied with my pack, I went back inside the post office and found a box that I could use to ship my bike in. They didn't have a large enough box, but we were able to tape two boxes together so the bike could fit. I then took the taped-up box outside and began taking the bike apart piece by piece and shoving everything into the box. It was about a hundred dollars just to ship the bike to Pennsylvania, so I didn't have much money left from the sale at that point. I thought it was a good trade, though, and went back outside to sit with my backpack. I looked at it for a few minutes, just trying to comprehend how much of a difference I was in for. Once I grasped the reality of the situation, I slung the sixty-pound bag onto my back, adjusted the straps, and began walking.

Loneliest Highway

Going from an average pace of twenty miles per hour down to only three was going to take some getting used to. However, I knew Highway 50, aptly known as the loneliest highway, would be the perfect place to get myself up to speed. I had already done my research and knew there were only a few small, unincorporated towns along the highway in Nevada, and most of them were close to one hundred miles apart. Since I was carrying three days' worth of water, that meant I had to walk at least thirty miles each day. I figured if dying from dehydration wasn't enough to keep me motivated, then nothing would. I also felt that if I could make it through Nevada, I would be ready for anything.

Before leaving Delta, I made my way to a gas station located in the center of town. From that point on, I decided that I would sit there any time I had access to an unlimited supply of water and force myself to drink until I had to urinate. Then, after relieving myself, I would drink one full liter and top everything off before leaving. So, that's what I did and began making my way for Hinckley's next small town. I only had eight miles to go and was already enjoying the feeling of the earth moving beneath my feet. As everything slowed to a crawl, I was able to see and study so much more. Every rock, bush, crack in the road, or piece of trash on the side- it all had a story to tell, and I was finally able to listen.

The clicking sound of my trekking poles hitting the road reminded me of a metronome, so I began using them to keep myself in rhythm. "Click. Clack. Click. Clack." I'd hiked with a single trekking pole before, but this was my first time using two, so it took some getting used to. I thought I probably looked a little funny using them, but I quickly realized several benefits to having them. Not only were they helping me to keep a steady pace, but they were also acting as an extra pair of legs and took quite the load off my knees. As I pushed through each step, I also noticed they were increasing my gate, which meant I was walking faster than I normally would. I then thought about how I could use them as weapons or to hold up a tarp shelter. So, as awkward as they were, I saw them as an invaluable asset.

It wasn't long before I'd made it into Hinckley, but there wasn't much to offer. Only a few small houses with rotting wooden fences, old rusted farm equipment, and a boarded-up gas station that looked like it hadn't been open in years. There was one last house on the right before there was nothing but barren fields as far as I could see, and beside it was a sign that read "Ely 153 Miles." When I was on my bike, that distance would've been a piece of cake, but my feet were already beginning to feel sore after only eleven miles. I began to have flashbacks from my Army days and remembered all the forced rucks they had us do and how the skin on the bottom of my feet would look like flip flops. I remembered how bad it hurt, but also how nothing could phase me once the wounds had calloused over. Staring down the long stretch of nothingness, with only mountains far away in the distance, I was ready to get to it.

After hiking just a few miles outside of Hinckley, I came across a large tree. Although it stood about fifty feet tall, it was undoubtedly dead. It was also decorated with nearly fifty shoes. It was the only tree for as far as I could see, but I wondered why there were shoes all over it. I began to imagine that the shoes were left there in case someone needed a pair to walk to Ely or a new pair after coming from there. I looked down at my boots

143

and said, "These still look pretty good. I think they'll do." I then continued walking and observing the things around me. After about five more miles, I realized that I'd passed by a few beer bottles that had been stuck into the ground. The necks of the bottles were shoved a few inches into the dirt and looked like someone had planted them. I found one and carried it with me for about a mile before planting one myself, taking part in the strange legacy.

The sun was just starting to set, and I'd already reached my goal of thirty miles. However, I still had quite a bit of energy, so I continued hiking for a couple more hours. After hiking about forty miles, I had reached Sevier Lake. I was hoping to camp next to some water, so I began walking out towards the lake. I thought it was much more convenient to get away from the road when I was on foot. I no longer had to worry about running my bike over sharp objects, such as the dreaded bullhead burrs, and getting a flat tire. I finally reached where the lake should have been, but it was all dried up, so I set up my tent on the smooth, flat desert floor. I must have been more tired than I thought because I fell asleep shortly after sliding into my sleeping bag.

I woke later than usual the next morning and sat up to look around and feel the cool breeze passing through the netting of my tent. After letting out a big yawn and stretching out my arms, I unzipped my sleeping bag to see how my feet were doing. As I had suspected, both had several blisters, but they weren't as bad as I thought they would be. I got everything packed up and began slowly limping back to the road. After about a mile or two, the pain went away, and I was back to hiking at about four miles per hour. I held that pace all the way until dark and decided to keep going. My feet were sore, but everything else about me felt great. The moon came up a little later and lit the desert so brightly that I didn't even need my headlamp, which I preferred not to use unless I had to. Not that I had seen more than five cars throughout the whole day, but I didn't like the idea of being seen unless I wanted to be.

However, I would still turn it on every thirty minutes or so, capturing a quick check of my surroundings.

It must have been about 1:00 a.m. when I looked towards the road behind me and noticed a pair of yellowish glowing eyes. Whatever it was, it appeared to be about thirty feet away and seemed to be keeping its distance. It also looked to be low to the ground, so I wasn't too worried about it. When I stopped, it stopped. When I walked, it followed. I didn't feel threatened by whatever it was, so I stopped giving it my attention. About an hour later, from the corner of my eye, I saw something move on the other side of the road. I turned towards it and switched on my headlamp to reveal a fox. Feeling a bit relieved, I laughed and said to it, "What's up, man?" It cocked its head when I said that, and I pretended that it knew what I was saying. I continued walking and talking to the fox until it disappeared into the brush just before sunrise.

It was about 5:00 a.m. when I finally claimed my Nevada sign. That meant that I had done fifty miles since waking up in Lake Sevier. I probably did half of those miles during the day and then the other twenty-five throughout the night. I sat next to the sign and took a two-hour break before getting back on the move again. I was beginning to feel a little tired but didn't want to waste a whole day sitting there and risk sabotaging my sleep cycle. Not too far from the Nevada welcome sign, I saw another sign that read "Ely 56 miles." I couldn't believe I'd already walked ninety-six miles since Delta! I was moving right along and felt very confident in myself. I decided to keep walking to see how far I could make it before dark. As the day went on, it felt like I was making little progress. All around me were open fields of nothingness, a few snow-capped mountains in the distance that never seemed to move, and absolutely no traffic. Eventually, though, I did notice some wind turbines that looked very far away, so I glanced back at them every hour until I finally passed them and had to find something else to work for.

I finally reached Ely around 11:00 p.m. and noticed an American Legion right off the highway. I figured since they were all about supporting veterans, they probably wouldn't mind if I slept under the pavilion connected to the building. I laid my sleeping pad and sleeping bag onto the cold concrete, using my tightly sealed bag of clothes as a pillow. I slept so heavily that night that I woke the next morning in a slight panic. It wasn't like me to sleep so deeply when I knew people were around, but all was well, and I packed up to make my way to the gas station.

I was walking through town just as the sun was coming up, and it felt great to see other people out and about. Although, most of them were giving me strange looks, which I wasn't surprised by in the least bit. However, I was surprised that no one stopped to ask what I was doing. It seemed like most of them just wanted to mind their own business, which probably explained why they lived in such an isolated place anyway. They seemed like the type of people you could count on when you needed them but would stay out of your way otherwise, and I respected that.

When I got to the gas station, I removed my water bladder and canteens from my backpack. I then realized I'd finished the last drop of water just as I was coming into town the night before. It looked like I'd made it just in time. Of course, I knew I could probably survive up to three days without water, but it was good to know I had correctly estimated how much I would need before running out. Although I was sure that I only had enough because it was winter, and the daytime temperatures were still comfortable enough to wear pants and a thin jacket without sweating. There was no way I would have attempted what I was doing if it had been summer, or even close to it.

After filling up on water from the gas station, I made my way across the street to the grocery store. I'd gone through most of my food and needed to resupply. I picked out a jar of peanut butter, several packets of tuna, a box of oat bars, a can of ravioli, a bottle of multi-vitamins, and a gallon-sized sports drink, which I took outside and finished before leaving the parking lot. As I was sitting there, having one of my snacks for breakfast, I opened my map and saw it was nearly eighty miles to the next town of Eureka. I shook my head when I saw that and decided to take a zero-day. I found a patch of grass to sit on, believe it or not, and sat there all day, sipping on water and resting my legs for the next long walk. As night fell, I felt comfortable enough with where I was that I decided just to sleep where I was.

I had some pretty bad leg cramps throughout the night, so when morning came, I made sure to grab a couple of packets of salt from the gas station. As I was drinking my pre-walk liter of water, I poured some salt onto my hand and licked a little between sips. I hoped that would help to prevent any cramps during my trek to Eureka. With the sun just beginning to light the morning sky, I got back onto the road and continued my hike into the loneliness.

It was 6:30 p.m., and I'd made it about forty miles, which was just over halfway to Eureka. I saw a gravel shoulder where vehicles could pull over and attach snow chains to their tires, so I decided to stop there and have dinner. Between two bushes was a rock that looked like it would make a good seat, so I sat on it and began looking through my food bag. I then stopped what I was doing because I thought I heard a vehicle slowing down. I looked up and saw an old brown van pulling off the road in front of me. The driver looked to be about forty years old with long blonde hair and was singing along with some punk rock music. He looked out of the passenger window in the middle of an air guitar solo and nearly jumped out of his seat when he noticed me. He turned the music down and shouted, "Hey, man! Are you all right?" I was thinking about asking him the same thing, but I lifted my backpack and said with a big smile on my face, "Yep! Just out for a walk!" He gave me a curious look for a few seconds and then began laughing as he crawled into the back. The side door then slid open, and the man continued, "Dude, you're insane. I'm about to cook dinner. You want some?" I looked inside and could tell he'd been living out of his van for a while. Not that it was unkempt, but he had all the amenities the average American would have in their house. I walked up to the open door and watched as he began rummaging through his mini-fridge. "How's about chili dogs? You cool with that, man?" he said as he lifted a pack of hotdogs. I laughed and replied, "Sure, man. I'm down for some chili dogs." He then pointed to a futon across from where he was sitting and said I could have a seat, so I made my way inside. He stuck out his hotdog juice covered hand and said, "Name's Kyle, by the way. Do you need a ride or anything? I'm heading to California." As we were eating our chili dogs, which he had cooked on a gas stove, I explained to him my backstory and that I wasn't looking for a ride but appreciated his company for the moment. After we finished eating, he was ready to get back to driving. I then hopped out of the van and thanked him for having me over for dinner. He wished me luck and pulled away, jamming out to his music again. I slung my backpack over my shoulders and continued walking, watching the red taillights fade into the distance.

I walked through the night again and made it into Eureka around 9:00 a.m. As I was making my way to the gas station to fill up on water, an older man in a white truck stopped in the middle of the road and shouted, "Jake!" I turned my head and waved at him as if I knew who he was. He pulled into the empty parking spot beside me and hopped out of his truck. He began talking about how he had been following my blog for a couple of months and noticed I was coming into town. He had brought me a plate of breakfast while he was on break from work. He couldn't stick around very long but wanted to grab a picture with me in front of the Eureka Opera House. After he'd left, I carried my plate to a small park that was in the center of town and sat on the grass to eat. I finally began to feel exhausted and couldn't fight the urge to sleep, so I pulled my bandana over my eyes and took a three-hour nap. When I woke up, I made my way over to the gas station to fill up on water before starting my seventy-mile hike to the next small town of Austin.

It was beginning to feel like I was stuck in an episode of The Twilight Zone. Day and night, it was just the same nothingness over and over again. The only difference was the towns in between, but even they looked similar to one another. I could understand how this stretch of Highway 50 had acquired the nickname "The Loneliest Road in America." I'd only seen a handful of vehicles pass me by, a couple of wild horses, and that one little fox. I also wasn't sleeping very much, so each day was kind of running into the next. However, not sleeping had been a personal choice, so I couldn't blame anyone or anything but myself for being on the edge of delusional. I'd finally made it to a set of mountains, which was about ten miles from Austin. I decided to go ahead and camp at the bottom and make my way through them after getting some sleep. Since I knew I wouldn't have to worry about waking up early, I set the alarm on my phone for 9:00 a.m. and pitched my tent behind a mound of dirt, which I assumed had been left by some construction company.

I woke the next morning and was happy to see the mountains before me. There were finally trees again instead of just flat desert and sage. I made it up the mountain and into Austin by lunchtime. There wasn't much to see in Austin, but I did think it was a little strange to see so many churches in such a small town. Almost surprisingly, I was able to find a gas station, but the cashier recommended that I buy my water because rumors were going around that the tap water was contaminated. I bought enough to fill up my water bladder and one extra to drink before leaving town.

As I made my way back down into the desert, I continued walking another fifty miles until I came across a small RV park. There was also a restaurant there called "Cold Springs Station." I decided to find a place to camp while I was there and would be able to grab breakfast in the morning. It was about 1:00 a.m., so

I decided to set my tent up behind the building and hoped that no one got upset about it.

The next morning, I packed my things and made my way to the front. It would be another hour before they opened, so I sat in one of the chairs on the front porch and waited. When the door finally opened, an older lady poked her head out and asked, "Was that you who was camping in the back last night?" I told her it was, and she waved for me to come inside. She knew I was out there and had already had breakfast made for me. As I was eating, she offered to have her husband drive me to Fallon the next day, but I told her I should already be there by then. She thought it was crazy that I was walking out there and would have her husband keep an eye out for me anyway. If he saw me on his way into town, he would stop to see if I needed anything. I appreciated the breakfast and the idea of someone being out there to help if I needed it.

About seven hours after I'd left the restaurant, I came across vast open fields of dunes and salt flats. There were quite a few people riding snowboards and four-wheelers on the large dunes. On the other side of the highway was a massive salt flat, lined with graffiti-covered stones. The colorful rocks went on for several miles, and reading all the names and quotes on them seemed to make walking through there go by faster. As the sun was going down, it appeared as though I'd made it past all the dunes and salt flats and was back into sagebrush territory. After a couple of hours of night walking, I came across the Grimes Point Archaeological Area. After noticing a pavilion near the entrance, I made my way over to it and decided I'd camp there for the night.

The next morning, I decided to explore a bit before making my way into Fallon. I made my way to one of the designated trails and started walking. To my surprise, there were petroglyphs everywhere! Some of which had been estimated to date back as far as seven thousand years! Most of the petroglyphs were bizarre designs, though I could make out a few of them, such as the snakes, deer, and people. The trail had taken me to higher ground, so I looked to the northwest and could see a naval station just before Fallon. I figured that would explain all the jets I'd seen and heard as I'd hiked that long stretch between here and Eureka. I then made my way back down to the pavilion, where I ate a granola bar that I'd smothered in peanut butter. And after having a quick snack, I was ready to get back on the move.

I made it into Fallon by noon and no longer felt so alone. With a population of eight thousand people, there were familiar chain stores and restaurants. I was also happy to see they had my bank there, so I was able to get rid of all the cash in my wallet. I was okay with carrying up to forty dollars at a time, but I didn't want to risk losing any more than that. Normally, I would've been in a hurry to get through a place like Fallon, but I decided to make the best of it and began searching for a cheap motel. I made my way to the west side of town and rented a room at the Budget Inn for fifty bucks. As soon as I entered my room, I grabbed a shower and tossed my clothes in there with me. I thought I was lucky to get a room located on the backside of the building because there was an empty field in front of it, and within that field was an old busted up fence where I could hang my clothes to dry. I didn't know what to do with all the extra time on my hands, so I got dressed the best I could and went for a walk into town. After being gone for about thirty minutes, I walked past a beer store and decided to buy a six-pack and brought it back to my room. Walking around in public wearing nothing but my waterproof pants and rain jacket felt kind of strange anyway, so I was ready to get back to my room sooner than later. Plus, my feet were already getting sore from wearing my boots without any socks.

When I returned to the motel, I noticed a woman sitting on the ground next to my room. I didn't think to say anything yet because I still had to hang up my clothes. But after putting my beer in the fridge and taking my clothes out to dry, I turned to ask the woman if she would like a beer. She then began pulling her hair and screaming all kinds of profanities. It didn't appear as though she was screaming at me, but more so in general, towards everyone and everything. The way she acted didn't seem normal, so I asked, "Are you okay?" She turned to look at me and screamed, "Don't call the cops! My mom is on her way!" I wasn't sure why she said not to call the cops, but I didn't. She didn't appear to be a danger to herself or anyone, but I was beginning to think she was on some sorts of drugs. I shrugged my shoulders and went inside to grab a beer for myself. I then took it back outside and sat in the chair in front of my room, trying to ignore the psychotic woman next to me, though I was still there to help if she needed it. Another woman, who I assumed was her mother, showed up about three beers later and took the unwell lady back into her room. I then finished off the rest of my beer and had the last one just as the sun was setting. I then collected my nearly dry clothes from the fence and went inside. As I was lying in bed, I decided to go online and order a different size backpack. The one I had was great but a bit too long in the torso, causing most of the weight to ride on my butt. I ordered the same pack, but in a smaller size, and had it routed to the post office in Carson City.

The next morning, I looked at my map and noticed I could shave off a few miles if I walked through the desert instead of taking the highway. Besides the fact it was a shortcut, I figured it would make things more exciting. I left the motel and began taking random roads, whichever ones appeared to lead southwest. I eventually found myself on an old dirt service road that I followed into the desert for a while. When I felt that I had gone far enough south, I stepped off the service road and began walking into unclaimed desert land. About a mile from the service road, I came across four old logs, half-buried and in the shape of a square. I figured it was likely an old and forgotten gravesite, but I didn't know for sure. Another five miles out, I came up to a circular clearing that was about thirty feet across.

There was a rock sitting in the center of the circle, so I walked over to inspect it. I had never seen one like it before, so I began searching the area and found about ten smaller pieces just like it. I collected the rocks and brought them back to the center, making sure they were the same. Then, out of curiosity, I unclipped the magnetic mouthpiece from my water bladder and held it to one of the rocks. Surprisingly, the magnet stuck right to it, so I began to wonder if I had stumbled across meteorites. I then decided to set up my tent within the circle and continued searching the area. By nightfall, I had collected almost twenty of the rocks. I knew if they were meteorites, they would be worth something, so I hid them and noted their location.

The next morning, I packed up and continued my way across the desert. A few hours later, I had accidentally found myself behind government property. I couldn't make it back to the road because it was fenced off. It looked like my best bet was to go back into the desert to try and make my way around it. I backtracked through the Lahontan State Recreation Area and eventually came across a trail. After crossing a few of them, I decided to follow it into the hills and found myself entering a small desert community. There were only about ten small houses, and the people who were standing outside began giving me strange looks as I passed through. Of course, I was sure it wasn't every day they saw someone pop of the desert with a backpack.

I continued following the dirt road towards the highway and found my way back to it just as it was getting dark. I continued walking along the highway and made it about ten miles from Dayton before looking for a place to camp. There were finally trees again, so I wandered off into them, hoping to find a good spot. I was about thirty yards from the highway and came across an old house that wasn't much more than the foundation. There was a large patch of soft grass in front of it, so I decided to set up my tent on it and crawled in for the night. I was finally awakened around 2:00 a.m. by the sounds of four-wheelers riding around. I stuck my head out and could see three sets of lights slowly making their way through the trees. I hoped they wouldn't see my tent and become suspicious enough to come over. For all I knew, that was their property, and they may not have taken kindly to strangers. After riding around for nearly thirty minutes, they disappeared in the opposite direction.

I had packed my things at the crack of dawn and made my way back to the highway. After walking about five miles, I noticed an older man with a long beard making his way towards me on the street's opposite side. Although it was comfortably warm, he was wearing a large camouflage coat with matching pants, a black beanie, and, oddly enough, he was playing a flute. As he continued to get closer, I began to feel anxious about how he was going to interact with me. He had finally made it right across from me and said nothing at all. He just skipped on by like I wasn't even there, jamming away on his flute and not giving a care about anything else. Once he had made it out of sight, I turned to see a large cave not too far from the road. I hopped off the road and made my way inside. There was soot all over the walls, a small fireplace, a few empty cans of food, a bag of clothes, and an old sleeping bag lying on the floor. The cave was probably large enough to sleep ten people, but I wondered if the man with the flute had been living there. I figured it wouldn't be a bad place for him if that were the case, but I didn't want to stick around to find out.

I made it into Dayton at 8:00 a.m. and decided to make a pit stop at a small coffee shop. I sat my pack down next to the entrance and heard a man's voice from behind, "Where ya headin'?" I turned to look at the man, who was on his way into the store, and said, "Alaska." "Alaska!" the man shouted. I laughed and replied to him, "Yeah, but it's kind of a long story." He then offered to buy me a cup of coffee if I sat and told him all about it, so I did. Carson City was only eleven miles away anyway, so I wasn't in any hurry. However, I did want to reach the post office before they closed because my new pack should be there by the end of the day. Also, a man named Tim lived in Carson City and said I was welcome to crash at his place once I'd made it.

I took my time getting into Carson City and made it to the post office just in time to swap out my new and old backpacks. I immediately fell in love with the new one's fit and didn't regret sending the other back. I then sent Tim a text and let him know I was available to meet up whenever he was. He texted me right back, saying he wasn't home, but I could go to his house and wait for him. As I was making my way to his house, he sent another text, "My girlfriend and I will be there in about an hour. Make yourself at home. We're going to head to the bar after. You're welcome to join us if you want. Drinks are on me." I was shocked that he had so much trust in me because I'd never met him before. However, he had been following my blog for a long time and probably felt like he knew me well enough.

When I got to Tim's house, I immediately threw my clothes in the washer, which was nice because I was so used to washing them by hand. It was probably about time for them to get a good soak in a machine, though. I got a hot shower while my clothes were washing and started to feel like a civilized person again. I made sure not to stay in there too long, though. As gross as it may sound, I didn't want to soften up the callouses on my feet. I'd already lost feeling in them and didn't want to start getting blisters again. I hopped out of the shower, feeling like a new man, and noticed a box of noodles sitting on the kitchen table. I felt like a wild animal that had just zoned in on its prey and texted Tim to see if I could have some. He replied to his text, "Yeah, man! Eat whatever you want!" I mumbled to myself, "Whatever I want, huh?" I opened the refrigerator and saw a pack of bologna, so I decided to make myself a sandwich instead. After spoiling myself with dinner, I tossed my clothes into the dryer and went back to the living room. I flopped down on the large, fluffy couch and reached over for the remote to the television. I didn't pay much attention to what was on, but it felt great to be in a house and feel normal again. Tim and his girlfriend showed up shortly after and thought it was strange to see me walking around with nothing but a towel on. I didn't even realize how unacceptable that was, so I knew something inside of me had changed. They didn't seem bothered by it but thought it was kind of funny. Tim then went to his room and brought me out a pair of shorts to wear until my clothes finished drying. Tim and his girlfriend, Alex, began getting ready to go to the bar while I continued sitting in the living room, remembering what it was like to have a house.

Once we'd made it to the bar, I realized he had invited several of his friends to meet me. They had reserved a table for us, and there were about ten people in our group. It was kind of strange being the center of attention as if I were some sort of celebrity. It got even weirder as time went on because nearly everyone in the bar found out what I was doing and began handing me free mixed drinks. Of course, as my anxiety began to increase, I eagerly accepted every shot the people tried giving me. As the night went on, I found myself surrounded by women and noticed several men were getting upset by it. I wasn't there to cause any problems, so I told Tim I was going to head back to his house and turn in early. He thought that was probably a good idea because he had also noticed a few guys giving me dirty looks. I made it back to his house around 11:00 p.m. and passed out on his couch as soon as I landed on it.

I woke the next morning and had no idea where Tim or Alex was. I assumed they had probably gone back to her place, so I left a handwritten letter on the table, thanking him for everything. I then grabbed my pack and made my way into town, searching for a place to eat and hopefully get rid of my hangover. I finally came across a restaurant called Red's Old 395 and was lured in by the large red letters "BBQ" that hung on the side. The fact the restaurant looked like a rustic cabin and had a windmill in front of it grabbed my attention as well. I took a seat on the outdoor patio and began looking over the menu. As

I was sitting there, I noticed one of the waitresses kept peeking around the corner at me. She eventually came over and asked, "Are you Jake?" I told her that I was, and she began laughing because she hoped she hadn't mistaken me for someone else. She then introduced herself as Alaina and said that she had been following me online. She couldn't believe I was sitting outside of the restaurant where she worked and offered to buy me lunch. I thought that was very kind of her and enjoyed our short chats as she gave me her time between the other customers.

After leaving the restaurant, I made my way into the mountains on the northwest side of town. It was very peaceful out there, alone, away from the busy city. The weather was also clear, cool, and slightly windy from the storm that had passed through during the early morning hours. The ground was still damp from the rain but had dried up by that evening. As the sun was going down, I climbed to the top of a hill and pulled out my sleeping bag to watch over the city before falling asleep. As I was lying there, I noticed a ball of white light appear in the mountains just northwest of town. At first, I thought it was a helicopter, or maybe a drone, but the more I watched it, the more I wondered. The light then quickly shot up from the mountain to about a hundred feet in the air and then back down again. After doing that a few times, it slowly made its way over the city, and the light began fading in and out until it finally disappeared completely. Suddenly, two other balls of white light came from the same spot in the mountains and went to the same location above the city before also disappearing. About a minute later, a single, larger ball of light reappeared in the sky and made a quick circle around the city before shooting straight up and out of sight. Luckily, I had caught it all on video and uploaded it to my Facebook Page. Otherwise, no one probably would have believed me. Hundreds of people began commenting on the video, and they were all just as stumped as I was.

I didn't know if sleeping in the mountains was such a good idea anymore, so I made my way back into town and tossed my sleeping bag down between two highway maintenance vehicles. Although I felt drained by the time I had made it back to town, I barely got any sleep because I couldn't stop thinking about what I'd just seen. The next morning, I grabbed a cup of coffee from a gas station and filled up on my water, preparing to go back into the mountains. I was so intrigued by what I had seen the night before that I was kind of hoping to get another video, though most people had warned me not to go back. I made my way to the same spot I had been the night before and took a seat on the ground, eating peanuts while I waited for the sun to set.

Just as the sun was going down, a man in a black suit appeared from the hill behind me. He approached me, and we talked for a minute, although I can't remember what we talked about. I just remember thinking it was strange for a man to be hiking out there in a suit. After he had walked away, I followed behind to make sure he was leaving, though I didn't see him anymore. I shrugged my shoulders and began walking back to where my pack was sitting. Before reaching my things, I turned and saw three children walking on the hill across from me. Within a few seconds of looking over at them, everything went black. I then reached out and touched what felt like a thin rubber bag. I immediately began to panic and tried to get out of whatever it was, but I was trapped, and it was too hard to penetrate. No holes or light were coming through, so I was scared I was going to suffocate. It only felt like I was stuck in there for about thirty seconds when I suddenly felt the bag come off and could feel the ground beneath me again. I turned over to see what was going on and saw a bright red light, which at first I thought was the brake light of a car. However, I quickly realized that I was looking up towards the sky, and the light shot straight up and disappeared. I began to panic again, so I jumped up to see if I was okay. I then checked to see if any of my things were missing. I appeared to be fine, and all my things seemed to be there, though one of my trekking poles was slightly bent. After collecting myself, I pulled out my phone and noticed it was 3:00

a.m. I had somehow lost about eight hours within what felt like only a minute. I then realized that nothing around me looked familiar, so I checked the GPS on my phone and realized I was about five miles away from Carson City on the opposite side of town.

Although I was only five miles from town, it took nearly six hours to make it there because I kept feeling sick and needed to sit. I thought maybe I had been poisoned, so I made my way to the emergency room. By the time I got there, I felt fine, so I sat there for a few hours to see if I would get sick again. After assuring myself I was okay, I left the hospital and began wondering if it was safe to stay another night in Carson City. Although I was tired and just wanted to rest, I decided to go ahead and start making my way for Lake Tahoe.

I was just outside of the city limits when the sun had gone down behind the mountains. It wasn't dark yet, but it was in that twilight phase where the sky had a soft magenta glow. I continued walking for a few miles and realized something just didn't feel right. For some reason, it still wasn't dark. I felt confused as to why, so I checked to see what time it was. 7:00 a.m.! But that was impossible because I hadn't missed a step, and it had never gotten dark. I thought something must be wrong with my phone, so I removed the battery and popped it back in. When I turned my phone back on, several messages began coming through. A few people had sent me the usual "good morning" messages. I then saw a message from Jody, which was a picture of the sunrise in Arizona. This confirmed that it was indeed morning, and I suddenly felt a massive amount of anxiety come over me. I then began to feel hot and got so dizzy that I nearly fell over. I didn't want any passing cars to pull over and check on me, so I got off the road and laid down behind some bushes. I began shaking and had a terrible case of vertigo. I tried to get up and go back to the emergency room, but I vomited and passed out before I could even stand.

I woke a few hours later, probably around noon, and I felt perfectly fine. I looked back towards Carson City and thought about going back to the emergency room, but I just wanted to get away from there. I checked to see how far it was to Lake Tahoe and saw that it was only twenty miles, so I got onto the highway and tried hiking out of there again. I made it about halfway when I felt an intense burning pain in my left knee. I pulled up my pants leg and noticed what looked to be a small cauterized spot on the inside of my knee, about the size of a pencil eraser. I stepped off the side of the road to wait for the burning pain to subside when a small blue car pulled over. The young man behind the steering wheel leaned across the passenger seat and asked, "Hey, man, do you need a ride?"

Not wanting to take any more chances, I replied, "No. Thanks, though. I'm actually walking across America and don't take rides unless I have to." With a concerned look on his face, he replied, "What? Really? That's crazy! Well, my name is Jacob. At least let me give you a ride to the top of this mountain, and you can tell me all about it!" After what I had just been through, I didn't know if I wanted to trust this man, but my knee was hurting pretty bad, and I really wanted to put some miles between myself and Carson City. I looked around for a moment, weighing my options, and said, "Okay. A ride up the mountain does sound good."

After reaching the top of the mountain, Jacob pulled over to let me out. I stepped out and grabbed my pack from the backseat, then stuck my hand in through the passenger window for a shake. He shook my hand and wished me luck before continuing his drive west for Sacramento. I then got off the loneliest highway and stepped onto Highway 28, making my way north towards the town of Incline Village. It felt great to be away from Carson City, but even more amazing to be back in the forest. I was astonished by how just one mountain separated all this beauty from the desert. As I continued hiking along, admiring all the trees around me, I could see the blue tones of

Lake Tahoe peeking through the branches. Seeing the water gave me a sense of peace that I hadn't felt in a while, so I smiled and eagerly made my way towards it.

__California__

As I followed the road along the ridge above Lake Tahoe, I couldn't resist making my way down the hill and through the forest to reach the water. Kicking at the football-sized pinecones and hopping over the fallen trees, I finally made it to the rock-covered shoreline. The cold wind was flowing steadily across the crystal-clear lake and seemed to blow away all my worries of Carson City. I took a seat on a large piece of driftwood and pulled out my phone to look over the videos I had taken of the UFO. I quickly realized the videos were no longer on my phone, so I decided to watch them from my Facebook Page. To my surprise, the videos had also been removed from Facebook, and several people had sent me private messages asking why I had deleted them, though I hadn't. So not only had I lost the proof of what I had seen, the fact that it had been erased from my phone validated that someone had physically gone through my things. I couldn't believe what had happened to me, and I felt so violated. At least, for whatever reason, I felt safe around the lake and began hiking north along the shore, making my way for the next town.

The path along the lake eventually turned into water, so I made my way back into the forest, where I came across a hiking trail. I assumed the trail would take me all the way to Incline Village, so I continued following it for the rest of the day. The sun was finally setting over the lake and put on a surreal show of natural beauty. The lake's vibrant blue colors reflected the orange and purple hues from the afternoon sky, an astonishing painting presented by the universe. The saturated green pine trees and pearly white rocks were an inspiring border to the canvas. I didn't want to walk into the night and miss the sunset, so I popped my tent up only a few feet from the trail and sat inside, enjoying the view. Once the show was over, I slid into my sleeping bag and fell asleep to the sounds of gentle waves on the lake and the breeze passing through the forest.

It was still dark out when I woke the next morning, but I got packed up and started walking anyway. A few hours after sunrise, I had made it into Incline Village. I knew this would be my last town before making it into California, so I stopped by a small restaurant to grab a victory breakfast. I was excited about making it across the country, but the people there weren't as social as the other towns I had been through, so no one asked what I was up to. Not that I really cared, but it would've been nice to have someone with me to celebrate. So, I sat alone at one of the picnic tables outside of the restaurant and enjoyed my sausage and biscuit, watching the people go on about their everyday lives.

After leaving the restaurant, I continued making my way around the lake with my sights set on claiming the California welcome sign. I had made it just outside of town when I came across a cell phone and wallet sitting on the side of the road. I picked them both up and immediately noticed the lady's driver's license was from Vermont. I thought it was a bit odd to stumble across a license from nearly three thousand miles away, so I called the local police station and waited for someone to arrive. An officer showed about thirty minutes later and took the items into custody. I didn't think they would take the matter seriously, so I was shocked when they gave me a call an hour later. It turned out the owner had recently moved to Incline Village and was working as a city bus driver. She and the police were both amazed that I, a homeless man, didn't take the cash and run, but I never even thought to check and see if there was any. I suppose that was another sign of me changing because normally, I would have been curious to see if there was. But I had enough money saved for food and a few more motel rooms, so I had no reason to care for it.

About an hour after returning the lost items, I had claimed my last state sign before officially making it across the country. Happy with making it into California, I slowed my pace and took the time to enjoy watching the forest grow greener and denser with each step. I probably could have made it into Truckee before nightfall, but I wandered off into the woods and stayed out there longer than I intended to. I was about a mile away from the road when I noticed a large cinnamon-colored black bear clawing its way through a pile of rotting trees. It was getting close to dark by that time, so it was easy to lose sight of the bear, but I was close enough to hear the trees being ripped apart. Since the sun had already gone down, and the canopy was so dense overhead, it was difficult to determine which way would take me back to the road. I turned with my back towards the bear and slowly, carefully, began walking. After I'd made it about fifty yards away, I found myself in a clearing and decided it would probably be a good idea to camp there. I sat my pack down and walked about fifty feet away to hang my food. As I walked, I called out to the bear several times, hoping it would hear me and leave the area. By the time I'd made it back to my pack, I felt it was safe enough to put up my tent and crawled inside.

After lying in the dark for a couple of hours, I heard several branches snap nearby. Although I had bear spray strapped to my side, I reached into my pack to pull out some tape and began securing my knife to the end of one of my trekking poles. I then stepped out of my tent and stuck my makeshift spear into a tree, testing its durability. Of course, I knew that would be nothing against the bear I'd seen earlier, but it still made me feel better knowing I had a weapon with some reach to it. I then heard a loud pop in the trees behind me and turned to see the bear

164

walking around. I began calmly talking to it, and it walked away, seemingly uninterested. I then stood with my back against the tree that was next to my tent and continued talking. After thirty minutes of rambling and no sight of the bear again, I placed my spear beside the entrance to my tent and crawled back inside to get some sleep. The crackling sounds went on through most of the night, though I never had any problems from the bear other than it being a noisy neighbor.

I made my way into Truckee the next day and immediately fell in love with the small mountain town. Since it was lunchtime, I stopped by at one of their bars, which was part of a ski resort. I made my way inside and ordered a burger and a couple of beers. I wasn't in any hurry to get out of there, so I took the time to enjoy it. As I was finishing up with my last drink, I slipped the pretty, blonde bartender my debit card. She turned to look at it and said, "I knew it! I knew that was you! I've been following you on Facebook!" She then handed the card back to me and said lunch was on her. I couldn't believe I had landed in another restaurant where someone knew who I was, and she seemed excited as well. She then handed me another beer and tried talking to me about my journey, but I dodged it. I was sick of talking about me and wanted to hear her story. She then asked the other bartender if she could cover her for a bit while we went outside to talk. We probably spent half an hour sitting at the outdoor picnic table, sharing stories, and enjoying casual conversation before getting a picture together and going our separate ways. Although, I didn't get too far before being lured to another lake.

I crossed the highway and found myself at Donner Lake. As I continued walking around the lake, admiring its beauty, and enjoying the cool weather, I noticed a large stone statue of a family and made my way over to it. Once I made it to the statue, I noticed a bronze plaque beneath the people's feet. The plague read, "Near this spot stood the brownish-green cabin of the party of emigrants who started for California from Springfield,

Illinois, in April 1846, under the leadership of Captain George Donner. Delays occurred, and when the party reached this locality, on October 29, the Truckee Pass emigrant road was concealed by snow. The height of the shaft of the monument indicates the depth of the snow, which was twenty-two feet. After futile efforts to cross the summit, the party was compelled to encamp for the winter. The graves cabin was situated about three-quarters of a mile to the eastward, the Murphy Cabin about two hundred yards southwest of the monument, and the Donner tents were at the head of Alder Creek. Ninety people were in the party, and forty-two perished, most of them from starvation and exposure." It was a beautiful lake but had some wretched history to it. Luckily for me, the snow had come lightly that year.

After camping in the forest next to Donner Lake, I got back on the move and continued walking along some backroads until I could go no farther. The road I was on had turned into an interstate, so I had to find another way to get through the mountains. It had been snowing for a couple of hours by then, so I was wary about going too far into the backcountry. I had no cellular service, so I couldn't check the weather and had to go by what my gut was telling me. There was an old, deserted gas station at the intersection, so I made my way over to it and stood under the awning, weighing my options. About thirty minutes later, I noticed a train was making its way through the mountains behind the gas station. It didn't matter to me where I came out at, so I made my way up to the train tracks and began following them west.

After following the train tracks for a few days and finding beautiful spots to camp in the forest, I'd made my way into the town of Nevada City. As I climbed down from the forest and landed back onto the road, I noticed a restaurant just up ahead. Not only was I hungry, but I also needed to charge my things. I made my way inside and quickly realized it was a vegan pizza restaurant. I'd never had vegan food before, so I was excited to try something new. I ordered a cheese-like pizza, which turned out to be delicious, and I plugged my phone into one of their power outlets. When I turned my phone on, I noticed I had received a text from my friend, Rob, the guy whom I'd spent two days visiting back in Texas. The text read, "Not sure when you'll get this, but I would like to meet up with you and join you in walking up the coast. It looks like it could be fun and may help me lose all this extra weight. Give me a call when you can." I was excited to know he wanted to walk with me and called him right away. I finished up with my meal and took our conversation outside. We agreed to meet up in Sacramento since it was the closest bus station to where I was. The only problem was that he wouldn't be there for five days, and I was only sixty miles away. I would have to slow down and find something to keep occupied until then.

As I was making my way for Grass Valley, the snow had turned into a cold rain, which slowly disintegrated into the mountains. I made it into town well after dark and immediately began searching for a place to sleep. Walking along one of the sidewalks, I noticed a small gap between a building and a parking lot. The opening was just wide enough for my shoulders, so I squeezed through and tossed my sleeping pad and sleeping bag down on the cold, wet ground.

The next morning, I made my way to a coffee shop and grabbed myself a warm cup. I then took a seat and began searching through the online dating site I had used back in Arizona. I wasn't interested in finding a mate, but I was hoping to find someone to hang out with while waiting for Rob. After swiping past several females, I landed on the profile of a pretty brunette girl named Megan. She had a backpack with her in most of her pictures, so I figured I would send her a message. It didn't take long for her to respond, and I quickly explained who I was and what I was looking for. She had recently finished a semester from school and thought it would be fun to do some hiking together, so we planned to meet up in her hometown of Auburn. She said she had some things to take care of but would be free within the next two days. Auburn was only a day's hike away from Grass Valley, so I decided to take a zero day and check out the town.

After walking around for a few hours, I came across a trail that led into the town's nearby forest. I made my way up a hill and came out to a clearing surrounded by pine trees. I noticed there were huge piles of pine needles, so I put my tent up and completely covered it with them. By the time I finished, my tent looked like it belonged there, so I threw my things inside and went back down into the city. It felt great being able to enjoy myself without having to lug around all my things.

As I made my way through town, I came across a young man playing guitar on the sidewalk, trying to make a little extra money. I thought he had a wonderful voice but could probably use a bit more practice on the guitar. I then pointed to his guitar and asked if he would mind if I jammed with him. He seemed excited that I wanted to play and didn't hesitate to hand me the instrument. As we sat outside of a bar, we played for nearly two hours before the manager came out and told us we had to leave. We were both satisfied with the eighty dollars we had made, though, so neither of us was going to complain. The panhandler then handed me my half and decided to look for another place to play. On the other hand, I decided to take my share into the bar to grab a few drinks.

After spending a couple of nights in Grass Valley, I began making my way for Auburn to meet up with Megan. As I was getting close to town, she sent a text that read, "Meet me at the statue of a man panning for gold. You can't miss it." Well, she was right about that. I had already spotted the statue and was heading over to check it out before she said anything. After sitting in front of the statue for about an hour, I stood to greet Megan as she approached me. Judging from her sense of humor, I picked up the notion that she would be good company. To get more acquainted, we made our way to the bar across the street to grab a couple of beers. As I began talking more about my quest for Alaska, Megan asked, "What if I were to tag along the entire way with you? Alaska sounds exciting!" Even though I knew having her around would slow me down, I told her I wouldn't mind. I figured the company would be worth adding a few weeks to my trip.

Before leaving the bar, we agreed to venture out and see how we got along before hiking long distances. I opened my map and noticed the North Fork American River was close by. I showed Megan and, since Auburn was somewhat of a busy city, she agreed that would probably be the best place to find a place to camp. We then began taking whatever backroads that lead in that direction until we came up to a dead-end at someone's house. Luckily, the owner was standing outside and said she didn't mind if we passed through her property. We continued through the forest until we came out at a clearing where we could see the river flowing through the green, tree-covered hills. I then set my tent up underneath a low hanging branch so we could have a great view but still be out of sight if anyone else was out there. After tossing our things inside, we walked down to the water, and I had the idea to give Megan a quick test. Without saying a word, I jumped into the river. When I lifted my head out of the water, I realized she had jumped in behind me, so I knew she would be wild enough to hang with me. After swimming in the cold water for about thirty minutes, we got out of the water and walked along the bank, trying to dry off before the sun went down.

We made it back to my tent just before dark, and I was kind of nervous about our sleeping arrangements. Since Megan didn't have a tent of her own, I was prepared to spend the first few nights sleeping on the ground. While she was back at the tent, getting ready for bed, I wandered off to hang my food bag. When I returned, I noticed she had put both of our sleeping bags inside the tent, which I assumed meant she was comfortable with me sleeping next to her. I slid down into my sleeping bag, and Megan asked, "Do you still have enough room?" She was a petite girl, so I laughed and replied, "Yeah, I think I can make this work."

When I woke the next morning, I realized Megan and I were cuddling. I wasn't sure how we ended up like that, but it sure felt nice, and so did the extra body heat. She was the first person to spend the night with me in my tent, and it had been a long time since I'd awakened with a woman in my arms. I liked it so much that I tightened my grip around her, and she did the same to me. I could feel her hand slowly moving around on my thigh, and I couldn't help but get excited about it. Once she noticed, she grabbed me and planted a kiss on my neck. It was obvious that we had both awakened with the same kind of feelings. So, after taking care of each other's romantic needs, we packed up and made our way back into town.

We were sitting outside of a coffee shop when a man named Ben approached us. He talked to us for a while and asked if we would like to hang out at his house in Sacramento. He seemed like a nice guy, so we accepted his offer. Once we made it to his house, we took some mixed drinks to the back yard and talked into the afternoon. Once Ben's husband got home, it was time for dinner, and they made me their honorary chef. Ben then handed me an apron and a chef's hat to wear while I prepared the food for everyone. It felt like we'd all been friends forever, though we were pretty much complete strangers. After we finished dinner, Megan and I went outside to camp in their back yard and was welcomed back in for breakfast the next morning. We then thanked Ben and his husband for having us over and made our way back to Auburn, where Megan wanted to introduce me to her grandparents.

After finishing our twenty-mile hike into Auburn, we decided to go back to the river and camp for another night. The next morning, we made our way to Megan's grandparents' house. I was a bit nervous about it since they already knew about her plans of going to Alaska with me, but she assured me that everything would be fine. We walked inside, and her grandparents took a quick liking to me. They figured if I'd made this long on my own that Megan was probably in good hands. We then helped her grandmother prepare breakfast and talked more about what we planned on doing once we made it to Alaska. Megan said she just wanted to stay for a couple of weeks, but I hoped to find a permanent home there. I just needed to make sure I was there before autumn, so I would have the time to find work and have a place to stay by winter.

Megan's brother, Alex, arrived a few hours later and immediately asked if I'd like to smoke with him. I thought it was a bit early to be smoking weed, but I figured it would be something for us to bond over, so I told him I would. I followed him to his room and expected to see a pipe or a joint, but instead, he had a strange bong-like piece. He then pulled out a torch and began heating the bowl. I began to wonder what it was that we were smoking, so I asked. He replied, "I smoke dabs, man. It's just the juices that have squeezed out of the marijuana." I shrugged my shoulders and thought that seemed kind of strange, but if that's all it was, then I wasn't scared to give it a try. He then placed the "dab" into the bowl and pointed the mouthpiece at me. I began inhaling the smoke, and my lungs felt like they were on fire, but I held myself back from coughing. After all the smoke was gone, I looked back up at Alex, and he had a surprised look on his face. I asked why he was looking at me like that, and he said, "I've just never seen anyone take a whole hit before." I didn't know dabs were concentrated and thought I was supposed to smoke it normally. Alex then smoked some, and his hit was about an eighth the size of mine. I felt fine, though, so I thought it might not be so bad.

Shortly after we had smoked, Megan stuck her head in the door and said, "Hey, Grandma needs us to run to the store to pick up some groceries. You guys want to come?" I was still feeling pretty much normal, so I told her I would go. When we arrived at the store, I began to feel a little dizzy as I was walking through the parking lot. However, it didn't feel any worse than any other time I had smoked. Then, the electric entrance doors slid open, and the high really hit me. I took a few steps inside, and everything appeared to be shrinking and growing, and I found everything to be hysterical. I then began to have a panic attack because I felt like I was going to have a hard time keeping my composure. I thought I behaved quite well, up until we were heading for the check-out. It was like time had come to a complete stop, but I was still functioning in regular time.

Then, I heard Megan say, "Jake, can you grab that pie?" I looked down at it, and, for whatever reason, I decided to show off my time-altering skills. I spun around, and karate chopped the pie off the table. As the pie was falling, I looked up and saw the shocked expression grow across a woman's face. I stared her directly in the eyes, spun around again, and caught the pie in one hand just before it hit the floor. I then turned to hand Megan the pie, and she had the craziest look on her face. It was the kind of face you would make if you had just witnessed some sort of miracle. Then, just as fast as it happened, it was over with. I still felt a little weird, but at least the altered sense of time was over.

We finally made it back to the house, and a second wave hit me. Everything began to sound huge, deep and drawn out. I couldn't even listen to the sound of people talk without laughing. Trying to hide the fact that I was high as a kite, I made my way to the bathroom to sit and wait it out. Several minutes had passed, and I heard knocks at the door, which sounded like large toms echoing throughout a cathedral. Megan then stuck her head in and asked, "Are you okay? Dinner is ready." Feeling unsure of myself, I replied, "I think so. I just needed a minute for that stuff to wear off. Let's go eat."

As I took my seat at the table, I quickly realized the effects of the dab were still in full swing. It was like every sound was hitting my funny bone, so I put my head down to prevent everyone from seeing the huge grin on my face. Then, to make matters worse, Megan's grandfather thought I was praying and invited everyone else to join in. I must have been in that position for a while because I heard Megan's grandmother whisper, "Does he always pray this long?" Wiping away my tears, I lifted my head and said, "Okay. Let's eat." I tried not to look at anyone but could tell they were all staring at me, probably wondering if I was crazy. The whole time I was eating, I never looked at anyone or said anything. Then, after everyone had finished, Megan's grandmother leaned over me and asked, "Would you like any more food?" A massive wave hit me when she asked that, and it was like her voice shook my entire body. I looked up at her distorted face and replied, "No. I'm good. Thanks, though." A few hours later, I woke up on the couch and asked Megan what had happened. She replied, "After you finished eating, you stood in front of the microwave for about an hour. Then, you turned to my grandmother and said, "Wow! You guys have a really nice microwave!" Then you came in here and went to sleep." Feeling kind of embarrassed, I put my hand over my face and fell back to sleep.

The next morning, Megan said she had a few things to take care of before she could set out on the road but would meet up with Rob and me later. After having one last breakfast with her and her family, I left their house and made my way to Sacramento to meet up with Rob. I made it to the bus station around 3:00 p.m. and began looking for a spot to camp nearby. Rob wasn't supposed to arrive until 2:00 a.m., but I wanted to make sure we had a safe place to sleep before he got there. That turned out to be more challenging than I thought because all the hidden spots had already taken by other homeless people, and most of them weren't too happy about being walked up on. I eventually found a vacant site, though, and put my tent up kind of early. It looked like someone and had recently camped there, and, if that was their usual spot, I was hoping they would come back during the day and decide to leave after seeing my tent. I sat inside of it for the rest of the evening, waiting to see if I ever saw or heard anyone. Rob's bus finally arrived, and since I never had any visitors, I assumed it would be safe to leave everything and made my way over to the bus station.

Rob had already arrived before I got there and was waiting for me on a bench. I walked up to him and had him follow me back to our spot for the night. While we were walking, I noticed he had a small school-sized backpack. I looked over at it and said, "Oh, man, that's not going work. Don't worry about it, though. I'll find a way to get you hooked up." As we approached my tent, I could tell Rob was a little uneasy about camping there. I laughed, then looked at him and said, "Don't worry, man. I do this all the time." We then crawled into my tent, and I watched as he began emptying his backpack, which he kept calling a "book bag." After he had all his things laid out, he asked what I thought he should get rid of. I laughed again and said, "Well, personally, I'd get rid of some of those clothes. Ideally, you'd want to wash one, wear one, and have one spare. Also, ten pounds of tortilla shells seems a little excessive. And, starting tomorrow, there will be no food allowed in the tent. We'll get you a bag to hang your food. Two full rolls of toilet paper? I usually just grab enough from public restrooms to last me three uses. You can carry whatever you want, though. You'll figure out what works for you. Everyone's different. Just start with what you need and then add the things you want. As long as you can carry your sleeping bag and water, you'll be fine for now."

When I woke the next morning, Rob was still in a heavy sleep. I had never been the type to lie there after waking up, so I began packing my things. Eventually, the only thing left for me to pack up was my tent. I slowly pulled off the rainfly and removed all the tent poles, causing the mesh portion to fall on top of Rob. I then sat on the hill beside our camp and waited about thirty minutes before he woke up. He sat up and swatted the mesh off his face, looking around in a panic. As I began laughing, he cocked his head back towards me and said, "Oh my God, dude! I thought you left me here!" I laughed and replied,

174

"No way, man! I just hate to keep lying around after I wake up. It makes my back hurt. You ready to get out of here?"

Rob had never done anything remotely close to what we were doing. I don't think he'd ever even been camping before, so living like a homeless person was going to be quite the experience for him. As we were making our way into town, I tried to get him into the feel of things and said, "Keep an eye out for any change you see lying around. Let's see if we can find enough to get a cup of coffee before we make it into town." After walking five miles, we had made it to the coffee shop and had collected nearly six dollars in change. Rob decided to sit outside and watch our things while I went in to order our drinks. When I went back outside, I noticed he was holding a large plastic bag and had a huge smile on his face. When he saw me walking towards him, he began laughing and shouted, "Dude! Look at what some lady just gave me! It's a bag full of food!" Excited for him, I patted him on the back and said, "There you go! Now you're officially a bum!"

After having lunch, we followed a trail next to a river that led us to the outskirts of the city. As the sun began to set, we decided to sleep right next to the trail. We couldn't pitch my tent because we were out in the open, where people could see us, so we just tossed our sleeping bags on the ground and turned in for the night. The next morning, I still had my head buried in my sleeping bag and heard Rob ask, "Dude, did it rain last night?" I didn't think it did, but I stuck my head out to make sure. I looked at Rob and watched as he ran his hand over his sleeping bag. He then said, "Everything is soaking wet, man. I think it rained." I laughed and said, "Oh! No, man. That's condensation. It's good for you." I then wiped some of the dew off my sleeping bag and ran it through my hair, trying to tame my cowlicks. I then tossed him one of my extra bandanas to dry off his sleeping bag and asked, "You ready to do some real hiking? It's twenty miles to Woodland. Think you can handle that?" Rob probably weighed about two hundred and forty pounds, so I was a bit worried if he would be able to make it that far. However, I felt he should be able to do at least that distance to make it to water, so we began heading west with an early start.

Rob's feet began to blister after only ten miles, so we had to take a lot of breaks. However, he kept trying, and we finally made it into Woodland about an hour after dark. I was proud of him for his determination, so I decided to stop at a Mexican restaurant and pay for dinner. As we sat to look over the menu, a man sat next to us and began asking about our backpacks. After telling him I was finishing up my walk across America, he offered to pay for our meal and asked if he could join us for dinner. We told him that sounded great and continued to talk throughout the rest of our time there. Before Rob and I got up to leave, the man asked if we'd like to come with him to the bar across the street and have some free drinks. I told Rob it was up to him because I figured he was probably exhausted. He then said he was down for a little bit of partying, so we followed the man across the street, and all three of us took a seat at the bar. After having a few drinks, Rob and the other guy went outside for a smoke break while I continued sitting at the bar. Right after they left, a tall, beautiful woman with long curly hair sat next to me and said, "So, you're the guy walking across America? My name is Christy, and I own a restaurant here in Woodland. If you're interested, you're welcome to stay at my place for a couple of days. There's going to be a food truck festival, and I could use an extra hand in exchange for free food and a place to crash." Rob walked in just as Christy and I had finished talking, so I ran everything by him, and we both thought it sounded like a good idea. Christy was ready to leave, so I found the man who had brought us to the bar and thanked him before we left. Christy, Rob, and I then took a taxi to her house, where we were able to get warm showers and decent sleep.

The next morning, Christy took us to meet her friend Eric. He was an artist and mechanic who lived and worked inside a large garage. His shop's interior looked like a museum, all done up with the different things he had made over the years. We hung out at his place for a couple of hours, and then we all made our way to Christy's restaurant, Mojo's Lounge, for lunch. When we got there, Christy gathered some of her friends and proposed a toast to me for making it across the country. She then told Rob and me that we could hang out there for the rest of the day and have whatever we wanted free of charge. The restaurant was also a bar, so we helped ourselves to a few drinks. Before we knew it, it was getting dark, and the bar had really livened up. The people there were excited for me to have made it across America, so a lot of them were handing me drinks and getting their pictures taken with me. The partying went on until it was time to close and head back to Christy's house for another night.

The next morning, Christy woke me up and said, "I have to go to a business meeting. I'll be gone most of the day. I was thinking I could drop you guys off at the wakeboard park and pick you up around closing." Although Rob and I had a bit of a hangover, we both agreed to it because we'd never been wakeboarding before and may never get the chance again. We grew up skateboarding together and thought it would probably be similar, so we loaded up into Christy's car and made our way to the wakeboarding park, Velocity Island. When we got there, it got brought up that Rob and I were making our way across the country, so the owner said we could ride all day for free. However, Rob was still feeling the effects of his hangover, so he decided to sunbathe while I hit the water. It was nothing like skateboarding, so it took me all day to be able to make a full run without wiping out. After being yanked around by an electric zipline all day and taking hundreds of slams, my body was sore, and I was happy to see Christy again.

After leaving Velocity Park, Christy asked if we'd like to go with her to a vineyard. Since Rob and I had never been to one before, we thought we would give it a try and see what it was like. As we were driving along the countryside, Christy explained that the vineyard sold their wine at her restaurant, so she could go there for free wine tasting whenever she wanted. I thought that sounded like a pretty good trade and felt better knowing it wouldn't cost her anything for Rob and me. After a couple of hours of relaxing and enjoying our ride through the hills, we arrived at the vineyard. When we walked inside, the owners handed us a glass of some new wine they were hoping to sell at Mojo's Lounge. Rob and I felt out of place being around fancy wine connoisseurs, but we enjoyed the free drinks and walking through the grape fields. After spending a couple of hours there, we made our way back to Christy's restaurant to pick back up on our drinking.

That morning, we left Christy's house and made our way to her restaurant. It was the day of the food truck festival, so we had to get there a few hours early to make sure everything was ready. Rob and I went around and helped to set up pavilions, tables, chairs, and whatever else needed to be done. As the festival went on, we walked up and down the streets, removing full trash bags and replacing them with new ones. We thought it was crazy how fast the trash cans were filling up, but it finally slowed down after lunch. As the crowd began to shrink, Rob and I made our way up to the restaurant's balcony to have a beer with Christy, where we sat watched one of the bands play in the park below. Once the festival was over, we made our way back down to the parking lots and helped to put everything away. We finally finished around midnight and made our way back to Christy's house for one last night.

The next morning, Christy offered to take Rob and me to a consignment shop to see if we could find him some better gear. She ended up buying him a cheap, used backpack, hiking shoes, trekking poles, patches for the blisters on his feet, and a tarp. Then, after leaving the store, she drove us to the bar where we had first met her. We thanked her for all the fun, help, and hospitality and began making our way for the next town of Guinda. Once we were out of the city and away from civilization, Rob said, "You know what it reminds me of out here? A level from Mario's World, with all the green hills and blue sky. It almost looks fake, doesn't it?" We continued walking until we were about five miles from the next town and wandered off into a field to look for a place to camp. After finding a nice patch of grass surrounded by trees, I had Rob pull out his tarp so I could show him how to make a shelter with it before it got dark. After helping him, I began setting up my tent when Rob asked, "Are there bears out here?" He looked worried when he asked, which I thought was funny because I had forgotten what that fear feels like. I replied, "Maybe. I'm not sure. If there are, they probably won't bother you. You can sleep with my bear spray if it makes you feel better."

The next morning, as we were making our way into Guinda, two police officers pulled over in front of me and ordered me to stop walking. I was confused about why they had stopped me, but not Rob. He was up ahead, which meant the police had passed by him first. He looked back when the cops pulled over, but I waved for him to keep walking because I knew I could catch up with him after dealing with them. One of the officers then demanded that I set my backpack down and step away from it. One of the officers took my pack and began going through it while the other asked me questions. When I told the officer that we had been staying in Woodland with Christy of Mojo's Lounge, they knew who she was and stopped harassing me. They finally told me they stopped me because I had a machete strapped to the side of my pack. I looked at them like they were crazy and asked what that had to do with anything. They then kept calling my machete a "weapon," which I corrected them each time by saying, "tool." I used my machete for chopping wood and digging holes to use the bathroom. I felt like I kind of embarrassed them after saying I had gone all the way across America with it and never had anyone say anything about it until now. It wasn't like I had access to it while I was wearing the pack anyway. If I had been carrying it for some illegal reason, I wouldn't have had it strapped to the side of my pack in plain sight.

After dealing with the police, I picked up my pace and caught up with Rob about thirty minutes later. I explained everything to him, and we joked about how uptight California was, although that was my first bad experience with the police there. We then continued into Guinda and stopped to camp at a river just before town. Jody had sent us a care package to the post office there, but it wasn't scheduled to arrive for a few days, so we were going to have to find a way to keep ourselves occupied. I didn't mind taking it easy, though. I could tell that I had a stress fracture in my hip and could really use the break. We went ahead and found a spot to camp for the night, and then I left Rob to watch over our things while I went into town to see what they had to offer.

There wasn't much to Guinda. All the town had to offer was a post office, one small restaurant, a firehouse, and a tiny grocery store. I walked into the restaurant to see if it looked promising enough to grab dinner for the night when the cook, Jessie, approached me. He said he had seen me walking earlier during the day and asked if I wanted anything to eat. He said he used to be a traveler himself, and I could have anything I wanted from the menu. I then told him I had a friend waiting for me at the river and asked if it would be okay if he ate too. I wasn't going to eat and leave Rob behind. Jessie said, "Sure, man! Go get him!" I went back to tell Rob the good news, and he was stoked! We threw our packs back on and made our way to the restaurant. We walked inside and saw Jessie standing at the back door, waving for us to come over. We followed him outside, where he said, "There are some picnic tables if you guys want to eat out here. You guys are welcome to camp back here, too, if you want. I figured you might like a yard to camp in, so you wouldn't have to worry about getting caught while stealth camping." Rob and I thought both of those things sounded great, so we went ahead and set up our tents while waiting for our

180

burgers and beer. After we finished our delicious dinner, we thanked Jessie and the owners for their help and turned in for the night.

The next morning, we were packing our things when Jessie came into the back to check on us. He asked where we would be going from there. I told him we didn't know because we were stuck there, waiting for a package. He then said, "Well, you guys can camp in my yard if you want. Come back around sunset, and I'll drive you guys to my house. It's about five miles up the highway here. I'd say you could go now, but my wife might freak out if she saw two guys hanging around the house." Rob and I thought that sounded like a good idea, so we made our way back to the river, where we could do some swimming and sunbathing in the meantime.

Once the sun started to go down, Rob and I made our way back to the restaurant to catch a ride to Jessie's house. Jessie was still finishing up with work when we got there, so we went to the back and waited. The owner then came outside with a guitar and asked, "Either of you know how to play? We have bands come through here every now and then, and one of them left this as a gift." I had been carrying a harmonica, which I used to occupy myself when I was alone, so I pulled it out of my pocket and tossed it over to Rob. He looked at it like he didn't know how to play, so I said, "It's in the key of G. Just follow my rhythm." I then took the guitar from the owner and began to play something from Tom Petty. After just a few strums on the guitar, Rob knew I was getting down to "Mary Jane's Last Dance" and tried his best to play along. The owner got a kick out of us playing and said we would be fun to have at their next concert if we were still around.

After about an hour of playing music with Rob, Jessie was finally finished with work. We tossed our packs into the back of his truck and began making our way to his house. When we pulled up, Jessie said, "Let me run in and tell my wife we have company, and I'll be right back outside to show you where to set up your tents." It looked like an old farmhouse, in the middle of nowhere and with no other neighbors. Rob and I knew we wouldn't have to worry about any other people out there. Jessie then came back outside and pointed to the shed in his front yard, "You guys can just set up camp in front of my shed if you want. Come check this out first, though." We then followed him over to the shed, and he cracked the door open before sliding inside. He then waved for Rob and me to follow him in. When we walked in, I saw kegs everywhere and then noticed Jessie was pouring beer into a couple of glasses. Handing Rob and me a glass, he said, "I've been trying to make my own beer for the past few years. It's kind of my hobby. Let me know what you guys think!" Rob and I were both surprised by how good it was! It was a dark and creamy beer, with hints of chocolate and bourbon. Jessie then went on to say he thought he had the recipe about right but still had to wait on all the legal stuff before he could get it into their restaurant. After having another glass, Jessie told us to have a good night and would see us in the morning for breakfast.

After having breakfast with Jessie, his wife, and two sons, Rob and I hopped into Jessie's truck again and took a ride back to the post office, which was right across the street from the restaurant. Since Guinda was such a small town, the post office was only open for a couple of hours, so Rob and I sat outside of it and waited for a worker to arrive. A worker finally pulled up around lunchtime and said our package wasn't there yet, so we had to find something else to do while we waited. We remembered Jessie had mentioned an old abandoned bridge that crossed over a great swimming hole, so we decided to go check that out. It was about a five-mile hike to the water hole, which made us want to swim even more by the time we got there. We got to swim for a few hours before the sun started going down and decided we should probably just camp under the bridge.

It was probably about 2:00 a.m. when Rob and I woke to the sound of a loud splash in the water. It sounded like someone had thrown a large boulder over the side of the bridge. We began to listen closely, curious if we would hear anything else. A few minutes had gone by without any other sounds, so we tried to fall back to sleep. Immediately after we closed our eyes, there was another large splash right next to our tent. The splash was big enough that some of the droplets even fell on top of us. I stuck my head out and turned on my headlamp, not knowing what to expect. I looked all around us, trying to figure out what could have made such a big splash. I thought maybe some debris had fallen from the bridge, but it was completely intact. I could see well enough into the water to know it wasn't a beaver. Then, I thought maybe someone was on top of the bridge, trying to mess with us. I turned my headlamp off and walked out of my tent, hoping to catch whatever it was. I stood in the bushes for about ten minutes before giving up and going back to the tent.

Although I was wide awake, Rob had fallen back to sleep and began snoring. A few minutes later, I heard a loud splash right next to the tent. I turned my headlamp on and stuck my head out, surprised to see there weren't even any ripples in the water. Rob then woke up and said, "I think maybe we should leave, man. Something just isn't right about this place." I agreed with him, so we began shoving our things into our packs. As soon as I stuck my foot out of the tent, rocks began flying all over the place. They were hitting the wall behind us, the tent, the water, the top of the bridge, the bushes, just everywhere around us. We didn't want to get hit in the head by one of them, so we put our packs over us and took cover. We were both too afraid to move and agreed not to until the sun came up.

As soon as we could see our surroundings, we jumped up and began packing the rest of our things to get out of there. Rob made his way to the top of the bridge while I stayed behind to finish putting away my tent. As I was stuffing the tent into my backpack, I noticed a man standing on the other side of the river. I ignored what he was doing because I assumed that he was fishing. Once I'd finished gathering everything, I threw my pack on and turned around to notice the man was gone. I looked around and didn't see him anywhere, so I made my way to the top of the bridge and asked Rob if he'd seen a man down there before he left. He said, "Yeah. Real weird guy. He was just standing there." I replied, "Yeah? I saw him, too, but when I turned around, it was like he had disappeared." We then both leaned over the bridge and waited for a few minutes to see if we saw or heard anyone, but we didn't and decided to head back into town.

We got back onto the road and had to walk by Jessie's house to get back into town. We noticed his truck was still there, so we sat outside and waited for him to leave for work so we could catch a ride back to the post office. As we were riding along, Rob and I began telling Jessie about what had happened during the night. He didn't seem too surprised, so I asked, "Have you had any strange experiences while camping down there?" Jessie replied, "Oh, I've never gone camping down there. I've only gone swimming a few times. I've heard stories about that bridge being haunted, though."

Out of curiosity, I pulled out my phone and searched online for "Cache Creek Yolo County Haunted." I read aloud the first article I found, "In the late 1940s, a young Nomelacki lady lived way out in the foothills and would walk the same trail into town every weekend to the dance hall. It's believed the town may have been either Rumsey or Guinda, both very small work crew settlements. One evening, during her walk to the dance, she met a young man who she described as dark-eyed, having well-groomed black hair, wearing a dark suit with a white undershirt, and carrying an overcoat. He was very handsome, with chiseled features and a cleft chin. He greeted her and offered to walk her into town. As they walked, he asked her all kinds of questions about herself. She thought he was very polite and wanted to bring him into town so everyone could see how good-looking he was. When they approached a wire fence, he cleared the way for her. When she bent down to go between the wires, she looked

184

down and noticed he had hooves for feet. She ran all the way into town and never looked back. She only told a few close friends and relatives about what she had seen. In the mid-1970s, a family saw the same man walking on a mountain road, miles away from the nearest town. Some say he is the devil, but elders said such an entity would use its charm as a weapon."

We pulled up to the post office just as I finished reading the article. Jessie thought it was cool and said he would like to spend a night down there to see for himself. However, Rob and I agreed that we would never go back, so Jessie would have to find someone else or go alone. We then hopped out of Jessie's truck, thanked him for everything, and then went to sit and wait for the post office to open. After waiting a few hours, a postal worker arrived and said, "Good news, boys! I got a package for you!" We both felt relieved to hear that because neither of us felt comfortable with spending another night there. We then sat in front of the post office and opened the care package to see all kinds of good stuff. There were probably enough snacks to last us a week and two twenty-dollar bills.

Reaching the Pacific

After leaving Guinda, Rob and I walked about thirty miles before deciding to set up camp within an orchard of walnut trees. The next morning, we only had ten miles to reach the town of Clearlake Oaks. As we were passing through, we noticed several people who were obviously on drugs. It didn't seem like the best city to be hanging around in, so we found a place to fill up on our water and continued following the road around the lake. Once we had made it outside the city limits, we found ourselves hiking through the nature-filled mountains. Although the view of the lake was nice, the road was very tight and curvy, unsafe to walk with the traffic. Rob was skeptical about walking along the highway because of how dangerous it was, but we really didn't have any other option. We had to continuously stop and put our backs against the mountain just so the passing vehicles could have enough room to squeeze through. Shortly after reaching the top, the road widened, and we noticed an RV park on the other side of the street. It looked like it would be a safe place to camp, so we made our way over to ask if we could set up my tent. The owner told us it would be fifty dollars to camp there, so we laughed in his face and continued walking, searching for a place where we could sleep for free. After about a mile from the RV park, we came across what looked to be an old abandoned building, so we set up camp next to it and had no problems throughout the night.

By the next afternoon, we had made it into the town of Calpella. It didn't take us long to realize the highway had turned into an interstate. Since pedestrians weren't allowed on the interstate, we decided to try and hitchhike to the next town of Willits. I wasn't happy about it, but the interstate ran north and south, so catching a ride wouldn't have made any difference to me as far as making it across the country on foot. We then made our way to the interstate on-ramp and stood there with our thumbs out. A couple of hours went by without anyone stopping, so we decided to make our way back into town to ask people for a ride while they were pumping gas. At least then we could explain ourselves and perhaps have better luck.

Once we made it into town, we noticed a bus stop in front of the gas station and began reading over the schedule. It appeared that the bus went up to Willits, and the next one should be arriving at any minute. It would only cost us two dollars each, so we decided to do that instead of bothering people for a ride. The bus pulled up a few minutes later, and we climbed aboard. Once we made it into Willits, the bus let us out in front of a grocery store. We both needed to run in to use the restroom, so Rob stayed to watch over our things while I went inside. As I was leaving the store, I heard a customer ask the cashier if she knew where he could buy some cocaine.

No one seemed surprised by the man's question, which I found a bit odd. I then went outside and told Rob about it. He laughed and said, "Oh, yeah? Well, I just watched a man punch a woman in the face. The cops are over there asking witnesses about it now." He then went in to use the restroom while I watched our bags. As I was sitting there, I heard a man's voice come from behind the store, "Psst. Hey, man." I turned to see what the man wanted, and he looked strung out on drugs. He continued, "You wanna come back here? We got drugs. We got women. What you want, man? You want some beer? You want some weed? Come on, man. We got some girls." I didn't say anything back to him, but he kept repeating himself until two cops came over to ask if I saw the accident. Rob then walked up to the cops and gave them a description of what he had seen. After the police officers walked away, Rob and I decided that Willits was a bit too sketchy for us, so we got out of there and began following Route 20 into the Jackson State Forest.

It didn't take long before the city had disappeared behind us, and we found ourselves surrounded by mountains and redwood trees. We made it about ten miles before the sun began to fade behind the hills. Since we were smack-dab in the middle of the forest, finding a place to camp was going to be easy. However, Rob was beginning to worry about bears again, so he wanted to continue walking until we found an area that was a bit more open. After hiking a few miles into the dark, we came across an emergency call box. Rob felt safe camping in the woods behind it because we could call for help should anything happen. Besides having a safety net, it was probably the best spot we would find anyway because there were steep cliffs everywhere else.

After hiking through the dark, moss-covered forest for two nights, we had reached the coastal highway by the third morning. We couldn't see the ocean yet because of how heavy the fog was, but we knew it was just up ahead. A large fence and heavy brush blocked off the beach, so we continued following the highway north into the town of Fort Bragg. As we entered the heart of the small coastal town, the sun had cleared away most of the fog, and the cold, salty sea air filled with the smell of sweet yeast from a nearby brewery. Our mouths began to water, so we followed our nose to the factory and went inside to try one of their freshly prepared beers. Shortly after leaving the brewery, we began walking along a paved trail that followed along the cliff, overlooking the Pacific Ocean. Once we'd made it to the north side of town, we came up to a bridge that crossed over a sandy beach, so we made our way down. We kicked our boots off and began walking barefoot through the cold, damp sand. I then stood where the last tide had retreated into the ocean and patiently waited for its return. It had been six months and twenty-two days since I'd left Florida, and the frigid water of the Pacific finally washing over my feet felt like it had set me free. Of course, I still had to make it to Alaska, but at least I could check one thing off my bucket list.

As Rob and I were putting our boots back on, a man walked up to us and asked, "Are you one of those cross-country hiker dudes?" I laughed and said, "Yep! Just finished today, and it feels so good!" With a big smile on his face, the man gave me a high five and said, "Hell yeah, man! Here! Take this!" He then reached into his cargo pocket and handed me a large sack of weed. Rob had a shocked look on his face, so I thanked the man for his gift and handed it over to Rob. He was obviously more interested in it than I was, probably because I was still a bit shaken from smoking that dab with Megan's brother. Ironically, she called a few minutes later and said she was ready to meet back up, so we had to come up with some plans for her.

Megan and I agreed that she would take a Greyhound bus to Ukiah, and I would take one from Fort Bragg to meet her there. Since she wouldn't be there for two more days, Rob and I began searching for a safe place to camp in the meantime. Luckily for us, Fort Bragg was small, and the people there seemed friendly, so we weren't too worried. We began following the coastal trail away from town until we came across what looked to be the perfect spot. A few large trees had grown closely together, with thick brush and dense leaves to keep us from being seen. The trees and their limbs had been permanently bent inland from years of constant wind, which we thought looked interesting. Once we approached the trees, we realized the ground was covered with squishy, succulent plants, which we imagined would be very comfortable to sleep on. Since we had an amazing view of the coast, we decided to hang around for a couple of hours to see if anyone ever came around. After assuring ourselves we had the place all to ourselves, we set up my tent, tossed our things inside, and made our way back into town.

About a mile from our camping spot, we came across a gas station. They had advertisements for beer hanging up in the window, so I asked Rob if he'd like to split a six-pack. We figured taking a few beers down to the beach sounded like a good way to celebrate and unwind. Since it was a cold and dreary day, we had the beach all to ourselves. We walked around for a few hours, sipping on our beer and checking out all the fascinating marine animals that had been living in the tide pools. After we had finished our beer, we made our way back to camp just in time to enjoy the sunset. We had an amazing view and joked about how it seemed like the kind of spot people would go to write inspirational poems. Rob then said with a poetic voice, "The view was astonishing and inspirational, so I felt inspired to write an inspirational book about feeling inspired by all of this stunningly beautiful inspiration." Joking aside, if you needed some inspiration Fort Bragg sure was the right place to find it.

The next morning, we made our way back into town and ran into another traveler. He informed us about a homeless shelter just a few blocks over, where we could get showers and do our laundry. We were both ready for a shower, so we took down the address and followed my GPS. We were a bit confused when we made it there because it looked like every other house in the neighborhood. We didn't want to walk up to a random person's house and ask if we could take a shower, so we sat in the field across from it and waited to see if anyone came or went that fit the part. After a few minutes of sitting there, we saw a couple who looked homeless enter the gate on the side of the house. Rob and I looked at each other, nodded our heads, and then made our way into the gate. After letting ourselves in, we saw about ten other people sitting at the picnic tables. They were either waiting for their clothes or waiting in line for a shower. A man then yelled for us to put our name on the list, so we did and waited with the rest of them.

After getting a warm shower and washing away days' worth of sweat and dirt, a man sitting outside of the homeless shelter told us there was a food bank just up the street. I still had a lot of food from the package Jody had sent, but Rob was beginning to run low, so we made our way over to it. From the outside, the food bank looked like a barn. We walked into the office area and saw several people through the window next door, standing in line with grocery carts. One of the workers then had Rob fill out a paper and told him to grab a cart and stand in line at the entrance. Once inside the building, there were several tables topped off with boxes of food. The tables zigzagged throughout the building like a maze, ending at the back door. I walked with Rob, watching him toss a ton of food into his cart. I could tell he was getting way more than he could carry, but I didn't want to say anything. I thought it was interesting to see how being hungry could cause a person to overreact when allowed free food. Once we made it outside, he began shoving as much as he could into his backpack and then asked if I'd like some of his leftovers. I took a few things for myself and then went over to give the rest to a group of three other travelers.

After we had loaded up on food, we decided to head back to the beach. As we walked along the coastal trail again, we noticed a sign that read "Glass Beach." I didn't know what to expect, but we made our way down and thought the name was very fitting. Millions of pieces of glass had washed onto the bank and completely covered the beach. There were all types of glass from all sorts of things, but most of the pieces appeared to be from bottles. All the pieces felt very smooth, so I took my boots off and began walking through them barefoot. Rob thought I was crazy for doing that, but it felt very soothing. We then took a seat on a large piece of driftwood and took out a pack of crackers. As soon as I opened the wrapper, a ground squirrel came down out of the rocks to investigate. I crushed one of the crackers and tossed the crumbs in its direction. Out of nowhere, about twenty squirrels had us surrounded, all begging for food. Every time I took a bite, I would hold the cracker out while I chewed. The bravest squirrels would then come up to grab a bite, and I was even able to pet one of them. After finishing my snack, it was time to catch the bus down to Ukiah to meet up with Megan. I told Rob it would be tomorrow before I made it back, so I asked if he wanted to go with me. He said he felt comfortable staying in Fort Bragg by himself, so I told him to enjoy himself and made my way into town to catch the bus.

I made it into Ukiah a few hours before Megan, which was good because it was about an hour's walk from the local bus stop to the Greyhound stop. I spent my time waiting for her by playing my harmonica and even scored enough money to pay for us to have dinner that night. The sun was just beginning to go down when Megan got there, so we made our way into the hills, hoping to find a safe place to camp. We walked around for a few hours and finally came across a church that looked promising enough. We then went back to a restaurant we had seen on our way through town and ordered a couple of burgers and beer. While we were waiting for our food to be served, the people sitting next to us left a plate full of fries, so I grabbed them and brought them back to our table. Megan looked at me like I was weird for doing that, but I didn't like seeing people waste food. After she realized no one seemed to care, she began eating them with me.

After Megan and I had finished dinner, we made our way back to the church and set up my tent next to the side of it. We woke up kind of late the following day and made our way to the bus stop to catch our ride to Fort Bragg. It was about 6:00 p.m. when we made it back, so I went ahead and showed Megan to our campsite. When we got there, I noticed Rob had laid out his tarp and was cozied up inside his sleeping bag, knocked out from smoking too much weed. I woke him up to introduce them and then helped Megan put her things in the tent. We then all made our way over to the cliff to sit and watch the sunset. While we were sitting there, Megan chuckled and said, "Wow! It's so inspirational!" Rob and I began laughing and had to explain to her why we thought it was so funny. Once the sun had gone down, Megan and I snuggled up in the tent while Rob wrapped himself in his tarp like a giant burrito.

The next morning, we were ready to start heading up the coast but decided to get some breakfast first. We probably would have kept walking but couldn't pass up the all-you-can-eat pancakes for five dollars. After filling our stomachs, we walked out into the parking lot and ran into two Swedish ladies. They began asking about our packs because they were hiking the Pacific Crest Trail and wondered if that's what we were doing. After explaining to them that Megan and I were headed for Alaska and Rob was going to Portland, Oregon, they invited us to their beach house for the night. Rob turned down their invite because he wanted to look for a vape shop but said Megan and I could go if we wanted. We thought it sounded like it could be a fun experience, so we hopped in the car with them and told Rob we would see him in the morning.

After we made it to the Swedish women's house, we just sat around and talked. Most of our conversation revolved around hiking gear until they heard that I had just made it across the country. They wanted to hear what it was like backpacking in America, and I wanted to know what it was like backpacking in Sweden. They then cracked open some beer they had brought from back home, and we began sharing stories until it was time for dinner. They ended up cooking Megan and me one of their favorite recipes, some sort of meatballs in a cheese sauce with a side of perfectly seasoned potatoes. After dinner, Megan and I were showed to the spare bedroom upstairs, which had its own bathroom. We took advantage of the shower and fell asleep, snuggled up on the large, comfortable bed.

After having breakfast with the Swedish ladies, they gave us a ride back into town. We then met back up with Rob, where we had camped for the past few days. We all decided to head over to the homeless shelter to get our laundry done and one more shower before getting back on the road. After everyone was cleaned up, I asked Megan if she wanted to see Glass Beach before leaving. She said she did, so we all made our way to it, and she loved it. We accidentally ended up staying there for a few hours, so we all agreed to spend one more night in Fort Bragg so we could have an early start in the morning. As the day was coming to an end, Megan said she wanted to try some beers from the brewery Rob and I had gone to when we first got there. She said she had enough money to buy us all drinks, so we made our way over to it. After finishing my third beer, I decided to head back to camp so I wouldn't be tired, hungover, or dehydrated for the hike to come. However, Rob and Megan decided to stay out and do some bar hopping. I woke up around midnight to the sound of Rob and Megan making their way back into camp. They sat outside of the tent and continued talking for a couple of hours before turning in for the night.

Since they had stayed up drinking all night, I was up much earlier than they were. I then got up to pee, and I noticed everything in my pack and been pulled out and scattered all over the ground. As I began collecting my things, I realized that five of my anxiety pills were missing. I hadn't taken any of it in a while, but I kept them for emergencies, and I knew exactly how many were left. Rob was the only person who knew about it because I had shown him everything I carried when he first got there. Since he also had a drug and stealing problem when we were younger, I woke him up and began asking questions. I shook him by his shoulder and said, "Hey, man. My stuff is scattered all over the place. Did you get into my pack last night?" He then replied, "Huh? Oh, yeah, I got some toilet paper out of there because I had to use the bathroom." I then woke Megan up and asked, "You didn't go through my pack last night, did you?" She sat up with a nervous look on her face and said, "We got some toilet paper out of there last night. Why?" Rob also had a worried look on his face, so I could tell they knew something. I then said to them both, "Someone stole some medication out of my pack last night. I'm not mad about it, but I can't be with you guys if I can't trust you. Either someone

194

confesses to stealing it, or I'm going to leave you both." Neither of them had anything else to say, so I finished packing up my things. After tossing my pack over my shoulders, I stood there for a few minutes, hoping one of them would own up to it, but they both stayed quiet. Before turning around and walking away, I looked down at them and said, "Okay then. Good luck to you both."

Killing Time

After parting ways with Rob and Megan, I checked my GPS and noticed it was sixty miles to the town of Garberville. I continued following the coastal trail for about another mile out of Fort Bragg, which I felt was a good warm-up exercise. Once I made it to the highway, I took off, mixing my pace between speed walking and a jog. I guess that was my way of letting off steam, but I hadn't pushed myself in about a week and missed the feeling of being exhausted by the end of the day. The coast was nice and cool, which meant I could push myself without overheating or losing a lot of water. As I progressed deeper into the dense forest, overgrown with giant redwood trees and bright green moss, I began to feel a sense of peace and belonging. Although, I could only enjoy that feeling for short periods because the road was extremely narrow, and I would have to jump out of the way of speeding vehicles periodically. For most of the day, there was barely any shoulder and lots of curves hidden by the large trees. A few times, I had to get behind a tree and hope a car didn't take my head off when I looked to see if it was safe.

The forest presented lots of fun and interesting things, such as the hundreds of wood carvings of bigfoot, a tree with a house inside of it, and the one thousand eight hundred-year-old "Grandfather Tree" that stood two hundred sixty-five feet and had a diameter of twenty-four feet. I also ran into a very unsuspected person as I was making my through. He was a scrawny older man, relaxing in a lawn chair outside of an old abandoned store. He had long white hair with a matching beard and was wearing a brightly striped jacket. I couldn't help but feel curious, so I walked up to ask what he was doing out there. His eyes squinted from the sun as he looked up and said, "What does it look like I'm doing? I'm working." I looked around, trying to figure out what exactly it was that he considered being work. I let out a small chuckle and asked, "What kind of work are you doing?" He then pointed at the old building and said, "I'm the window cleaner." However, the building had no windows. There were only boards where the windows used to be. The man then pointed towards my hip and asked, "What's that? Is that some of that of bear spray stuff?" I pulled it out to show him and replied, "Yep. It is. I'm headed up to Alaska and figured I'd carry this until I made it up there." He then laughed and said, "Oh! Yeah, there's probably a lot of bears up there! Look here, and I'll show you what I carry." He then reached into the pocket of his loosely fitted camouflage pants and pulled out a laser pointer. Flicking the light on and off, he said, "I just shine this in the bears' eyes, and they hate it! The same bear comes down to the river over there every morning. Well, one morning, I woke up, and he was about as close as you and me, so I shined this in his eye, and he took off! He doesn't bother me anymore." The man then started coughing a lot, so I reached into my pack and pulled out a bag of cough drops. He then shook his head and cleared his throat, "It ain't that kind of cough, brother." I then asked if he needed me to call anyone for him, and he replied, "Nope. Everyone who needs to know that I'm here already knows." I began to feel like the man had come here for his final resting place, so I shook his hand and told him to enjoy the rest of his evening.

Once I'd made it about five miles from Garberville, two state troopers stopped me and said I wasn't allowed to be on the interstate. I never knew the highway had turned into an interstate because I had been walking on it since Fort Bragg.

197

The only signs for it would've been located at the on-ramps. Therefore, I wouldn't have seen them. I tried explaining to the officers that I had just finished walking across the country and was capable of making it to town. However, they seemed persistent about enforcing the pedestrian laws and forced me to take a ride into town. After patting me down and searching through my things, they told me to get into the back seat and tossed my pack into the trunk. As we were riding along, the officers began saying things like, "Why did we have to pick up this piece of shit? He's back there, stinking up the car." Their attitude kind of reminded me of the state troopers from the comedy movie Super Troopers, but they didn't seem to like the fact that I was laughing at them.

We finally pulled up to a bus stop in Garberville, and one of the officers said, "If we see you on the interstate again, we will arrest you. We will take you to jail, and we will confiscate your backpack. If you want out of here, you'll have to take the bus." I looked around after the police drove off and decided it would probably be a good idea to take a bus out of there anyway. There were tons of transients everywhere who looked like they were either drunk or some other hard drugs. Normally, I wouldn't have minded them, but I had only been there for a few minutes and had seen a few fights break out. Most of them were hanging out in groups, so I felt like they might single me out because I was alone and had some quality hiking gear. The bus finally arrived about an hour later, so I climbed aboard and caught a ride to the town of Eureka, which was sixty-seven miles away.

After the bus had dropped me off in Eureka, I began searching for a place where I could use the restroom. Feeling like I was on the verge of having an accident on myself, I walked into a gas station and noticed a sign on the bathroom door that read, "See attendant for the key." I walked up to the cashier and asked, "Excuse me, could I have the key for the restroom, please?" The cashier smirked and replied, "Sorry. It's for customers only." I then grabbed something off the shelf and told her to ring it up. The cashier smirked again and said, "I'm not going to sell you that. You just want to buy something so you can use the bathroom. I'm sick of homeless people coming in here all the time, shooting up needles and making a mess." Feeling a bit irritable, I replied, "Ma'am, I'm not going to do drugs in there or make a mess. I'm about to shit my pants and need to use the bathroom. May I please use it?" She then shook her head and called for the next customer. As I was walking out the door, I turned around and yelled, "Well, what do you want me to do then? You want me to shit out here in the parking lot?" The cashier looked up at me and said, "That's up to you, sir. Not my problem." I felt humiliated, but I couldn't hold it in anymore. I walked across the parking lot and squatted inside of a small bush. It was the only cover I could make it to, but it didn't do much to keep me from peoples' view. As I was wiping myself, I looked across at the gas station and could see everyone inside, pointing and laughing at me. I pulled my pants up and walked away, giving everyone the middle finger. By that point, I already hated Eureka, so I got back on the move and continued for the next town of McKinleyville.

McKinleyville seemed to be a much nicer town than Eureka. Although, I didn't exactly interact with enough people to find out. I was exhausted by the time I got there, and since it was starting to get late, I immediately began searching for a place to get some sleep. I took one of the side roads that led towards the ocean and came across a field that was for sale. There was a tree in the middle of it, so I made my way over to it and figured it would do for the night. The next morning, I continued making my way towards the ocean, which turned out to be more difficult than I thought it would. The coast was lined with houses, fenced-off government property, and thick vegetation. However, I managed to find a coastal trail and decided to follow it through the forest. After hiking through the dense forest for a few miles, I finally came out at the shoreline. I made my way down the cliff and walked out onto the cold, muddy beach. I looked up and down the beach and saw no other people. I figured it was probably just too early, or perhaps too cold for other peoples' liking. I began walking north along the beach and realized there were no other human footprints. It looked as though I had the entire beach to myself, so I decided to enjoy it and began searching for a place where I could set up camp early. I could see a grass-covered bank just off to the side, so I made my way over to it and climbed up. The grass was green and soft, and there were no signs of other humans or their trash. It looked like the perfect spot, so I set up my tent and sat there for the rest of the day, where I enjoyed the cool breeze and watched the orcas and seagulls.

Later that night, as I was getting ready to fall asleep, my phone began to ring. I noticed it was my mother, which kind of had me worried because we barely stayed in contact anymore. Expecting to hear some bad news, I answered the phone, "Hey, mom!" She didn't even know I was in California and was happy to hear I had made it across the country okay. After spending a few minutes getting all caught up, she said, "Since you're heading up to Alaska with intentions on living there, I thought I'd call to let you know that Akin and Porter are looking for workers to pick okra. I thought you might like to come home and save some money before heading up to Alaska." I thanked her for letting me know and told her I would think about it, and I'd give her back a call later.

Shortly after hanging up, I realized Mother's Day was just a few days away. I then looked at the bus schedules and saw that I could be there in time to spend it with her if I left tomorrow. I also figured that making some money before I got to Alaska would probably be a good idea, so I called my mother back and told her I would see her in a couple of days. Before turning over and going to sleep, I went ahead and ordered my bus ticket. The next morning, I made my way to the town of Arcata and waited for my bus back to Tennessee.

After three days of watching the country pass by in reverse, I'd finally made it into Jackson, Tennessee. It was the day before Mother's Day, May 10, 2015, and my mother was at the bus station waiting for me. After collecting my pack out from underneath the bus, she ran over and hugged me. The first thing she said was, "Wow! You've lost a lot of weight! When was the last time you ate? I'm hungry. Are you hungry? Let's go find somewhere to eat!" After stopping by my parents' house to grab a shower and do some laundry, my mom and I went out to enjoy dinner together. While we were eating, I filled her in on just about everything I'd been through since the last time she had seen me, which was about six months ago. She admitted to worrying about me and was always scared something would happen, and no one would ever know, but since I was doing fine, she was beginning to have more faith in my ability to survive. During the drive back to the house, she said, "Something about you is just different. I can't really put my finger on it, but you seem a lot happier. I just want you to know that's all I ever wanted for you. If traveling is what makes you happy, you have our support."

After staying with my parents for a few days, I began working in the okra fields for twelve dollars an hour. Every day for the next month, I picked those prickly veggies from 6:00 a.m. to 6:00 p.m. Since I was getting paid cash and was so used to not spending my money, I was able to save up five thousand dollars before I had to start thinking about Alaska again. Since I knew I wouldn't be able to hike through Canada before winter, I gave myself two options. The first option was that I could buy a vehicle, maybe a cheap van, and drive to Alaska and live out of it for a while. The second option was that I could catch a plane and continue living out of a backpack. If I got a vehicle, I would have to worry about gas, breaking down, finding places to park at night, insurance, oil leaks, engine overheating, flat tires, registration fees, traffic violations, and having accidents. The thought of dealing with a vehicle gave me anxiety, so I decided to look at plane tickets. After spending several hours looking over all the flight schedules, I realized my cheapest option was to fly from Nashville, Tennessee, to San Diego, California, and then fly from San Francisco, California, to Anchorage, Alaska, in the next two weeks. I realized that meant I would be on a tight schedule, but I was confident that I could hitchhike if I had to, so I went ahead and purchased the plane tickets for two hundred dollars.

With only four days to make it to Nashville, which was one hundred and forty-five miles away, I said my goodbyes to everyone and began walking away from Greenfield. I'd only made it about ten miles from town when the heat had already become unbearable. I took my pack off so my back could cool off and began holding out my thumb. After standing there for a few minutes, a small red car pulled over. He was your typical middle-aged redneck and removed his cigarette to say, "Get in." Like a lot of cars in the south, the air conditioner didn't work, so he had the windows rolled down. The outside air flowing in felt like a hairdryer and was so loud that we had to yell so we could somewhat hear one another. He said he could drop me off in Milan, which was halfway between Jackson and Greenfield. The goal was to get to Jackson and then hitchhike to Nashville along Interstate 40, so I was already making great time.

After hopping out of the little red car, I made my way inside the gas station, where I had been dropped off, and bought a couple of sports drinks. I took my drinks to a tree beside the convenience store and sat down to enjoy them in the shade. As I swallowed the last few drops of my drink, I looked towards the gas pumps and saw a short blonde girl filling up her van. I thought she looked familiar, so I yelled across the parking lot, "Sydney!" When she turned around, I noticed it was indeed Sydney. She screamed from excitement and yelled for me to come over to her. We couldn't believe we had just run into each other! She asked what I was doing there, so I told her I was hitchhiking to Nashville to catch a plane to San Diego. She then said, "My boyfriend and I just got a new apartment in Memphis. You can stay with us for a few nights, and I'll take you to Nashville." That sounded like a great idea to me, so I hopped into the van and took the ride to Memphis.

Once we arrived at Sydney's new apartment, she, her boyfriend, and I began drinking to celebrate my return to Tennessee. As the night went on, Sydney and her boyfriend went out to buy more alcohol, while I decided to stay at their house. After waiting for them for a couple of hours, I ended up falling asleep and didn't wake back up until about 9:00 a.m. I then realized that they still hadn't made it back and began to worry that they may have been in an accident or gone to jail. I tried calling Sydney a few times over the next couple of hours but got no answer. I then gave Sydney's grandmother a call and told her about Sydney's disappearance so she could start calling around and make a report if she wanted to. I didn't know what else to think or do, but I began to worry that I was going to miss my flight because I had lost my ride.

After leaving Sydney's apartment, I made my way through the city and finally reached the interstate around noon. It was extremely hot outside, but I was desperate for a ride, so I sucked it up and stood in the relentless heat with my thumb out. After standing there for four hours, dripping with sweat, I finally began to feel the effects of heat exhaustion. As my vision began to blur, I noticed a patch of trees about fifty yards away. I then made my way over to them and collapsed as soon as I reached the shade. I woke up around 10:00 p.m. with a terrible headache and noticed a pool of blood where my face had been. I assumed that I had gotten so hot that the capillaries in my nose had ruptured. It was a scary thought, but at least I was alive. I then sat up and drank a gallon of water before pulling out my sleeping pad and going back to sleep.

The next morning, I made my way to a nearby gas station to fill up on water before spending another day at the on-ramp. As I was shoving my hydration bag into my backpack, a police officer pulled up and asked if I was okay. I told him about how my friends had disappeared and how I was trying to hitch a ride to Nashville. The police officer then offered to buy me breakfast from the gas station and said, "How's about I give you a ride to the Greyhound station so we can get you a ticket to Nashville? We have a program set up here to help pay for transients to leave the city." I thought that sounded like a much better idea than trying to hitchhike, so I hopped into the officer's car and took a ride to the bus station. He then followed me inside, and everyone began looking at me like I'd done something wrong since I was being escorted by a police officer. Once we made it to the counter, the cop handed the clerk a pre-paid ticket from the city. The clerk then printed my ticket out for Nashville, and I thanked them both for the help before taking a seat and waiting for the bus.

I ended up making it to Nashville two days before my plane was scheduled to leave. After getting off the bus and collecting my things, I took a seat in the terminal and tried to come up with some ideas on how to spend my extra time there. I made a post on my blog, asking people what they thought I should do. Just a few minutes after making the post, I was contacted by an old high school acquaintance, Samantha. She said that she and her husband, Drew, had moved to Nashville a few years ago, and I was welcome to stay with them until my flight. I felt so relieved to read her message because I really didn't know what else to do besides waste money on motel rooms. She was at work when she messaged me but came to pick me up during her lunch break. She then dropped me off at her house on her way back to work. As soon as I walked inside, I tossed my sweat-crusted clothes into the washer and hopped into the shower.

For the next two days, I spent my time relaxing on Samantha and Drew's living room couch, seeking refuge from the relentless heat. Since my visit with them was during the week, they were gone to work during the day, but I did get to have dinner with them twice before having to leave. Then, on the morning that my plane was scheduled to depart, Samantha gave me a ride to the airport. As I was walking away from her car, she yelled to get my attention, "Hey, Jake. You might want to do something with those knives and bear spray!" I had been traveling with them dangling from my pack for so long that I had forgotten most people saw them as dangerous weapons. I shoved them into my backpack, which I handed to the airline as checked luggage, and hoped security never gave me any problems about it.

After my plane had landed in San Diego, I nervously made my way to the baggage claim area. My pack never dropped down onto the carousel, so I had to talk to the airline attendants. After giving one of them my information, she said my bag was being held by security, but it should be released shortly. I had a bad feeling they were going to confiscate my knife, machete, and bear spray, but I really hoped I wouldn't be in any legal trouble. A security guard then walked out, handed the attendant my pack, and said it was good to go. No one ever said anything to me, but I carried my pack outside before looking through it. As soon as I opened it, I saw a "letter of inspection due to dangerous items." It was obvious that it and been gone through, but everything still appeared to be there. I didn't know how San Diego's police would react to those things, so I decided to just leave them inside of my pack and began making my way to the beach.

As I was walking along the beachfront sidewalk, I took several pictures of all the boats in the dock. I then uploaded a few of them to my Facebook Page and let people know that I had made it. Shortly after sharing my whereabouts, I was contacted by a Navy woman, Shannon, who said she had been following my Facebook Page and would like to hang out. I didn't know anything about San Diego, so I thought it would be nice to spend some time with someone who could show me around. She met up with me about thirty minutes later and asked if it would be okay if we drove to her house so she could change out of her uniform. It wasn't like I had any other plans, so I tossed my pack into her trunk, and we began driving. The city began to disappear behind us, and she just kept driving, so I said, "I guess I should've asked first, but you live pretty far out here, huh?" With a grin on her face, she looked over and replied, "Yeah, it's about forty miles out. That's not a problem, is it?" What I said was, "No. It's fine. I was just wondering." But the voice in my head said, "It's not a problem as long as you give me a ride back."

We finally pulled up to Shannon's house after about an hour-long drive. I grabbed my pack out of her trunk and followed her into the house. As soon as we walked into the door, Shannon's drunken roommate handed her a large mixed drink, which she chugged like it was water. Shannon then went to take a shower. While she was in there, her roommate brought her two more mixed drinks. As the roommate was fixing Shannon her fourth drink, I said to her, "Excuse me, but Shannon has to give me a ride back into San Diego. I don't feel comfortable with her having any more drinks." She looked at me in disgust and stomped into the bathroom with Shannon. I couldn't tell what they were saying, but it sounded like they were arguing, which slowly turned into drunken laughter. They finally walked out of the bathroom about thirty minutes later and looked surprised to see that I was sitting on the couch. Shannon then began laughing and said, "Oh, I forgot you were here! Hold on a second!" Shannon's roommate then grabbed her by the arm and pulled her into their bedroom. A few minutes later, Shannon comes out and says, "Sorry, but my roommate said you need to leave." I looked at her in disbelief and said, "Are you serious? You just drove me forty miles from San Diego, and now I have to walk back?" She then smiled, shrugged her shoulders, and said she was sorry. Although, I was pretty sure her apology was insincere. As I was walking out the door, I turned to see her roommate's head hanging out of her bedroom door, glaring at me with an evil, ugly smirk. I walked outside and felt like such an idiot for not listening to my intuition about Shannon. As I started making my way back to San Diego, I felt so overwhelmed by being betrayed that it triggered a full-blown panic attack. As I began shaking from head to toe, tunnel vision and a rapid heartbeat soon followed, and before long, my whole body felt numb. I then began to feel short of breath and thought I was about to die. I couldn't take the feeling anymore, so I dropped my pack and began searching for my Klonopin, which was the anxiety medication Rob had stolen. I tossed two of the little blue pills into my mouth, salivating from their delicious minty flavor. Within about twenty minutes, I completely forgot about what had happened. However, I quickly remembered how good those pills made me feel and was glad I got another prescription while I was in Tennessee.

I made it back into San Diego around 11:00 p.m. and had a difficult time finding anywhere to sleep. All the hotels were close to three hundred dollars for one night, which I refused to pay, and the city was still full of life. Everywhere I turned, there were hordes of people, traffic backed up with people shouting and honking at each other, mentally ill people screaming at everyone, homeless people begging for money, and drug addicts searching for their next fix. I continued walking up and down the busy streets, trying to find an escape from all the chaos. I finally said, "screw it," and took two more of my Klonopin. I then continued walking, waiting for the pills to kick in. Slowly, it was like everything around me faded to silence, and my worries disappeared. I then came across an air conditioning unit located behind a commercial building and thought it looked like a great place to get some sleep, so I tossed my sleeping bag down on the concrete, and everything went black.

I woke the next morning, and it took me a few minutes to even remember that I was in San Diego. I then understood why a lot of homeless people were on drugs. It was so much easier to deal with everything when I didn't care. Most people seemed to think that people were homeless because of addiction, but I began to think it was probably the other way around. Being alone in a big city, full of danger, and stuck on high alert, who wouldn't want an escape from that? I probably wouldn't have slept a wink had I not taken those pills. With a new outlook towards life on the city streets, I made my way towards the beach, hoping to find some interesting people to hang out with.

Once I had made it to the beach, I walked out to the ocean and took a seat to watch people play fetch with their dogs. I sat and enjoyed the nice weather for about an hour and then made my way back towards the city. Once I made it to the beach's parking lot, I ran into a group of gutter punks. They reminded me of myself except for their clothing style, which looked like a mix between punk-rock and hippie. I noticed one of the girls with them was holding a sign that read, "Tell you a joke for a quarter," which I thought was a positive way to make some money. I then introduced myself to a few of the guys and began asking where they were all from and how they ended up in San Diego. Although, their attention span only lasted until someone walked by that looked like they might have money or weed, so I felt pretty much useless to them. I decided to stop trying to talk and just sat back to hear some of the girl's jokes. Surprisingly, a lot of people came up and paid to listen to some, and they were actually quite funny. I'd watched a lot of comedy shows but never seen anyone who had as many jokes as she did. After watching her show off her talent for about thirty minutes, she looks over to her friends and shouts, "Okay! Let's go get some liquor!" One of them invited me to come with them, but I turned down the offer and decided to continue my walk.

After walking around aimlessly for about an hour, I received a message from a lady named Shany. She said that she and her husband, Jim, had been following me on Facebook for a couple of years and would like to host me at their house in El Cajun for a couple of days. She said Jim was working in San Diego and could pick me up after he got off work. I didn't want to make the same mistake as before, so I looked over their Facebook

208

profiles to make sure they seemed like trustworthy people first. After seeing they appeared to be good, honest people, I told her that sounded great and gave her my phone number where Jim could reach me after he got off work.

I ended up meeting Jim at the beach, where I'd spent most of the day, and he seemed like a real laid-back kind of guy. After shaking his hand and tossing my packing into the trunk of his car, we made our way out of San Diego. Once we made it to their house, I was able to get a shower and then helped them prepare dinner. Once the food was done, we took our meal to the living room, and they handed me the remote to the television. Since I was their guest, they said I should pick out a movie for us to watch. I hadn't watched television in a few years, so everything that was popping up looked strange to me. I tried clicking things that sounded interesting, but they all turned out to be horrible B movies, which Jim and Shany thought was pretty funny. After finishing dinner, Shany and Jim went upstairs to their bedroom and left me to get some rest on the couch.

I spent the next day trying to figure out how I was going to get up to San Francisco. After looking over my map, I realized that interstates connected most of southern California, so I decided to get a bus from San Diego to Santa Maria. The ticket was only thirty dollars, which I figured would be worth it when my only other option was hitchhiking. Then, for the rest of the day, I took the six-pack of beer that Jim had given me out to their pool and tried to keep cool. Later that evening, while we were preparing dinner again, I told Jim that I'd decided to get a bus from San Diego. He said I could catch a ride with him in the morning on his way to work so that panned out well.

My bus wasn't scheduled to leave until 9:00 a.m., but Jim had to be at work by 8:00 a.m., so we left their house around 6:00 a.m. to be sure we had enough time to add me to his route. Once we made it to the transit center, I grabbed my backpack out of the trunk. I then reached through the passenger window to scoop up the breakfast sandwich Shany had made for me and thanked Jim for all their help.

Shortly after Jim drove away, I began walking down the sidewalk, looking for the Greyhound station. Once I made it to the bus stops, I saw a homeless man sleeping next to one of the benches and noticed he had a bag of food sitting next to him. I then wondered why I didn't see a Greyhound sign anywhere, so I searched for the address on my phone and realized Jim had dropped me off at the wrong bus stop. The Greyhound station was twenty miles away, so I gave Jim a call to see if he had enough time left to give me a lift. The Greyhound station turned out to be just a few blocks from his work, so picking me back up wasn't going to be a problem. Feeling relieved that I wasn't going to miss my bus, I took a seat and waited for Jim to return. As I was sitting there, I saw a sketchy-looking man walk up to the sleeping homeless man. He stood in front of him for a few seconds, then reached over to grab his food and walked off with it. There was a large group of people standing around him, but no one said or did anything. I then made my way through the crowd and woke the homeless man up to tell him someone had just walked off with his food. Before the man had time to react, I'd already given him the sandwich Shany had made me. Disgusted with everyone for not sticking up for him, I turned to walk away from the crowd so it would be easier for Jim to find me.

A couple of hours after catching a ride to the correct bus station, I was on my way to Santa Maria. I didn't know what to expect of Santa Maria, other than the fact that it looked like a good starting point to follow the coast up to San Francisco. After hopping off the bus, I could tell right away that I should have continued a bit farther north. The people all seemed a bit on edge, and as I continued walking into the city, I noticed several small groups of people who were all wearing blue and white shoes, which was a trademark of the MS-13 gang members. Since it was beginning to get late, I made my way to the outskirts of town and came out at some large dirt fields. I saw a large shipping container sitting in one of the fields, so I set my tent up behind it and began searching for the next bus out of there. After doing a bit of research, it looked like my best bet would be Santa Cruz, so I purchased a ticket for the following evening.

The next morning, I made my way back into town and took a seat in a parking lot. As I was sitting there, a truck pulled up and parked right next to me. I thought it was a bit strange for them to stop so close because the whole parking lot was empty. A heavyset man with a long, straggly beard stepped out and began making his way over to me. Standing directly in front of me, the man casually says, "Hey, Jake. Name's Matthew. I was just on my way to work and saw you sitting over here. Thought I'd see if you wanted one of these drinks." He then reached back into his truck and pulled out a couple of canned teas. I pointed to one of them and said, "Thanks, Matt. I'll take that one off your hands." He then handed me the drink and said, "Well, I have to get to work. It was nice meeting you. Try to keep cool out here." He then got back into his truck and drove away just as casually as he had come. I then sat back and enjoyed the drink he had given me, waiting for time to pass before making my way to the bus station.

Once I made it to Santa Cruz, I got off the bus and took a short walk down to the pier. As I walked along the beach storefront, the enchanting aromas coming from all the restaurants were too much for me to ignore. I then made my way into one of the bars and noticed everyone staring at me out of my peripherals. They were probably wondering why some homeless bum was coming in, perhaps assuming I would ask someone for a hand-out or dine and dash. To assure everyone I was a paying customer, I pulled out my wallet and began tapping my debit card on the table, trying to get the bartender's attention. I could feel the tension in the room lighten up, and all the judging eyes began to move away from me.

After having lunch, I made my way across the street and walked out onto the pier with all the panhandlers, people fishing, and tourists. Once I made it to the end of the dock, I looked over the edge and saw several seals hanging out on the boards below. After watching them for a few minutes, I looked out into the bay and saw a large group of surfers, all lined up and waiting for their turn to get the perfect wave. Then, as I was making my way back towards the beach, I noticed some large concrete columns supporting a building. Since it would be getting dark soon, I decided to make my way over to them, hoping I had just found a good place to sleep. After following the beach for as far as it would go, I finally made it to the columns just before the beach turned into a cliff. It appeared someone had recently camped behind them, so I figured it would probably be safe enough. I then tossed my sleeping gear onto the sand behind one of the columns and crawled in for the night.

The next morning, I made my way back over to all the little shops and bought a cup of coffee before making my way north. After hiking for a few hours, I had made it between the towns of Davenport and Pescadero. When I stopped to take a break, I noticed some log steps that led up to some train tracks. Although there was no sign, there were a few cars parked across the street, so I figured there was probably a beach on the other side of the hill. I made my way up to the tracks and heard what sounded like someone walking through the bushes. I turned to look and saw a naked lady walking towards me. I didn't want to make the situation any more awkward than it already was, so I turned my head down towards the beach to give her some privacy. I then saw about fifteen other naked people walking around on the sand below. The naked lady then walked past me and continued down to the nude beach. I wasn't interested in taking my clothes off, so I began following the train tracks out of there.

I continued into the small town of Davenport and made my way down to an unoccupied beach, searching for a place to wash all the dried sweat from my hair and face. The ocean waves were too violent to get close enough, but I was able to find a large, horseshoe-shaped cave that was full of water left from high tide. I made my way inside the cave and dipped my head into one of the frigid tide pools. After getting cleaned up, I made my way back up to the highway and continued walking for a couple more hours. Although it was only 3:00 p.m., I decided to go ahead and stop when I came across what looked to be a great spot to set up camp. There was a grassy clearing at the cliff's bottom, surrounded by dense brush and on the edge of another cliff. It was kind of difficult to get to, but I knew no one would be able to see me and probably wouldn't deal with all the trouble to get there.

After making it to the clearing, I decided to pull out my sleeping pad to relax. As I was lying there, looking up at the grey, fog-filled sky, I noticed a black spot lingering directly above me. I thought it was a bird at first, but it didn't appear to be moving at all. After staring at it for a few minutes, the wind finally cleared out enough clouds that I could see there were actually three of them sitting in a triangle formation. I immediately pulled out my phone and uploaded a few pictures of them to my Facebook Page. I remembering the videos from Carson City had been deleted, I began sending the images directly to people just in case that happened again. After lying there for nearly three hours, the black spots still hadn't moved, so I put my tent up and began collecting wood for a fire. After collecting enough wood, I kneeled and began picking out small pieces of kindling. The next thing I knew, I woke up in my tent and realized it was morning. I stuck my head out and saw the sticks were still sitting there from last night, so I knew I never started the fire. I then looked up at the sky and noticed the three black spots were gone. Other than feeling perplexed, I didn't know what to make of the situation, so I collected my things and continued heading north.

As I was walking along, I took a picture of myself to let everyone on my Facebook Page know I was back on the move.

Someone then left a comment on the photo, "What happened to your earrings?" I'd had my ear lobes stretched for the past couple of years, so it must have been obvious when there was nearly an inch hole near the side of my face. I couldn't answer their question, though. Even I was baffled that they were gone because I'd had them for a long time, and they'd never fallen out before. They were designed to prevent that from happening, so I began to wonder if those black dots had anything to do with it. I then began to feel unusually dehydrated, so I went to take a drink and realized that all my water was gone. It wouldn't have surprised me if it was just my water bladder, but even my canteens were bone-dry, and I knew I never drank from them. I still had about fifteen miles to the next town of Pescadero and hoped I could make it there before my body shut down.

Once I made it into Pescadero, I was feeling extremely dehydrated but couldn't find water anywhere. I started to feel a bit nervous at that point, so I continued walking and stuck out my thumb to every passing motorist. After hiking for about ten miles with my thumb out and not having any luck, I noticed a half-empty bottle of orange-flavored sparkling water. Because of the lack of color and condensation, it looked like it had been sitting there for a while. I picked it up and began to inspect it, wondering if it would be safe to drink. I held onto the bottle and continued walking with my thumb out, hoping someone would stop before I got desperate enough to drink it. After carrying the bottle for about five miles, I finally gave up on anyone giving me a ride and took a few sips of the questionable liquid. My tongue began to swell to its normal size, which felt so good that I couldn't help but drink the rest. It wasn't much, but I could feel my entire body absorbing it and thought the chances of getting sick would be worth making it to the next town alive.

I had made it a few more miles when a car pulled over. I had given up on begging people for a ride, but I was happy to jump in when the man offered it. As we were riding along, I told the man about my plans to get to Alaska. He then said he was headed for San Francisco, and if I wanted, I could catch a ride all the way. I thought that was a generous offer. However, I still had a week before my plane was scheduled to leave, so I asked if he could let me out at the next town that had a place where I could fill up on water. He then replied, "Half Moon Bay is only about eight miles up ahead. They have a few stores there. Honestly, I'd recommend just hanging around there before your flight out. San Francisco is kind of whack." I laughed when he said that because I had already been thinking the same thing. I didn't want to be in San Francisco any longer than I had to.

After making it into Half Moon Bay, I went into the gas station where the man had let me out and filled up on a bunch of sports drinks. From what I could see, I thought the town would be a great place to stay low for the next week, but I needed to walk around to be sure. After leaving the gas station, I followed some back roads towards the beach and passed through the quiet neighborhood, filled with coastal houses. So far, it was beginning to feel like the friendliest town I'd ever been to. The few people I had run into seemed very friendly and weren't giving me strange looks just because I had a backpack. The air was also much colder there, and the fog was denser than in the surrounding areas, which was probably why the town had a cozy feel to it. It was the kind of place where I could imagine people probably spent a lot of their time inside, sipping on hot clam chowder and reading the newspaper.

After following the roads as far as I could, I made my way through a grassy field and came out to a cliff overlooking the ocean. There was a paved trail that followed alongside the cliff, so I walked it until I saw a path down to the beach. I was happy to see that I was the only person on the cold, windy beach and began following it south, looking for a good place to set up camp. After walking through the sand for about half a mile, I came across a corroded area in the cliff. It looked like it would make a great place to camp, so long as the cliff didn't come crashing down or the tide didn't come up too high. Although it

215

was still kind of early, I went ahead and put up my tent, then climbed to the top of the cliff and began tossing firewood down onto the beach. I then sat there for the rest of the evening, enjoying my view of the sunset dropping into the ocean. Once the sun had finally gone down, I built a fire and fell asleep to the sound of the howling wind and the echoes of the waves bouncing off the cliff walls.

I walked back into town the next morning and found a welcoming coffee shop. As I was sitting there, I wondered what I could do to pass the time over the next five days, so I went out for a walk to get some ideas. Shortly after leaving the coffee shop, I saw a sign that read, "The relay for life will be held at the high school this weekend from 8:00 a.m. on Saturday to 8:00 p.m. on Sunday. Come out and help kick cancer's butt!" That sounded like a great way to pass the time, but it was only Friday, so I decided to go into the forested mountains just southeast of town. I followed as many side streets as I could and exited into the forest after reaching a dead end. It was so lovely and peaceful out there that I wondered what more Alaska could have to offer. I slowly strolled through the mountains until dark and sat up camp beneath all the cajeput trees, the ground covered with pieces of their spongy, paper-like bark.

The next morning, I made my way back down to the coffee shop I'd gone to the day before, and, after finishing my drink, I went into the restroom to get cleaned up for the cancer relay. I then made my way over to the high school and checked in under the name "Road Warrior," and vowed to complete a hundred miles. The ladies at the check-in desk, their eyes swelled in disbelief as they prepared my entry bracelet. I then turned to start walking on the track when one of the check-in ladies laughed and said, "You can leave your backpack with us if you want. I don't think you could do a hundred miles with that." I was so used to my pack that I completely forgot that I was even wearing it, so I smiled and said, "Sounds like a bet to me."

As the day went on, people began to question who I was and why I was carrying a backpack. A little later into the evening, it seemed like everyone there knew about my Facebook Page and began getting their pictures taken with me. By 9:00 p.m., I had already walked sixty miles, so I decided to take a break and finish the rest on Sunday. As I was sitting there, watching one of the bands perform, a beautiful blonde lady sat next to me and introduced herself as Jennifer. She sat and talked with me for a couple of hours, and she had the sweetest, most sincere, innocent smile. She was so bubbly and full of laughter that I couldn't help but flirt to try and get more laughs from her. It was probably around midnight when she decided to leave, and I made my way to a shaded side of the school to set up my tent for the night. Just before falling asleep, Jennifer sent me a text saying I could come to her place after I finish with the walk tomorrow.

I woke the next morning around 4:00 a.m. and finished the other forty miles by 3:00 that afternoon. Just as I claimed my hundredth mile, a man walked up to shake my hand and donated five hundred dollars to the American Cancer Society on my behalf, which helped me to feel like all that extra walking was worth it. I then sent Jennifer a text saying I was ready to hang out whenever she was. She came by to pick me up shortly after, and we made our way back to her house, where I would be able to grab a shower and do some laundry. After getting cleaned up, Jennifer said I could lie on her bed and get some rest while waiting for my clothes to finish. My body was sore from the past two days, so I didn't hesitate to take a load off. She then got into the bed next to me and began showing me funny videos from her phone. All the laughing and squirming around led to some accidental touching, which was like tossing a match into a pile of dry leaves. Since I was only wearing a pair of loosely fitted basketball shorts, it was kind of hard to keep my feelings for her a secret. Luckily for me, the feelings turned out to be mutual.

A few hours later, I gathered my clean clothes and hopped back into the car with Jennifer. We then drove down to the beach, where we walked out onto the sand and enjoyed the sunset. Once the sun had gone down, I walked her back to her car and hugged her goodbye. It was a bittersweet feeling because we seemed to get along great, but we both knew it would probably be our last time seeing each other. It was hard for me to not catch feelings for someone so beautiful and fun to be around, even though our time together had been so brief. It wasn't normal for me to catch feelings so quickly, so I attributed that to being alone for so long and would just have to deal with the pain of being alone again. Wanting to get my mind off of her, I made my way back down to the beach and began collecting old, dried-up driftwood to build a fire. I hadn't started a bow drill fire in a while, so I decided to do it that way to make sure I still had it in me. It took a lot of focus and energy to get the fire going, so it turned out to be a great distraction. Although I was still missing Jennifer's company, as I was lying in my tent, I knew the feelings would eventually pass and forced myself to stop thinking about her.

The next morning, I went back into town for another coffee and ran into an old homeless man named Bill. We sat outside of the coffee shop and talked about all sorts of things, but he was kind of a hippie and mostly talked about health-foods and natural healing. As our conversation went on, I mentioned the assumed meteorites that I had found in Nevada. He was very intrigued about it and began trying to think of ways we could get a vehicle so we could go back to pick them up. After I brought up the idea of buying an old school bus and turning it into an RV, Bill began laughing and said, "No way, man! Charles Manson came through here in the 60s and asked if I wanted to go down to Los Angeles with him. He had the craziest look in his eyes. I'd never seen anyone with eyes like that. I was too scared to go with him, but the group of people he was with seemed cool with it. He had a bunch of girls with him, man. But, yeah, man, that Charlie guy was something else. I wasn't surprised when they arrested him for those murders. I don't know if he did it or not, but, man, he really had everyone that was with him under control. They'd all come, go, and do whatever he said. It was so weird, man. But if he ever told them to kill someone, I wouldn't doubt they would have. They must have been on a shit-ton of acid or something to be hanging around that guy, though." I thought maybe Bill was a little delusional about meeting Charles Manson, but the more he went on about it, the more I believed him. I guess I just found it hard to believe I was sitting there talking to someone who had run into him, although I knew it wasn't impossible.

After parting ways with Bill, I made my way over to a small bookstore he had recommended. It was in a different part of town than I'd been to, and while I didn't care much for the bookstore, he mentioned there were several other small stores and restaurants. I crossed over a small bridge and entered the old uptown area, lined with small businesses. This side of town had a calm, welcoming sense to it.

As I was walking along and doing some window shopping, I came across a bar and grill called the San Benito House. I noticed they had a lovely outdoor seating area with a fire pit, so I made my inside and ordered a Bloody Mary. As I was sitting near the fire pit and enjoying my drink, I overheard a lady tell someone on the phone about how she was feeling nauseous. Once she got off the phone, I introduced myself and offered her a few of my activated charcoal tablets. She said her name was Elsa and had never heard of activated charcoal before. I explained how I always carried them with me in case I had any stomach problems, and they always fixed me right up. She took a few of them and then asked if I'd be interested in coming over to her house for dinner. I told her that sounded great and gave her my number so she could contact me later.

After finishing my drink at the San Benito House, I made my way to the hardware store and picked up some copper wire. I had picked up several interesting rocks and thought Elsa seemed like the type that would appreciate it if I put one of them into a necklace for her. I took the copper wire out into the parking lot and pulled a small, flat green rock from my pack. Elsa had green eyes, so I thought it would match her perfectly. I then took out my needle nose pliers and began twisting the copper wire around the rock, creating an elaborate housing with an archaic, Celtic design. Just as I was adding some finishing touches, Elsa gave me a call and said dinner was ready. I told her where I was and waited a few minutes for her to pick me up. Once we made it into her house, she began setting the table with a large variety of delicious, home-cooked foods. She then lit a candle and poured us both a glass of red wine. I thought it was kind of strange to have such a fancy dinner, being a dirty traveler, but she didn't seem to mind at all. Just before we sat down to eat, I reached into my jacket pocket and pulled out the necklace I had made for her. As I smiled and handed it over to her, I said, "I figured it was the least I could do in exchange for dinner. It will look great on you." And it did. Glowing in the candlelight, she looked sophisticatedly beautiful, which I knew was too far from my standards. Still, I enjoyed being in the company of someone so elegant and caring anyway.

After having dinner with Elsa, I thanked her for the date and made my way back into town. As I walked past a motel on the highway, I decided to go ahead and rent a room since it was going to be my last night in Half Moon Bay. Shortly after checking into my room, I received a text from Jennifer, asking if I was still in the area. I really wanted to see her, but I was afraid that I would have those bad feelings of missing her again. However, I couldn't resist her company and told her she was welcome to stop by at my motel room if she wanted. She seemed excited about seeing me again and showed up about fifteen minutes later. When I opened the door, she asked if I'd like to go with her to pick up some beer so we could have a little going away party. I thought to get a little buzz together sounded like fun, so we hopped into her car and made our way to the grocery store. As we were shopping for beer, her bubbly and giggly personality came out again. Her positivity was so infectious that I was already missing her, but I couldn't tell her that. Instead, I waited until we got back to the motel and showed her just how crazy I was about her.

I woke the next morning to the feeling of Jennifer's warm, soft skin wrapped around mine. Her soft, blonde hair lying across my chest smelled like strawberries. I knew it was time for me to get going, but I hesitated to wake her because I wanted to enjoy her company for a little longer. After preparing myself to be alone again, I slid out of bed and went to grab one final, civilized shower, not knowing when my next one would be. After getting cleaned up, I walked out of the restroom and saw Jennifer getting her things ready to leave. We didn't say much, but I think it was because we both felt a bit of sadness about it being our last day together. However, neither of us admitted to it, so those feelings could have been mine alone. Either way, we walked outside and gave each other a quick, meaningless kiss before we parted ways, and I began my lonely hike towards San Francisco.

I still had one day left before my plane was scheduled to leave, so I decided to take the day kind of slow. Maybe ten miles from Half Moon Bay, I came across a large reservoir and decided to end my day there. It was located halfway between Half Moon Bay and San Mateo, which had a train station where I could catch a ride straight up to the airport. It looked like a good place to camp and would be an easy hike the next morning. I then walked around the lake, just taking in all the natural beauty. After walking through the forest for about an hour, I came across a five-foot rattlesnake and decided to have it for lunch. Although I'd never killed or eaten a rattlesnake before, I had studied how to do it and wanted the experience.

I actually had a phobia of snakes, so even being close to it made me feel extremely uncomfortable. As a matter of fact, I was terrified and probably should have just let the snake be, but I already had my boot on its head, and it was too late to go back. I gritted my teeth as I reached down to grab the tail end of the snake and quickly pulled it up and away from my boot. Preparing to whip the snake and break its neck, as I knew that was the proper way to do it, I remembered being in the army and popping one of my buddies with a towel, accidentally tearing open his scrotum. I then imagined popping him with the towel again and quickly snapped the snake, killing it instantly.

Even though the snake was dead, I still felt uncomfortable holding it. However, showing respect for it being my meal, I carefully removed its head and began pulling its skin down the length of its body, revealing the pinkish-white meat and guts beneath. I then ran my finger along the spine, and all the guts came out in one long, solid piece. What I was left with looked kind of like fish with a lot of tiny rib bones. I then prepared a small fire to cook it on, and the flavor kind of reminded me of a fish as well, but a bit gamier, sort of like a rabbit. While it wasn't the best-tasting thing I'd ever eaten, my stomach did feel full, and I appreciated the opportunity to try something new.

The following morning, I made my way back out to the highway and followed it east through the hills towards San Mateo. By 8:00 a.m., I was on a train headed up to San Francisco. Since I'd never been to San Francisco before, I was a bit anxious about taking all the trains and subways. Everything was moving so fast, and everyone else was in sort of a routine, so it was a bit difficult to ask anyone for help. It looked like all the subway workers had been replaced by security cameras, so I just had to sit for a few minutes to watch how everyone went about doing everything. I was beginning to worry that I would miss my flight, so my brain kicked into overdrive, and I began observing how everyone else purchased their tickets. I quickly put together what I needed to do and made it to the airport just in time to check in.

Alaska

It was July 29, 2015, and my plane was preparing to land in Anchorage, Alaska. The clouds were so dense that I couldn't see anything from the window, which added to the suspense of what I was getting myself into. After going through a rough patch of turbulence, the plane broke free from the clouds just a few hundred feet from the airport. I could see the tall buildings of downtown Anchorage, the sun glistening on the gulf, and what looked to be an infinite supply of rugged mountains, thick mist, and saturated forests in the distance. Just as our aircraft wheels contacted the rain-soaked runway, I felt a simultaneous sense of relief and anxiety. It was an unsettling feeling of being alone, mixed with being astounded by a naturally beautiful and unforgiving world.

After collecting my backpack from the baggage claim area, I made my way outside and filled my lungs with the cool, clean air that smelled of salt and moss. I then took a picture of myself standing outside of the airport and posted it to my Facebook Page. Shortly after beginning my walk into Anchorage, I received a message from a beautiful young lady named Katie. She said that she wanted to hang out and could meet me at one of the nearby stores. I just needed to pick one and wait there for about thirty minutes, and she would be there to pick me up with her friend's truck. It was about 6:00 p.m. when she showed up, and we greeted each other with a hug, which I thought was a great way to kill the ice and become friends almost instantly.

She then said, "Throw your pack in the back and let's go celebrate." I did as she said and didn't even bother to ask what the plans were because it didn't matter to me. As a matter of fact, my plans for Alaska were very vague, which is what I told Katie as we were driving along the coast. She then brushed her long, curly wind-blown hair from her smiling face and said, "I think we've made it far enough away from the city. Reach behind the seat. I got you something." I felt a plastic bag and pulled it into the front seat with us. I opened the bag and noticed it was a six-pack of my favorite beer. Katie then laughed and said, "I've been following you for a while. Figured you might like that."

After driving along the coast for about an hour, we stopped a gravel turnout and decided to enjoy our beer and wonderful view. I then grabbed the beer from the truck and followed Katie across the street and up into the mountains. As we were sitting there drinking our beer and overlooking the gulf, Katie began telling me about how she also had PTSD and had come to Alaska to get away from everything. Although our reasons for having PTSD were different, it seemed as though our reason for being there were pretty much the same. We both wanted to get away from large crowds of people and surround ourselves with nature. Alaska just so happened to be the farthest we could get away without needing a passport. With a better understanding of each other, it seemed like we were probably going to be friends for the rest of my time in Alaska, which felt much better than being completely alone. However, she was living with a friend in Anchorage and needed to get the truck back home soon. We packed up and made our way back into town around 9:00 p.m., although I wouldn't have known it was so late if I hadn't looked at the time. It was still so bright out that I probably would've been off by about four hours if I were to guess.

Katie wished she could bring me back to the apartment with her. However, her friend didn't feel comfortable having a stranger over, so she dropped me off at a gas station and told me

224

to be safe. I had no idea where to go to get some sleep, but I was so tired that I knew I would give up looking soon and just flop down wherever I had to. I finally came up to a house with a fence running along the back yard, so I placed my tent between it and some thick bushes. Even though the sun didn't seem to set until midnight, which was difficult to ignore, I still woke the next morning feeling rested. As I was taking my tent down, I noticed a young man walking around in the yard beside where I had camped. He then noticed that I was up and moving around, so he walked over to the fence to where I was and said, "I wondered who the hell was camping in my yard. You didn't seem to be bothering anything, though, so I didn't wake you." I apologized for crashing on his property and explained how I had just flown in the day before. I hadn't had the time to get out of the city yet. The man laughed and said, "Oh, it's no problem. You aren't from around here, huh? Well, we get a lot of crazy homeless people coming through here, so I just wanted to make sure you weren't a threat or anything. What are you doing in Alaska, if you don't mind me asking?" I continued packing my things and replied, "You know? That's a good question. I've come here intending to stay, but I'd like to do some exploring first to see where I think I fit in. I definitely don't plan on staying here in Anchorage, but I need to get some stuff taken care of here before I go venturing off." After I finished packing my things, the man asked if I'd like to come inside and have breakfast with him. I thought that was a very kind offer and wish I would've taken it, at least for the chance of making another friend, but I felt like he'd already done enough by being polite about me camping next to his house.

I needed to find a place where I could camp without intruding on people's property, so I made my way through the city, headed for the forest on the north side of town. As I was making my way along, it quickly became apparent that Anchorage had an enormous homeless population. I didn't mind their business, but I knew so much of us being there was going to cause problems between myself and the non-homeless people. Every time I'd been through cities with a large number of transients, I had a difficult time because everyone always associated us with being violent alcoholics and drug-addicted thieves. All they had to see was my backpack, and I'd be just as guilty as the last person who came through and did them wrong. My theory was proven only a few minutes later after I decided to stop at a gas station to buy something for breakfast. I left my backpack at the door, hoping the cashier would see that as a sign of respect, but he kept watching me anyway, probably assuming I was going to steal something. As I was paying for my coffee and microwaved burrito, the cashier was giving me a look of pure hatred and didn't reply when I told him, "Thank you. Have a nice day." I then took my food outside and walked around to the side of the gas station, so I could sit and eat while trying to decide on where to go next. As soon as I sat down, the cashier yelled at me from around the corner, "No! You cannot hang around here! Leave now, before I call the police!" I tried to explain my situation, but every time I opened my mouth to talk, he would continue to scream over me.

After dealing with the rude cashier, I wanted to give up on people for the rest of the day, so I pulled up my map and began looking for a place where I could get away. I noticed a large green area on my map on the northwest side of town, not too far from where I was, so I followed the sidewalk through the crowded downtown area until I reached the gulf. There was a park there that had a paved trail that went into the forest and circled the city. There didn't appear to be too many people on the trail, so I began following it until I was almost entirely alone. The only other people I saw were a few homeless people who had set up their tents, but they seemed to keep to themselves and didn't pay any attention to me. Eventually, I made my way off the trail and turned to walk towards the beach. Once I made it to the muddy shore, I began looking around for signs of people. As it appeared that I was alone, and it was such a beautiful location, I decided to claim that area as my temporary camp. I then took a seat in the grass and began crafting a longbow out of the wood of a yew tree. It seemed like a great way to pass the time and could come in handy later.

After spending two days in the forest, which I used to focus on building a couple of bows and some arrows, I made my way back into town to find a place to use as my mailing address. I checked in with the post office, where the worker recommended filling out an address form with the homeless shelter, which operated under the name of Bean's Café. The postal worker then wrote down the address on a small piece of paper and slid it over to me, "That's the address to the cafeteria, but they have a package center as well. Just tell them you'd like to receive your mail there, and they will probably let you use their address." I then made my way back through the city, towards the northeast side of town, and made it to Bean's Café just in time for lunch. However, after seeing a dead body on the sidewalk, I didn't feel much like eating. It was apparent there was nothing anyone could do, so, like all the other people who were waiting for the kitchen to open, I took a seat on the curb. A few minutes later, the paramedics arrived and scooped up the dead man's body as if it were just another day. As they drove away, the kitchen doors flung open, and all the homeless people began to shuffle their way inside. Even though I was in that group of people, and I was indeed homeless, I felt very out of place.

After filling out the address form at Bean's Café, I was told I would have to wait a few days to receive a confirmation letter, which I needed in order to get an Alaskan identification card. Knowing I would be stuck around Anchorage for a couple of weeks wasn't the best feeling, but I decided to make the best of it and began hiking towards the forest on the west side of town. After following the road along the woods for nearly ten miles, already void of human existence, I decided to step away from the road and ventured out into the bush. I'd only been in the forest for an hour when I received a text from Katie. She informed me that she would be off work and asked if I'd like to meet up to have dinner somewhere. I knew the forest would be there when I returned, so I told her that sounded great and made my way back to the road.

Katie and her friend, Danica, pulled up in their small gray pick-up truck as I was walking towards town. Danica would have to use the truck soon but had enough time to drop Katie and me off wherever we wanted to go. Katie then asked, "How's beer and pizza sound? There's this place called Moose's Tooth that has some great options." I didn't know of any restaurants in the area, but I thought "Moose's Tooth" sounded interesting and gave Katie a nod. After Danica dropped us off, I realized it would be a long wait before we could eat. Normally, I would have avoided crowded places like that, but I decided to stick around anyway because it seemed like it could be kind of romantic.

After finishing our dinner date, Katie and I walked back into the forest where I had been when she came to pick me up. Once we were deep in the forest, we came across a creek and began following it for quite a while. After getting tired, we decided to sit in the grass and take a break. Soon after taking a seat, we were bombarded by a massive swarm of mosquitos, so we decided to clear an area for a fire, hoping the smoke would get rid of them. Once we had the fire going, the mosquitos seemed to disappear. However, we decided to keep the flame alive much longer for its warmth and sociability. Since the ground was damp from all the rain, I had to collect all the dead branches, which were still connected to the trees. Since they were dead, my machete was knocking them down rather than cutting them. I then saw a thick branch that looked like it would burn for a while, so I sat my machete on it to see if the weight alone would bring it down. It appeared to be hanging tightly onto the tree, so I gave my machete a swing, and it went flying right through like butter. I wasn't expecting it to go through so easily and had my hand placed on the tree, just beneath the limb. Since I kept my knife and machete razor-sharp, I immediately grabbed my finger, scared of what I might see. It didn't hurt much, but it stung just enough that I knew it had done something. Still holding my finger, I asked Katie to reach into my pack and pull out my medical bag. I then looked down at my left-hand's middle finger and saw that I had filleted the flesh down to the bone. My fingernail had caught the blade and stopped the machete from completely removing the skin from my finger. Blood quickly began pouring out onto the ground, so I took some water from my canteen and washed it off, put the skin back over the bone, and wrapped it up tightly with a bandana.

After nearly cutting my finger off, I walked Katie back to her apartment and began searching for a place to camp. There was a church not too far from her apartment, so I made my way over to it and decided it seemed safe enough. There was a small alley to its side, which was between the church and someone's house. I figured it would be okay to camp there, so long as I made sure to get up early and be gone before anyone had the time to notice. However, I accidentally slept longer than I meant to and woke to the sound of a man's voice, "Excuse me. Is someone in there? Hello?" I unzipped my tent and stuck my head out to see what the person wanted. The man continued, "Sorry, sir, but this is my church, and you can't be sleeping back here. Nothing against you, but if someone sees you camping back here, I'll have every homeless person in Anchorage doing it." I understood what the man was getting at and apologized for being there. He hung around as I began packing my things and said, "You don't look homeless. Why are you sleeping out here?" I laughed and replied, "Well, technically, I am homeless. I just try to take care of myself. Anyway, I walked my friend to her house over here last night and thought this looked like a safe place to sleep." After I had finished packing my things, the man invited me into his church, where we sat and drank coffee as I filled him in on my travels across the country.

After leaving the church, I made my way back into the city and followed the old trail back to where I had stashed my bows and arrows. Once I made it there, I put my tent up and got back to crafting my hunting gear. I stayed there doing that for two more days and then made my way to Bean's Café on the third morning. My address confirmation had arrived, so I took it over to the DMV and had them prepare my Alaskan identification card. When they went to take my picture, I gave them the largest, proudest, most sincere smile. They then handed me the temporary copy printed on a sheet of paper, and I immediately compared it to my old driver's licenses. It was mind-boggling how much I had changed over the years, but it was kind of sad to see how cold and miserable I looked before. It was evident that all the traveling I'd done had changed me both physically and emotionally. I just hoped that I could stay positive over the next week while waiting for the permanent card to arrive.

After leaving the DMV, I made my way back to my campsite near the beach. When I got there, I noticed a small group of homeless people had decided to set up camp nearby. I figured I would just try to ignore them since I really liked that spot, but as the night went on, their violent nature made me question my safety. The next morning, I hid my bows a little better and then made my way into town. I didn't really know where to go or what to do, so I decided to buy a six-pack of beer and took it off behind some bushes to try and enjoy myself. Compared to everywhere else I'd been, Alaska was much more lenient about public intoxication. Every time I walked through the city, I saw at least twenty people walking around and drinking beer or whiskey. However, I was used to people getting fines for that, so I decided to try and keep it a secret.

After finishing my beer, I got a call from Katie. She asked if I would be interested in riding up to Fairbanks with her and Danica for the weekend. She didn't have to ask me twice! I was more than ready to get out of Anchorage! I told her where I was and waited for them to come and pick me up. However, I was a bit nervous about going on such a long ride, especially with people I barely knew, so I took a Klonopin to help me relax. By the time I remembered I'd just finished a six-pack, it was too late. I knew I'd be okay, but I hoped I wouldn't pass out or act too loopy. They picked me up about thirty minutes later and went to fill up the gas tank before heading out. Katie then walked out of the store with a big smile on her face and a twelve-pack of beer in her hand, "You think you can drink without me? I smelled it on you!"

Driving north towards Fairbanks, it didn't take long to be away from the city and completely enveloped by Alaska's enormously wild state. After making it about sixty miles from Anchorage, I reached over and grabbed one of the beers from the case Katie had bought. Then, I had another. And another one. After having three beers on top of the six-pack and Klonopin, we decided to pull over and stretch our legs. I wasn't out of my mind yet, but I was certainly more carefree than usual and decided to follow a nature trail into the Alaskan bush. Danica wanted to stay behind and take a quick nap, but Katie, feeling adventurous as usual, tagged along with me. After following the trail through the thick forest for about a hundred yards, we came out at a massive field full of blueberries. We continued walking along, picking and eating the berries as we went. Caught up in the moment, we ended up walking about two miles from the vehicle when I felt like we should turn back. The open field had turned into a forest so dense that I couldn't see more than three feet into it. However, Katie said she wanted to walk just a bit more, so I followed. After walking only a few more feet, I noticed something brown sticking out of the brush and onto the trail up ahead. I thought it might be a bear, so I put my arm out in front of Katie, stopping her in her tracks. Then a giant moose stepped out onto the trail with its calf following close behind. Once the moose and its calf had disappeared back into the bush, we decided it was probably best to turn around and make our way back to the truck.

After enjoying a nice walk in the woods, Katie and I made it back to Danica and loaded up into the truck to continue making our way up to Fairbanks. As we were driving along, it felt like my buzz had worn off, so I secretly took two more pills and got back to drinking. About thirty minutes later, I had pretty much lost my senses, meaning I didn't care about anything. We could have had a wreck, been attacked by a bear, had a wildfire roaring towards us, and been caught in a tornado all at the same time, and I wouldn't have given a damn. My short-term memory had also gone down the drain, so, without realizing I'd already taken two pills, I took two more just to be sure. We then pulled over at a gas station to top off and get some snacks, and I purchased another six-pack, which I made last for the remainder of our drive.

Once we made it into Fairbanks, Danica said she wanted to swing by a bar to meet up with some of her friends. For some reason, I felt nervous about meeting more strangers, so I took two more of my pills to help take the edge off. Once we'd all made it inside, Danica began talking to her friend while Katie and I continued drinking with each other. After having a few more drinks, I reached into my pocket and pulled out my pill bottle. Katie immediately snatched it out of my hand and yelled, "Jesus! No wonder you've been acting so weird! How many of these have you taken?" By that time, I really couldn't remember, and I began to feel myself slipping away. Katie then helped me outside to the truck, and everything went black.

Shortly after passing out, I began to have the strangest, most vivid dream I'd ever had. It felt as though I was being sucked through a warm vacuum hose that was changing colors and playing music. I eventually landed in a field full of colorful flowers, and the grass felt like satin sheets. A strong gust of wind then came flowing through the meadow, and the sky began to change to water. The water slowly made its way down over me, but it didn't feel wet, and I could still breathe. I looked around and realized the ground was no longer there, but I was just floating. It was then like someone pulled the plug on a drain, and I began to get sucked down towards a bright light. The next thing I knew, I woke back up in the truck and had no idea where we were, other than the fact that the forest surrounded us.

I looked over and saw Katie and Danica were still sleeping next to me, so at least they hadn't ditched me. I quietly exited the truck to use the restroom when I realized I had pissed myself during the night. I then turned around and saw that we were parked next to a church, so I took a pair of clean clothes inside to change. When I walked into the restroom, I was surprised to see there was a shower. I hadn't had a shower since I'd been in Alaska, so I couldn't resist the urge to take one. When I turned the water off, I heard someone violently beating on the bathroom door. I hurried to get dressed so I could see what was going on. When I opened the door, I saw a young girl standing there in a dress. She looked up at me and said, "Oh, you're going to be in trouble. The bride needed to get in there to do her hair." I had no idea there was a wedding about to take place, so I held my hand up to signal to the girl to keep quiet, and I made my way back out to the truck. As I was making my way down the church's steps, I saw Katie and Danica walking around as if they were looking for something. As I got closer to them, Katie ran up to me, screaming, "Oh my god! There he is! Jake, we thought you were dead!" I laughed and said, "Chill out. I just needed to use the restroom. I think we should get out of here, though. I accidentally held up a wedding because I took a shower."

We all got back into the truck and began making our way up to one of their friend's house in the town of North Pole. As we were riding along, I noticed Katie and Danica were acting kind of strange, so I asked if something was bothering them. Wide-eyed, they looked at each other for a few seconds, and then Katie turned to me and said, "You were dead last night." I laughed and asked what she was talking about. "You were dead. You weren't breathing, and you had no pulse. We didn't realize it until after we had a lot to drink, so we were going to take your body to the hospital when we woke up." I laughed again out of disbelief, "Well, I'm alive now." Katie replied, "Yeah? How's your head feel? We hit a bump last night, and you smacked your head on the dash. That's when we realized you weren't just sleeping." I looked out the window, admiring all the beauty around us, and I replied, "Actually, I feel amazing. I don't have a hangover or anything." Danica had remained quiet the whole time but finally burst into laughter, "Man, this is crazy! I swear on my life, you were dead. I work in hospice. You were dead as dead could get. I can't believe this!" They then began asking me questions about what it was like to die, but I wasn't really prepared to explain it. I thought that I'd just had a weird dream, so I needed some time to think that was what death felt like. However, I could tell they wanted an immediate response, so I just said, "Well, I guess it just felt like I was asleep." They seemed a little let down by my answer. I could tell they were hoping I had just uncovered some sort of mystery to life, but I was still trying to figure that out myself.

We finally made it to their friends' house in North Pole a couple of hours later and made our way to the back yard. There were about five other people there, getting everything ready for the outside dinner party. After introducing myself to everyone, I was given a list of choirs that I could do to help. We were going to have a barbecue and a bonfire, so I went behind the shed and began pulling out some old boards to cut up into firewood. Katie and I then worked together to prepare a fire ring with stones and set out all the lawn chairs for everyone. As the sun began to set, a few more people had shown up, and I tossed a spark onto the firewood, a symbol that the party had started.

After we had finished eating, we were all sitting around the fire and sharing stories when one of the children walked up to me and asked if I knew how to ride a unicycle. I told her I didn't but wondered why she asked. She said, "We have one over there, but no one knows how to ride it." I asked her to bring it over, and I'd see what I could do. The first time I tried to ride the one-wheeled stick with a seat on it, I landed flat on my back. Everyone began laughing, and the girl looked at me and said, "That's why no one rides it. They all fall off." I then laughed and said, "Well, yeah, it was my first time. I knew I was going to fall." I then hopped on for a second try and almost fell, but I caught myself just before hitting the ground. The third time, I got a few pedals in before I got bucked off, and the girl said, "Oh! You almost got it!" I turned to the girl and said, "I think I got this time!" I got on for the fourth time and slowly began pedaling my way through the grass. The little girl began yelling, "Everyone, look! He's doing it!" I probably only made it ten feet before getting bucked off again, but the girl seemed impressed and took it away to try and learn how to ride it herself.

After sitting back at the fire and sharing a few beers with everyone, the time had come to turn in for the night. I put my tent up next to the side of their house, and Katie asked if I would mind her sleeping in the tent with me. I felt it would have been preposterous to deny such an exquisite young lady from reposing within the walls of my finely woven, polyester castle. "Yes," I said with a smile, "of course you may!" Katie laughed as I greeted her into my tent, "After you, my lady." We had spent quite a bit of time together, so it didn't feel awkward to be cuddling up with her. Although we were sharing my sleeping bag, there didn't appear to be any sexual feelings going on between us. Instead, it was more like we both just wanted to feel someone there, a mutual desire to feel warm and safe.

The next morning, we made our way back south for Anchorage. I wasn't looking forward to being back in the city, but I still needed to claim my Alaskan identification card before I could leave the area for good. If I'd had it with me before catching that ride up to Fairbanks, I probably wouldn't have gone back with them. As we passed by Denali National Park, I had Danica pull over so I could step out and get a sense of what

I was going to be up against. The vastness was almost overwhelming, terrifying to imagine being out there alone and without a rifle. I figured that should be my next goal and knew Anchorage would probably be the best place to acquire one. After stretching our legs along the bank of the Susitna River, we got back into the truck and finished our ride back into Anchorage.

Once we made it back into the city, Danica said I was welcome to come inside to get a shower and do some laundry. After getting cleaned up, I left their apartment and began walking towards the city. There was a long bridge that separated downtown Anchorage and Katie's rural neighborhood. I stood at the edge of the bridge for a moment and began to feel sick of the thought of going into the city, so I got onto a dirt trail that went through woods instead and found a secluded area to set up camp. I wasn't sure why, but I woke the next morning feeling extremely depressed. I didn't even have the motivation to get up, so I just laid there for the rest of the day. That one day of lying in my tent was enough to take me out for another week. During that time, all I did was walk to a nearby gas station, fill up my water, and then go back to my tent to lie down. It was a rough week, for sure, but I finally forced myself out of the funk and made my way to the DMV to pick up my identification card.

After picking up my new card, I wandered off into the same forest where I'd almost chopped my finger off and decided to build a small cabin. It wasn't like I planned on staying out there permanently, but winter was on the way, and I knew I would need something better than my tent if I were going to make it through the cold. After working on my squatter's cabin for about two weeks, the only thing I had left was the roof. I needed to get some supplies for that, so I made my way into town and began searching for a hardware store. After finding one and purchasing the stuff I was going to need, I loaded it all up on a small trailer and began pushing it back to my little cabin in the woods.

Once I'd made it back to my site, I noticed there was a girl in my tent. She hadn't seen me yet, so it startled her when I asked, "Can I help you?" The skinny blonde scrambled out of my tent and nervously replied, "Oh, I'm just trying to find my phone." I cocked my head to the side and asked, "Why would your phone be in my tent?" She tried to run away but ended up tripping over some logs I had lying about. I then pulled out my bear spray and aimed it at her face while I looked around the inside of my tent. I immediately realized that my pack was missing.

Full of rage, I turned back to the girl and screamed, "Where the fuck is all of my gear at!" Quivering in fear, the girl replied, "I don't know. Please don't hit me." I yelled at her again, "Bullshit! I know damn well you aren't out here by yourself! Where are your punk ass friends, and where did they take my stuff!" I then looked up when I heard some rustling in the woods and saw two men running towards me. One of them had my knife in his hand, and the other had my machete, so I hid my bear spray down by my side and waited for them to get closer. Once they had made it about ten feet away and could tell it wouldn't go peacefully, I lifted the bear spray and began hosing them down. I was so angry and fearful for my life that I continued spraying them both until the can was empty. I then reached into my side pocket and pulled a couple of zip ties to cuff the two men, which was pretty easy because they had their hands covering their faces. While the two men were rolling around in pain, I took my tent down, threw everything that was left inside of it, and tossed it over my shoulder. I then looked over at the shaking girl and screamed, "Take me to my stuff! Now!"

After following the girl through the forest for about a hundred yards, we finally came across my backpack. Although everything had been strewed about, it all appeared to be accounted for. As I began shoving everything back into its rightful place, I turned back to the girl and noticed she was still crying and begging for me not to hit her. Trying to calm her, I changed my tone and said, "Listen. There's a creek on the other side of that cabin. Go back over there and lead your friends to it. You're going to have to help them wash that bear spray out of their eyes, or they're going to go blind." The girl nodded and ran back towards her friends while I finished packing my things before starting my hike back into the city.

I began shaking as I was making my way back into Anchorage. It wasn't because I was cold, but because I was so angry about those bastards following me out there and trying to steal my things. All the hard work I had put into that cabin was gone because I couldn't go back. I knew they would return to it with more of their homeless friends and have it taken over in no time. I'd also just lost a whole weeks' worth of time, and winter was coming quickly. Wanting to relax and destress without having to pop some pills, I decided to make my way into a restaurant to grab a bite to eat. I'd passed by a place called Humpy's a few times and thought it seemed like a nice place to have dinner and relax. As I approached the rear entrance, a security guard stepped in front of me and said I'd have to leave my backpack outside. I figured it would be safe since he was guarding the area, so I tucked it away into the corner and went inside to take a seat.

After I'd made my order, I was waiting for my food to come out when the security guard walked up to me and said, "I'm going to have to ask you to leave." Becoming frustrated, I asked the man, "What? Why?" He began to look irritated and continued, "Look, we know you're going to dine and dash. Now, are you going to leave, or are we going to have to make you leave?" Disgusted with their judgment, I pulled out my wallet and said, "No, you look. I have money to eat here. I already ordered my food. I'll leave when I've finished eating." The security guard then called over two more security guards, and all three of them carried me through the restaurant and tossed me out into the parking lot, causing me to bust my head open. They then threw my backpack and trekking poles at me, and the impact from the landing ended up breaking the camera I had bought at the airport, as well as bending one of my trekking poles. One of the security guards then yelled, "Now get the fuck out of here before we call the cops, you homeless piece of shit!" I was on the verge of going back inside to fight the security guards, but I didn't want to go to jail. I was just so close to a breaking point, and everyone kept pushing my buttons. I was still hungry, though, so I began walking up and down the sidewalks, peeking into all the trash cans for any good food. As I passed by a bus station, I saw several slices of pizza had been thrown away, so I began pulling them out. The bus station security guard then came out and yelled, "Hey! You can't be taking food out of the trash!" However, I ignored him and continued to dig the slices of pizza out anyway. I then had the idea to play deaf, and the man finally tapped on my shoulder. I jumped back, acting surprised. He then continued talking about how I couldn't be digging food out of the trash, and I made motions with my hands to make him think I couldn't hear anything. He looked away and said, "Oh, my God. I can't tell some homeless, deaf man he can't eat. I'll go to hell for that." Before walking away, he waved one of his hands at me as if to say continue what I was doing.

After eating a full meal's worth of garbage, I made my way back across the bridge and into Katie's neighborhood to set up camp for the night. The next morning, I made my way over to the homeless kitchen and had one last meal before making my way for Denali. A part of me wanted to stick around in Anchorage a bit longer so I could get a rifle or wait for my bows to finish setting, but I couldn't deal with the people anymore. However, I did purchase a new can of bear spray before heading out. It wouldn't be able to provide me with food, but at least it offered me some protection.

As I was entering the smaller town of Wasilla, which was about forty miles northwest of Anchorage, a middle-aged lady, who was wearing a large, puffy jacket and sunhat, pulled up beside me in an SUV. The lady then leaned over to roll down the passenger window and asked if I needed a ride. As far as passing a quick judgment goes, she seemed nice, so I hopped in and asked how far she was going. It turned out she was driving all the way up to Fairbanks, so I said, "Perfect! You can drop me off at Byers Lake if you don't mind." The lady looked over at me and replied, "Byers Lake, huh? Yeah, they have a nice campground. How long you plan on staying? I have to come back through in a few days if you need a ride back down." I thought, judging by the tone of her voice, she probably assumed I wasn't going to any campground. I replied anyway, "Hmm. They have a campground there? I'll probably stay there tonight and then leave for Denali tomorrow." Her tone quickly changed from cheerful to concerned, "I had a feeling you might be doing something like that. And you're going out by yourself?" I nodded, so she continued, "Do you have a gun? There's an awful lot of bears out there." Although I knew not having a gun out there was risky, I just smiled and replied, "I'm not too worried about the bears. I'd rather deal with them than all the crazy-ass people back in Anchorage." Although she didn't exactly know what I'd been through, she probably had a good idea because she began to laugh and nodded her head in agreeance. I figured she'd probably had some kind of bad experience herself, though neither of us went on to elaborate.

Once we reached the campground at Byers Lake, the lady popped open her glovebox and revealed a high-powered handgun. She then looked over at me and said, "You can take it if you want. I can get it back from you when I come back through here." I hesitated for a moment because I knew I would feel safer if I had it, but I just smiled and replied, "No. I can't take that. You might need it, and I don't know how long I'll be out there for. Thank you, though!" Seeming to respect my choice, the lady smirked and said concerningly, "Be careful out there. I'd hate to read that something happened to you after I dropped you off." I truly felt her concern, which made me feel like I should be a bit more careful. I then smiled and waved goodbye as I turned away from her vehicle and began walking towards the campground.

Once I'd made it to the camping area, I realized there were quite a few people there and barely any sites available. Since I felt like I needed more space, I left the campground and crossed the highway, where I began searching for a way to cross the raging river that separated me from Denali. After hiking along the river's edge for about an hour, I came across a footbridge that would lead me straight into the wilderness. I looked around for a moment, trying to gather my courage before entering the dark, damp, colossal forest. I continued across the bridge, and it felt like I was in an entirely different world. I then felt the realization that no one knew where I was except for the lady who had just dropped me off. It was a great but eerie feeling- a mixture of peaceful solitude and fear. I began to wish I had invested in a search and rescue beacon, but it hadn't crossed my mind until I was already making my way deep into the Alaskan bush.

After a couple of hours of navigating my way through the thick brush and shallow creeks, I could hear the unmistakable sounds of bears roaring in the distance. They sounded kind of far away, but it was hard to be sure because the forest was so dense. However, I could tell the forest was thinning just up ahead because I could see the water from a lake passing through the trees like a roll of film. Once I had made it to the edge of the tree line, I saw two grizzly bears fighting over a dead moose. Although they were only about a hundred yards away, I could tell they were so preoccupied with each other that they wouldn't pay me any mind, so I stepped out of the forest and began looking for where I'd like to head from there. I noticed some accessible mountains towards the northwest side of the lake, so I started walking in that direction and away from the raging bears.

After hiking through miles of dense brush, I finally reached the top half of the mountain, and the brush began to thin out. I had a pretty good vantage point at least and could see where the highway was a few miles off in the distance. I could also see the lake down below and noticed the bears had already gone off somewhere. Since it was getting late, I decided to set up camp and prepare a fire, which was a bit difficult because everything was so damp. However, I managed to get a fire going and appreciated its warm company throughout the night.

The next morning, after getting rid of my fire pit and hiding any other trace of my being there, I made my way higher up the mountain to get a better view of everything. Once I made it to the top, the beauty that I was presented with left me speechless. I then decided to spend the rest of my day sitting there to take it all in. As I looked towards Mt. Denali, which was where I was hoping to end up, it was apparent there was way too much snow on it for me. I also realized it would be much more treacherous to get to than I previously thought. There were several sets of mountains in front of me, which all appeared dangerously steep and jagged, and the forest below was mesmerizingly dense. However, the mountains were vast around the base, which meant I could probably make it to the bottom of Mt. Denali within a week. I thought about making the trek for a few minutes and finally decided where I was at would be good enough. All I wanted was to get away from everyone, and I thought I'd done a pretty good job at that.

After camping on the mountain for another night, I made my way down to a river, hoping to collect water and do some fishing. As I was making my way down, the open field quickly turned back into a dark, thick, and eerie brush. As I made my way lower, the wind began to pick up. I began to feel nervous about my scent being carried away and how all the rustling leaves were drowning out the sounds of my footsteps. Not wanting to sneak up on a dangerous animal, I began to sing random parts of whatever songs would pop into my head.

I finally made it to the river without any trouble and dropped my pack down onto the rocks. I then reached down to remove one of the canteens from my pack, eager to fill it with water. As I lifted the canteen, the elastic band that held it in place slapped against my tightly packed backpack, creating a loud thumping sound. Almost immediately, I heard a violent splashing sound coming from the other side of a fallen tree. I quickly threw my pack over my shoulders and turned to climb back up the bank, almost afraid to see what was causing all the noise. When I turned around, I saw a massive grizzly bear making its way up the bank just behind me. It was insane, the size of it! It was like someone had tossed a big, wet carpet over a small car and lined it with teeth and claws! Luckily, the bank was soft, steep, and muddy, so it gave way underneath the bear's weight. I knew that was probably the only good chance I'd have at this, so I took out my bear spray and leaned over the edge. The bear's face was only about six feet away, and I'd never seen anything look so intent on killing me. Before thinking anything else, I held down the trigger, and a puff of orange smoke hit the bear directly in its face. The bear then turned its head away, which I hoped was going to be the end of it, but it turned back and began making its way for me again. I let out another burst of spray, but the same thing happened. After the fifth time, the last bit of spray fizzled out of the can. Thankfully, at that point, the bear turned to walk away, huffing and rubbing its face into the mud along the bank. I then used that time as my chance to escape, so I began making my way back towards the top of the mountain from which I came.

After I'd made it back to the top of the mountain, I thought about how I had used up all my bear spray on that one grizzly. I knew I would have to go back into Anchorage to buy some more, and maybe even a handgun, but I was okay with making the trip if I could get it done quickly. Knowing it would be dark before I could make it to the highway, I went ahead and set up camp on top of the mountain again. As I laid in my sleeping bag that night, I couldn't stop thinking about how intense that bear looked and how close it had come to killing me. I then wondered why it decided to come after me anyway and what would have happened if I had done things differently. No scenario I could imagine ended any better than it did, so I guessed I had done the best thing possible. I finally drifted to sleep and woke several times from having nightmares of the bear. Every time I woke up, I would think there was one right outside of my tent, so I'd grab my knife and stick my head out to look around. Although I knew my knife would be pretty much useless in the case of a grizzly attack, it was all I had left.

I made it back to the campground at Byers Lake around noon the next day and hoped to catch a ride back down to Anchorage. However, the campground had been completely deserted, so I began walking south along the highway. About an hour later, a man in a truck pulled over and asked if I needed a lift. I could tell he had been drinking, but I decided to take the risk anyway and hopped inside. I figured if I tried waiting for someone who hadn't been drinking, I'd be walking the whole way. As we were riding along, I told him how a bear had almost attacked me in Denali. The first thing he asked was, "Did you shoot it?" I laughed and said, "Nope. Didn't have a gun with me." He looked over at me like I was crazy and said, "Man, you got some balls going out there without a gun. Either that or you're stupid. Everyone carries a gun out here, man. You better get you one if you're going to be hiking out here." I couldn't have agreed with him more and decided I would try to look for one soon.

About an hour later, the man pulled over into a parking lot in Wasilla. He then looked over at me and said, "This is the end of the line for me, brother. I don't go into Anchorage. People are crazy over there." As I was getting out of the truck, I laughed and said, "Yeah, I know. Thanks for getting me this far, though. I don't mind walking the rest." I then went inside the nearby hospital to fill up on my water and began hiking back into

Anchorage. Once I made it back into the city, I decided to go into a bar and grill called McGinley's Pub to grab some dinner before heading to my campsite. As I sat there enjoying my meal, a young native lady named Ashley decided to sit with me. After having dinner and a few drinks together, she asked if I'd like to come back to her place. She said I could get a shower there and was more than welcome to camp in the back yard. I accepted her offer, and we made our way to her house. At the time, she was living with her nephew, mother, and her brother, Chris. I was a bit nervous about meeting them, but they seemed to take a quick liking to me and made me feel right at home.

After staying with Ashley and her family for two nights, she asked if I'd like to go to a concert with her and Chris. I thought that sounded fun, so the three of us and their dog loaded up into their car the next morning. It was about a six-hour drive to wherever it was we were going, but I was preoccupied with their dog, who loved to sing along as I played the harmonica. Once we arrived at where the concert was supposedly being held, I thought maybe they had made a mistake because of how small the town was. Feeling a bit skeptical, I asked, "Are you guys sure there's a concert here?" They both laughed and assured me we were at the right place; that we had just arrived earlier than we needed to. We then pulled up to a large cabin in the woods, and Chris killed the engine in the parking lot. I then asked, "Are we picking someone else up?" They both laughed again, and Chris replied, "No, man. This is the town's high school. You see that building over there? That's where the bands play." I looked over to where he was pointing and saw a young man setting up a drum set underneath a small pavilion.

We then got out of the car and decided to walk around while waiting for the show to start. As we were walking back towards the school, I could hear what sounded like heavy metal music. Chris began banging his head to the thrashing noise in the distance and took off running towards the school. I looked over at Ashley with a confused look on my face, "What? It's a metal concert?" She began laughing and replied, "What did you expect? Bluegrass? Come on!" I scooped up their short-legged dog, and we began running towards the music.

Surprisingly, the crowd consisted of about forty people. I wouldn't have guessed there were even that many people in the whole town. I figured that must have been close to all of them. The adults didn't seem to enjoy the metal music so much, but the younger people seemed to like it. I had played in a few metal bands growing up, though, so it was kind of nostalgic for me. I just wasn't expecting that kind of music from such a small town, buried deep in the Alaskan bush. However, where I was from, the crowds got kind of crazy at metal shows. The people here were just standing around like Eskimo zombies, which I thought was funny. The bands were surprisingly good, though.

After watching the bands play for a few hours, it was time to head back to Anchorage. As we were walking back to the car, Chris asked if I'd mind driving back so he could take a nap. I hadn't driven in a while, so I was kind of excited about it. However, I was a little hesitant because I had no idea where we were or how to get back. Chris then laughed and said, "You can't really get lost here, man. Just follow Glenn Highway all the way back to Anchorage. Just keep an eye out for moose."

We finally arrived back at Ashley's house around 2:00 a.m., and I crashed on the couch. The next morning, I thanked them for having me over and made my way back into Anchorage. As I was walking back into the city, I felt a strange zapping sensation in my brain. I then began to feel nauseous, dizzy, and even a little spaced out. The feeling came and went a few times, so I made my way through the city and crossed the bridge back into Katie's neighborhood, and set up my tent in the place I had before. I then crawled inside and took a nap, hoping the feeling would pass. However, I woke a few hours later and realized the feeling was still there, as well as a few more symptoms. My whole body was sore from head to toe, a deep-bone kind of pain. I tried to get out of my tent to walk it off, but my legs were too wobbly, and my vision began to distort. Then, it felt as though someone had shocked my brain with a taser, and I passed out.

I woke the next morning feeling drained, achy, and confused. I then began searching online to see if I could find anything that matched my symptoms, and I finally came across Klonopin withdrawals. Although I hadn't taken them daily for an extended time, every symptom was matching up perfectly. I assumed it must have been from the accidental overdose I had done a few days prior, which made sense given the time it takes for the drug to leave your body. I then decided to lie in my tent for the rest of the day, hoping tomorrow would be better.

After lying in my tent for nearly two days, my withdrawal symptoms appeared to be getting worse, and I was beginning to feel extremely anxious and depressed as well. I then read it could take up to two weeks for the symptoms to pass, so I made my way over to a nearby grocery store and stocked up on water, vitamins, dehydrated fruits, and nuts. After a week of lying in my tent, I noticed the season was changing very fast. It was almost like overnight that the leaves had all turned from a vibrant green to a dull orange. The first light snow had already fallen as well. I knew if I was going to be staying in Alaska, I was going to have to hurry up and find a place to stay. I began searching online to see if I could find an affordable place to rent. I came across an ad for a tiny cabin in Wasilla for only three hundred dollars a month. I still had enough saved to cover that for the winter, so I gave them a call. Unfortunately, they had already rented it out to someone else, so I continued my search. Unable to find anything I could afford, I purchased a refundable plane ticket back to Tennessee, two weeks in advance. If I couldn't find anywhere to stay by then, at least I knew I had a way out of there.

Another week had passed, and I was finally feeling like my normal self. However, I had yet to find any affordable living arrangements. I knew my time in Alaska was probably going to be cut short, so I decided to make the best of what remaining time I had. I then packed up my things to prepare for exploring the forest just east of Anchorage. As I was crossing the bridge back into the city, I noticed there wasn't any traffic. Not that there was ever a lot of traffic coming across the bridge, but this time there was absolutely none. Halfway across the bridge, I saw several helicopters flying around the city, and one of them began making its way towards me. I began to wonder if something was wrong with the bridge, so I stopped walking and began to check my surroundings. I then saw a police car heading in my direction and was curious to see what they had to say. The officer stopped next to me and said, "Get in the car. President Obama is about to come through, and the bridge has to be clear." Although the streets leading up to the bridge were barricaded, I had no way of knowing because I had been camping in the woods before the last intersection.

The officer dropped me off just on the other side of the bridge and told me not to move until after the president had passed. I felt a bit awkward standing there as the president and his security guards slowly drove by. I was standing next to the bridge by myself, so I knew I probably had snipers and news cameras watching me. After the president had passed, I made my way across the bridge and asked one of the officers what Obama was doing in Alaska. The officer then said that he was headed out to Denali National Park to rename Mt. McKinley back to Denali.

Before making my way out of the city, I decided to swing by Bean's Café for lunch. I hadn't eaten much in the past couple of weeks and felt like a good-sized meal would help get my energy back up. After standing in line with about fifty other homeless people, I was handed a tray and watched as the workers loaded it with rice, carrots, mashed potatoes, a small piece of salmon, and a stale sugar cookie. As I was sitting there eating, I looked around at all the homeless people and wondered what their stories were. I wanted to go up and ask each one of them, but I figured I would just focus on the lady sitting next to me in a wheelchair. Without trying to sound rude, I turned towards her and asked, "How did you end up where you are?" She then looked at me and said, "Well, my husband died a few years ago, and he did all the work. Now, I just get a few hundred dollars a month from social security. Not enough to rent anywhere around here, so I just stay over at the shelter." We were then interrupted by a fight that broke out, and the security officers forced everyone to leave.

After leaving Bean's Café, I began looking over my map to get an idea of where I'd like to go. I then noticed Flattop Mountain was only fifteen miles southeast of downtown Anchorage, so I figured that would be an easy escape out of the city. Although there was a road that led to the mountain's trailhead, I decided to shave off a few miles by walking through the forest instead. I'd made it about halfway by lunchtime and decided to sit on a log while I ate a granola bar. As I was sitting there, I heard something making its way towards me through the brush. I had a feeling it might be a bear, so I took the rest of my granola bar and scattered pieces of it all over the ground. I then turned to walk up the hill behind me and waited to see what popped out from the bushes. About a minute later, a black bear appeared from the dense forest. It then began sniffing around and searching for all the small pieces of granola I had left behind. I watched him for a few minutes, snuck a couple of pictures, and then slowly made my way out of there while the bear was still distracted.

Although I had taken a shortcut, it took much longer to make my way through the forest than if I had taken the streets. By the time I had made it about a mile from the trailhead, I had reached the road leading up to it. Since it was starting to get late, I decided to go ahead and set up my tent behind a church and would finish my way up the mountain in the morning. As I was lying in my tent, I began to think about how fast the seasons had changed. When I first arrived in Anchorage, it would get dark at midnight, and the sun would come up just a few hours later. Now, it was getting dark at 8:00 p.m., and the sun was coming up twelve hours later. I'd never experienced such a rapid change in the seasons as I had in Alaska. I knew there would be no way I could find a place before winter was in full swing, so I began to think about what I was going to do once I'd made it back to Tennessee.

The next morning, I followed the narrow road up the mountainside and made it to the trailhead parking lot around lunchtime. I was surprised to see so many people there, although it made sense because it was the easiest mountain to reach from Anchorage. Most of the crowd only hung around the trailhead, though. Only a handful of people were on the trail to the top, and that number began to fall as I made my way farther up. The trail finally turned into a steep rock climb, and since a person had recently fallen to their death, I was the only person out there. Ice was beginning to accumulate as I made my way higher, and the strong winds passing through the mountains made the hike even more treacherous. As I began to second-guess my decision, I continued pushing on, though I hoped the risk would be worth it. Once I had reached the top, I noticed an American flag had been erected within a large pile of rocks. After getting a picture of myself with the flag, and Anchorage far away in the background, I grabbed my pack and continued hiking farther into the mountains. Since I still had a few days before my flight was scheduled to leave, I decided to spend the rest of my time out there in the wild.

I made it back down into Anchorage the day before my plane was supposed to leave and set up camp in the woods only a few miles from the airport. Despite the heavy rainfall that night, I woke around 2:00 a.m. to a man screaming. He kept yelling, "Hey! Hey, you! Yeah, I see you!" Thinking someone had spotted my tent and was going to come over to start some trouble, I grabbed my knife and continued listening. "You want to fuck with me," the man screamed, "I'll fucking kill you!" He just kept repeating that, so I finally decided to poke my head out

250

to see what was going on. There was a light on the trail where the man was standing, and I could see there was no one else with him, and he wasn't looking in my direction. After watching him for a minute, it was obvious that he had been screaming at himself or his imagination. He finally continued walking along the trail and made his way out of there, his own violent screams following him through the forest. I shook my head and fell back to sleep, feeling glad my time in Anchorage was nearly over.

The next morning, I made my way to the airport and made it just in time to board my plane. Since I had to hurry to catch my flight, I didn't have the time to feel any regrets until I was in the air. Once the pilot had turned on the internet, I got online and messaged one of my friends from back home, "Hey, Mike. I'm heading back to Tennessee now. I should be there in a few days. Do you want to join me for a walk across America? I've been thinking about doing it for St. Jude Children's Research." As my plane flew over the mountains in Canada, I received a text back from Mike, "Yeah, man! I'll walk with you! I just got laid off and will be out of work for a few months. Been living with my dad, so I have no obligations to stick around." He had mentioned that he would love to join me several times but was always too busy with work, so I was glad to know he finally got the opportunity. I was also happy to know I'd have company from someone I could trust.

<u>An Old Friend</u>

After my plane had landed in Tennessee, I spent the next three days hitchhiking to Mike's house in the small town of Dresden. Once I made it to his house, we walked to a nearby store to pick up some beer. We then brought them back to his house and had a bond fire in the back yard, where we discussed our upcoming walk across the country. After tossing up some ideas, we decided to start our journey from my uncle's house in Fort Walton Beach, Florida. There wasn't much hesitation there, as we quickly pulled out our cellphones and purchased our bus tickets two weeks in advance. We were eager to start earlier, but the tickets were cheaper that way, and Mike still needed to order his hiking gear. Because I'd had some outdoor companies make me an ambassador, I was able to get most of his things for free. After shuffling through all the offers I'd been given, Mike's setup was beginning to look a lot like mine. I was a bit jealous that he was getting all new equipment, but most of my things were still in pretty good shape, minus the one trekking pole that had been broken in Alaska.

Mike's new hiking supplies arrived just a couple of days later, and we immediately began our twelve-mile hike to my parents' house. Once we made it, we ventured off into the woods so I could prepare Mike for living outside. Although he was an outdoorsy person, he said he hadn't done any camping in a few years. I figured we could spend a week out there before heading out, which would be enough time for him to adjust. As the days went on, I helped pass the time by teaching him all that I knew about survival. He seemed eager to learn more as I began sharing some survival skills and my seemingly endless knowledge of plants in the area.

After staying in the woods for a week, Mike and I began our forty-five-mile hike to the bus station in Jackson. We gave ourselves three days to make it, which I figured would be a good endurance test for Mike. That would also give us enough time to take things slow or even hitchhike if we fell too far behind. However, everything went well, and we camped just a few miles from the bus station on the night before it was scheduled to leave. The next morning, we finished up our hike to the bus station and sat outside of it to wait for our bus to arrive.

After riding along and dealing with three bus transfers, we finally made it to Florida thirty-five hours later. Luckily, my uncle only lived a few miles from the bus station, so we made our way to his house and sat up our tents in the back yard. We then crawled inside to take a nap until the sun made our tents unbearably hot, which was about noon. Since Mike had never been to Florida, or any coastal state for that matter, we left our gear behind and made our way to the ocean. My uncle only lived about a mile inland, so it was a convenient walk. We then sat at the beach for the rest of the day and decided to stay in Fort Walton Beach for a week before starting our hike across the country. Besides giving us some time to enjoy ourselves, that would also give the weather some time to cool off.

After spending a week camping in my uncle's back yard and bumming it on the beach, we started our hike across America on November 1st. Following along the coast, we ended our evening in Navarre Beach, which put us right at twenty miles. However, the last two miles were pretty slow because Mike had developed some blisters on his feet and could barely walk. Once we found a place to sleep on the beach, Mike kicked his boots off and began pulling at his bloody socks. He began complaining and was already thinking about giving up, but I told him the pain would go away within the next day or two, and he wouldn't have any problems after that. We would just have to take it slow until then, and I allowed him to set the pace. He then asked if it would be okay to soak his feet in the ocean and was heartbroken when I told him no. Although it probably would have soothed his feet, the risk of contracting some flesh-eating bacteria just wasn't worth it. Instead, I gave him some ibuprofen and told him to keep his feet elevated throughout the night. We then tossed our sleeping bags right down on the sand and turned in early enough to watch the sunset.

The next morning, after drying off our things and shaking them free of sand, we began our fifteen-mile hike for Pensacola Beach. Mike had a tough time walking on his new blisters, so I pointed out a hotel in the distance to give him something to focus on. As the day went on, it felt like we weren't getting any closer to our landmark. However, we finally reached the hotel in Pensacola Beach just after dark and parked our sleeping bags on the beach again. Mike was really starting to lose hope at that point, thinking the pain would never go away, but I continued trying to keep him motivated.

The next morning, we crossed the bridge from Pensacola Beach and made our way into Gulf Breeze. Although we had only covered about six miles, Mike wanted to take an hour-long break before crossing the four-mile bridge into Pensacola. His feet were beginning to feel better after his break, so we tossed our packs back on and began making our way across the intimidating bridge. There was a lot of traffic and only a tiny shoulder for us to walk on. Mike was nervous about the cars zooming by so closely, so he just focused on my feet as I marched on in front of him. I then turned to look over into the water and saw a school of stingrays being ganged up on by sharks. I turned to tell Mike about it, and when he turned to look, a car came within about an inch of hitting his backpack. Another car then passed by, and the mirror grazed my shirt, so we decided to pick up the pace and get off the bridge as quickly as possible.

After we had made it across the bridge, we made our way into a small veteran's memorial park. We had only planned to stop there for a break but decided to wait and see if it would be a safe place to sleep. About an hour later, an older man walked up to us and began talking. After telling him we were walking across America for St. Jude, he offered to take us out for dinner. He seemed like a decent guy, so we followed him back to his truck and went for a ride to one of his favorite barbeque restaurants. After we had finished eating, he tried convincing us to go for a ride, but Mike and I had already given each other some distrusting looks. The man then dropped us back off where he'd picked us up, and Mike said, "Man, I'm glad you told him just to drop us off. I saw him put a gun in a brown paper bag, and then he sat it in the back seat next to me. I kept my hands on my head the whole time, so he wouldn't think I was trying to reach for it." I believed every bit of what Mike was saying because the man did seem a bit out of touch, and he had shown us both the pistol in his side door panel. After watching the man drive away, we began searching for another place to sleep in case he decided to come back.

After parting ways with the strange man, Mike and I did some night walking. We ended up making it about fifteen miles and found a place to set up camp in the Big Lagoon State Park. We put up our tents beside a building next to a boat ramp and passed out from exhaustion. The next morning, we noticed that we had set our tents up next to a sign that read, "Beware of alligators." We thought that was funny because we had made jokes about alligators being out there right before we had fallen asleep. We then got back on the move and crossed into Alabama just in time for lunch. We found a restaurant that served one-dollar tacos, so we got our fill there and continued another ten miles into Gulf Shores. There was still plenty of daylight left after we got there, and Mike's feet didn't seem to be bothering him anymore. While we both had the energy to continue, we decided to stay there for the night and enjoy the beach since we would be inland for the remainder of our walk across the country.

The next morning, as we were making our way into the town of Foley, I remembered Sydney and her boyfriend had recently moved there. I sent her a message letting her know Mike and I were in the area and that we'd like to meet up if she was available. She called me right back to ask where we were, and it turned out we were standing at the gas station right across from her apartment. She then ran outside to greet us and was about to cross the street when I yelled for her to stay where she was. I still had nightmares about her getting hit by that car and didn't want it to happen again. Mike and I then made our way across the street, where I gave Sydney a big hug and introduced her to Mike.

Once we had made it into Sydney's apartment, Mike and I took turns getting a quick shower and then followed Sydney down the street to her favorite bar. As we were sitting there having drinks, Sydney and I got each other caught up on where we were in life. She was surprised that I had come back from Alaska but thought it was probably for the best after explaining why I left. However, we both agreed that walking for St. Jude was very noble and would be something to keep me motivated. Mike wasn't as enthusiastic about the whole charity thing, though. He was just looking for some adventure, which I completely understood. Trying to keep all my followers entertained so they would make donations took quite a bit of work. I was always on my phone: posting this, sharing that, replying to all my messages, and uploading pictures and videos. Just trying to keep my things charged was challenging enough on its own, but I couldn't complain since it was all for a good cause.

After leaving the bar, Sydney led us down a hiking trail, where we were hoping to find some alligators. We searched the bayou for a few hours, and even a couple of hours after dark, but never had any luck. After making our way back to her apartment, I asked about the cages I'd seen sitting outside. Sydney said she had gone crab fishing just about every night since she had been there and ate them for dinner most nights. Mike and I were feeling hungry for some fresh, home-cooked crabs, so we took the cages down the nearby pier and tossed them over into the water. Within an hour, we'd captured a dozen healthy looking crabs and brought them back into the apartment to prepare for dinner. The lemony fresh, butter-soaked crab legs sure paired nicely with great friends and some cold beer.

The next day, after having lunch with Sydney, Mike and I got back on the road and began heading west. Shortly after leaving Foley, a heavy rain came pouring down. Even though it was raining, it was too hot and muggy for me to put on my rain jacket. However, Mike didn't like getting wet, so he put his on. After hiking for a couple of hours, I heard Mike yell from behind, "Man, I think my jacket is leaking!" When I turned around to look at him, his face all red, he lifted his arm and showed me the stream of water that was dripping from his jacket sleeve. I began laughing and said, "That's not rain, man. That's sweat, and it looks like you're overheating. Just take that thing off and enjoy the rain while it lasts." He then removed his jacket and let out a sigh of relief, "Oh, man! This feels so much better! No wonder you weren't wearing yours!"

After slowly hiking through the rain for twelve miles, we decided to end our afternoon in the unincorporated community of Barnwell. We noticed a small grocery store as we passed through and decided to camp behind it since it was closed. It seemed like a safe place to set up our tents, so we both fell into a deep sleep. Sometime around midnight, I woke to the sound and feeling of something sniffing near my head through the wall of my tent. I thought it might be a bear, so I swatted at it and yelled for it to get out of there. I stuck my head out to see what it was, but it was already gone. Mike then woke up and asked what was going on, so I said, "Something was just over here, sniffing at my tent, but I'm not sure what it was." We then heard a loud whistle and the voice of a man calling out for his dog. I then saw two sets of flashlights appear from the front of the building, heading in our direction. As the lights popped out from around the corner, I could make out two police officers. Preparing myself for them to ask us to leave, I sat up and waited for them to come over and talk to us. Once they had made it in front of our tents, they took a few seconds to assess us when one of the officers said to the other, "Holy shit, man. If your dog had attacked them, we'd be so fucked." The other officer replied, "Yeah, I know. Why do you think I'm shaking right now? We're all lucky my dog didn't attack you guys. He probably would have killed you. We come out here all the time to let him use the bathroom. Never seen anyone out here before. What are you guys up to?" After explaining to them that we were walking across America for St. Jude, they decided to leave us be but said we'd need to be gone by 6:00 a.m.

We woke early the next morning and walked into a nearby gas station to fill up on our water. We then hiked eighteen miles north into the town of Spanish Fort. Since the morning was nice and cool, we were able to make it there by lunchtime. After taking a short break and having a couple of snacks, we crossed the eight-mile-long bridge into the city of Mobile. However, we didn't stick around there too long because of all the dirty looks we were getting. After pushing our way through the city, we found ourselves halfway between Mobile and Semmes, where we were able to find a forested area to camp in, right off the highway.

We got an early start the next morning and crossed into Mississippi after walking about fifteen miles. Shortly after crossing the state line, we noticed an older man on the opposite side who was waving for us to come over. Once we made it over to the man, he told us he was the pastor of the church behind him. He then invited us inside, where he told us we could eat as much of the leftover food from their Thanksgiving lunch as we wanted. We were both pretty hungry, so we thanked him for the offer and scarfed down about two plates each. The pastor had no idea who we were or that we were walking across the country for St. Jude, so it felt great to know we weren't just receiving any special attention. However, I did show him my Facebook Page before leaving, which he got a kick out of. Mike and I then walked outside and got a picture with the pastor. We thought it was funny how we all looked like "The Lord of the Rings" characters. Because the pastor greatly resembled Gandalf, Mike and I sort of just fell into place as Frodo and Samwise.

After leaving the church, we continued hiking along until dark, where we ended our night deep in the De Soto National Forest. Feeling completely drained, we put our tents up and decided to eat a snack before heading to sleep. Since I had a much smaller stomach than Mike, I was satisfied after having only one granola bar and was ready to turn in. Since Mike was still eating, I handed him the food bag and asked if he would find a tree to hang it up once he was done. He said he didn't mind, so I slid into my sleeping bag and drifted off to sleep.

I woke up a few hours to the sound of something large making its way through the woods. Whatever it was, it was obvious that it was heading in our direction, so I grabbed my knife and bear spray and jumped out of my tent. As soon as I turned to shine my headlamp into the forest, I saw a black bear standing about ten yards away. I began yelling at it to get out of there, but it didn't seem too bothered by me. Along with screaming, I also started throwing sticks at it and smacking some of them against a tree. Mike finally woke up and calmly asked from inside his tent, "What are you yelling for?" "There's a bear out here! Get out here and help me scare this thing off," I screamed back at him. I then ran a few feet towards the bear, still yelling and throwing sticks. Thankfully, it started to walk away after I charged at it. I then turned back around and noticed Mike was still in his tent. "Mike! What the hell, man," I asked in disbelief, "Why are you still in your tent? We almost got ran up on by a bear, and you're just lying in there like it's nothing." Mike then replied, "What? It was probably just a car or something." I then figured he had taken something to help him sleep, so I gave up trying to talk and crawled back into my tent. Just as I was getting ready to zip the flap closed, I noticed Mike had left my food bag sitting on the ground, along with several wrappers from the food he had eaten before going to bed. It was no wonder why the bear had come up to our tents, so I picked up all food and trash and took the bag to hang it myself.

The next day, Mike and I were making our way into Hattiesburg when I received a message from a local girl named Jessie. She said that we could crash at her place for the night if we wanted, so we picked up the pace and made it to her house around noon. Jessie and her roommate, Lauren, were sitting on the front porch waiting for us when we got there. After everyone had introduced themselves, Mike and I tossed our packs into their house and hopped into the car to ride with them into town. A few minutes later, we pulled into the parking lot of a beer store when Jessie turned to me and said, "Go ahead and get whatever you want. We're having a party tonight!" I looked over at Mike and saw he had a shocked look on his face. I'd ran into several people like Jessie on the road before, so I wasn't nearly as surprised as he was, but I was still excited about it and eagerly followed Jessie inside.

Once we'd made it back to their house, we all opened a beer and began talking and drinking into the afternoon. As the sun was going down, we decided to put a movie on and continued working on our buzz. About halfway through the movie, I heard a knock at the door. Since I was sitting right in front of it, I stood up and opened it. I looked down and saw a little boy standing there. He began trying to peek into the house, so I had a feeling someone may have sent him to go around the neighborhood and look for things they could steal. I then stepped out onto the front porch and shut the door behind me.

"Are you looking for someone," I asked? "No," the boy replied, "My daddy told us to go to every house and ask people for money." I looked at him suspiciously and asked, "What do you need money for?" The boy laughed and replied, "I don't know. He told us to say we needed money for food." I then asked where his father was, and the boy said his dad was back at home. It appeared the kid was being honest about his whereabouts, so I told him to do twenty pushups, and I'd give him five dollars. He seemed to have a hard time with them, but he eventually finished all twenty and stood up with his hand out. I then gave him the five dollars I'd promised and went back inside to finish watching the movie.

After the movie had finished, everyone went out to the front porch to play a drinking game. After a few rounds of beer pong, Jessie and I went back into the house to watch another movie, while Mike and Lauren stayed outside to continue drinking. After the movie had finished, Jessie and I went back outside to see what Mike and Lauren were up to. When I opened the door, Mike was lying there, passed out on the porch. Lauren was sitting there laughing and said, "I told him to slow down. He finished the whole bottle of Captain." I rolled my eyes and said, "Well, let's get him into the house. Doubt he'll be awake again before morning." Mike probably weighed about two hundred and fifty pounds at the time, so getting him into the house took quite a bit of work. The girls didn't really know how to help, so I just grabbed him by his legs and pulled him through the front door, leaving him lying on the living room floor.

It was still kind of early, so Jessie, Lauren, and I went back out onto the front porch to just sit and talk. Jessie then reached her hand over into my lap as we were sitting there and began giving me an erotic massage. I was really surprised because she didn't take me as the type to do something like that, but I didn't say anything. After a few minutes of rubbing me down, Jessie says, "Oh, my God, Lauren. He's huge!" Lauren then looks under the table and laughs when she realizes what Jessie is doing. Jessie then smacked me on the leg and said, "Take it out. Let us see." I didn't really know what to make of the situation. I kind of felt like she was joking, so I laughed and said, "What? Out here on the porch?" Jessie then replied, "Yeah! It's dark out here, and no one is around. Pull it out!" I was kind of nervous, but at the same time felt like doing something a little spontaneous, so I gave in to their request. After about thirty minutes of messing around on the porch, Jessie grabbed me by the wrist and pulled me into her bedroom to finish what she had started.

Jessie and I walked out of her room a couple of hours later when I noticed Mike was no longer lying on the floor. I then heard him and Lauren talking outside on the front porch, so we went out to join them and took a seat. Mike and Lauren gave us the look of shame, which Jessie and I thought was kind of funny. We then sat around and talked for a few minutes before Jessie and Lauren decided to turn in for the night. As Mike and I were sitting on the front porch alone, he began laughing and said, "Man, when you were in there getting some, I tried to make the moves on Lauren, but she was on her period. She let me make out with her, though!" I laughed and said, "Oh yeah? She and Jessie both went down on me earlier. How did those kisses taste?" Judging by the look on his face, Mike didn't think that was as funny as I did, but I knew he'd get over it soon enough.

The next morning, after accidentally setting off their security alarm, Mike and I thanked Lauren and Jessie for having us over and made our way back into town. Not surprisingly, Mike had a terrible hangover, so we stopped at a fast-food restaurant to get him something heavy and greasy, hoping to ease his symptoms. After grabbing breakfast, Mike wanted to take a nap, so we made our way behind a building and laid down on the ground for a couple of hours. After getting some rest, Mike was ready to get back to walking, so we began making our way for the town of Seminary.

After hiking about twenty miles, we came across a church that looked like a great place to spend the night. Since we didn't have too much longer before dark, we figured we would go ahead and end our day there and then take some back roads for Monticello in the morning. We made our way over to the church and set our tents up in the back, just in time to watch the sun go down behind the forested hills of Mississippi. We then crawled into our tents to turn in for the night when we heard two cars pull up in the gravel driveway just beside the church. Both cars' engines turned off, followed by a few seconds of silence. Then, I heard several doors open and slam shut. I could hear people talking and their footsteps making their way closer to us. I then heard a set of keys jingling and then unlock the door on the side of the church. Hearing that was a relief because I assumed it must have been the pastor. However, I was still nervous about them seeing us and telling us we had to leave. Not that it would have been hard to find another place to camp, but we had already settled and gotten comfortable. Luckily, once the people exited the church, they walked straight back to their vehicles and drove away.

We packed up early the next morning and began making our way for Monticello. However, after hiking thirty miles, we decided to end our day next to a small river called Silver Creek. Next to the river seemed like a good place to camp because it was between towns and we'd be hard to see from the road. We still had about three hours of daylight left, so we set up camp early and began gathering firewood. As we walked around and collected sticks, I told Mike about the time Rob and I had camped under the creepy bridge in California. Mike was a little freaked out by my story and jokingly said, "Man, if you had told me that before we got down here, I would have said just keep walking. I ain't trying to get possessed or have rocks flying all around my head!" I laughed with him because I was sure we were fine. I just wanted to get him a little worked up.

Once we had our fire going, Mike and I sat next to it and took turns playing my harmonica. Just as the fire was beginning to die down, and we were getting ready to get into our tents, we heard a loud splash in the water nearby. Since I had just told Mike the story of what had happened in California, we were both a little freaked out. I turned my headlamp on and walked into the woods along the river, trying to figure out where the sound came from. I couldn't find any reason for it, though, so I returned to Mike and suggested we build the fire back up. We didn't want to be out there in complete darkness if things started getting too weird. It looked like our fire would burn for a couple of hours, though, so we went ahead and turned in for the night.

A few hours later, something hit the water again, and the sound woke me up. I then heard Mike whisper, "Jake, did you hear that?" I laughed and replied, "Yeah, man. It was probably just a branch falling or something. Go back to sleep." About an hour later, we woke to the sounds of things constantly slamming into the water. We then jumped out of our tents to try and get the fire going again, but we'd already used all the dry wood earlier that day. Everything else was alive and wet from the rain earlier that morning, so we had a hard time bringing our fire back to life. We could hear what sounded like trees snapping just on the other side of the river. At the same time, it was like someone was throwing large boulders into the water as hard as they could. As the noises continued around us, we packed up our things and made our way back up to the road.

As we were crossing the bridge over the river, the noises finally stopped. I then leaned over the concrete rail and shined my light down towards the river, but I couldn't see anything that would explain the noises. Although we were tired, we decided to put down a few miles between us and whatever was lurking in woods near Silver Creek. As we were following the empty highway through the night, Mike looked over at me and asked, "Do you believe in Bigfoot?" I laughed and replied, "Man, I don't know what that was back there! Your guess is as good as mine!" Once we'd made it about three miles from Monticello, we got off the highway and walked up a large hill, where we stopped to set up our tents. It was obvious that we would be visible from the road come morning, but it was likely that no one would bother us since we were between towns. Either way, we were so tired that we really didn't care and fell straight to sleep.

We woke up around 9:00 a.m., which meant we had been able to get about five hours of sleep. We slowly packed up our things and made our way back down to the road. We then took a few seconds to prepare ourselves for another long day and began making our way for Monticello. After walking for about a mile, a lady pulled over up ahead and began walking towards us. She had a couple of paper bags in her hand, which she held up as she began getting closer. Just before I reached out for the bag, the lady asked, "Are you the two who were camping up on that hill last night? I saw some tents up there on my way into town and figured I'd bring whoever it was some breakfast." Mike and I were shocked that someone had gone out of their way to bring us food and thanked her for her generosity. After the lady drove away, we took a seat on the damp grass next to the highway and devoured three sausage and biscuits each.

After finishing our breakfast, Mike and I quickly made it into Monticello and only stopped long enough to fill our water. We then began following the highway north for the next town. It was kind of a slow day because there was no shoulder next to the road, and we had to spend most of the day walking through fields of waist-high grass. By the time we had finished our twenty-five-mile hike into Georgetown, we probably had about two hours left of daylight. As we continued into town, I pointed out a gazebo sitting in a park across the street. We made our way over to it and began preparing our dinner, which consisted of a tuna packet, a spoonful of peanut butter, and a granola bar. After eating, we contemplated pulling out our sleeping bags and sleeping underneath the gazebo, but we would have to wait until dark to see if the park got busy.

We then began to pay attention to the white truck with tinted windows sitting just across from us. It had been sitting there since before we arrived, and we wondered if anyone was inside. Out of curiosity, Mike looked over at me and asked, "Do you think if someone's in there, they would give me a cigarette?" I replied, "I'm pretty sure if anyone's in there, they're either an undercover cop or a drug dealer. If you want to risk interfering with a drug deal, then sure, go ahead." Mike then started walking towards the truck, and as he got closer, a man rolled down the window and began yelling for him to go away. Mike then walked back to me with a confused look on his face. I then looked up at him said, "See. They're up to something, man. No one would just be sitting behind a building like that for no reason."

A few minutes later, the man stepped out of his truck and made his way over to the gazebo. He then asked Mike, "Yo, man, what do you want? You can't just be walking up to people's vehicles like that. I got some business going on. Cops are gonna see you walkin' up and think I'm sellin' to you, man." Mike, a little naïve to the situation, quietly laughed and replied, "I was just gonna ask if I could get a cigarette." The man shook his head, then pulled a cigarette out of his jacket pocket and handed it to Mike. Just before walking back to his truck, the man shook his head again and said, "You can't just go walkin' up to people's vehicles round' here, dude. You gonna get shot. Lot of people runnin' business around here. Just sayin.' Not everybody gon' be chill like me, dawg." Mike then looked over at me and said, "Okay, maybe we shouldn't sleep here." I agreed, so we grabbed our backpacks and walked into a nearby wooded area.

The next day, as we were making our way through the small town of Utica, a man yelled for us to come over to him at a gas station. When we approached the man, he asked if we were hungry. I nodded my head, and Mike said, "Yes! Very!" The man laughed and said, "Well, go on into the store and get whatever you want." We didn't want to be too stingy with the man's offer, but we both got a small order of chicken livers, a roll, and a drink. We thanked the man for his help and took our food to a church just across the street. We then took a seat in the shaded grass underneath a tree and tried to cool off while enjoying our free lunch. Even though it was nearing December, the South was still hot enough to wear shorts and t-shirts.

As we were finishing up our meal, I received a message from both Holiday Inn and Candlewood Suites in Vicksburg. They had each offered us a complimentary room for one night. I then gave them a call and set up a reservation for the weekend. We then continued hiking north until dark and found ourselves camping behind another church. After sitting in our tents for about thirty minutes, a car pulled around to the back of the church, and the man inside rolled down the window, "Can I help you, gentlemen?" Sitting in my tent, I looked up at the man and replied, "No, sir. We're walking across America for St. Jude and just taking a break for the night." The man looked us over for a few seconds, "Oh. Okay. Well, this here is my church. I don't guess I mind if ya'll sleep here. Is that what ya'll usually do, camp behind churches?" Mike then replied to the man, "Well, we would camp in the woods, but they're dark and scary." I looked over at Mike like he had just said the most ridiculous thing I'd ever heard. No way was the pastor going to buy that. However, the pastor then turned to look at the woods and said, "Yeah, you're right about that. Them woods are dark and scary. I wouldn't be camping out there. Well, ya'll have a good night and be safe on your walk tomorrow." After the pastor drove away, I looked at Mike and asked, "Really? The woods are dark and scary?" Mike started laughing and replied, "Well, it worked, didn't it?"

I woke the next morning and realized my tent was covered in a thick layer of ice. I began smacking the pieces away from my tent and heard Mike groan, "Dude, it's so cold!" I started laughing and asked, "What? No way, man! This is the best!" Excited about the freeze, I jumped up out of my tent and began getting everything packed up to leave. However, Mike wasn't as thrilled about it as I was and had a hard time getting up. He wanted to sleep in until it warmed up outside, but I made him get up anyway because there were kids standing around outside, waiting for the school bus, and we had a hotel room waiting for us in Vicksburg.

We started walking around 7:30 a.m. and made it to the Holiday Inn in Vicksburg around noon. They recognized us as soon as we walked into the lobby and immediately wanted to get pictures with us. A few other customers in the lobby were giving us strange looks, probably wondering why the hotel was so excited to see two homeless guys. After talking with the hotel managers for a few minutes, we thanked them for their help and made our way up to our room. After making it to our room, we took turns taking showers and got our laundry done. After getting all cleaned up, I looked over at Mike and saw he was laid up in the bed and watching television. I jokingly said, "Don't get too comfortable, man. It'll make you miss home, and you'll want to give up." He laughed back at me and asked, "You think Domino's would donate a pizza?" I looked at him like he was crazy and said, "Probably not. The hotels are only helping us because they can mark it off on their taxes. I don't think Domino's will do that." He decided to give it a try anyway and gave Domino's a call. As he asked if they would be interested in donating a pizza, I sat there, shaking my head. Then, I heard Mike say, "Really? Awesome! Jake, what kind of pizza do you want?" I was kind of thrown off by the fact that they'd said yes, so I replied, "Just get whatever, man. I'm not picky. I mean, I've eaten pizza out of the trash before."

After we had finished eating, Mike decided to make a sign out of the pizza box, hoping to take it out to the street and make a little money. I said jokingly, "No one is going to give you money, man. Although, you do look kind of rough, so maybe they will." He then laughed and made his way outside while I stayed in the room and did some stretches. He finally walked back into the room about two hours later and said a police officer made him leave. I shrugged my shoulders and asked, "Well, how much did you make?" I was guessing he was going to say something like five dollars, but then he pulled out a wad of cash and counted out one hundred. Surprised by how much he'd collected, I laughed and said, "There you go! That's food for a while!"

The next morning, we went downstairs to eat breakfast and then made our way up the street to Candlewood Suites. Since we had nothing else to do, we just sat around and relaxed for the rest of the day. Although Mike enjoyed it, I was already starting to get cabin fever after just a couple of hours. I knew he probably needed the break, but I hoped he wouldn't get used to it and start getting lazy. I remembered back to when I first started traveling and how much staying in a room would make me miss home. I had a feeling that was happening to Mike, although he never said anything about it, and I never asked.

The next morning, we grabbed some breakfast from the hotel and got back to walking. As we were making our way out of Vicksburg, we came up to a long bridge that crossed over the Mississippi River. There was a sign overhead that read, "No pedestrians," so we stood there with our thumbs out. A truck pulled over a few minutes later, and the man driving signaled for us to hop into the back. Since traffic was kind of heavy, we didn't bother talking with him. We figured it must have been obvious that we just needed to get across the bridge, so we quickly tossed our packs into the back of the truck and climbed over with them.

After crossing the Mississippi River, the truck pulled over to let us out, and we continued hiking west. Not too far from the bridge, we had made it into Delta, Louisiana. It felt great to have another state under my belt, though Mike didn't seem to be as enthusiastic as I was. He had developed a heat rash on the inside of his thighs, causing him to walk kind of bow-legged. I'd been in that position before and knew how bad it felt, so I didn't mind taking a break. Since he'd already used all of his body powder, I gave him mine and a couple of ibuprofen. We then took a seat on the ground and waited for him to start feeling better. After sitting there for about ten minutes, enjoying the cool breeze flowing across the recently harvested cornfields, Mike picked up a small stick and drew a line in the dirt. He then said, "I think I'm done, man. If I cross this line, I'll keep going." I wasn't surprised when he said that, so I couldn't act like I was. I'd noticed he had been slowing down over the past week, probably from losing his motivation. That was sort of the reason why I had chosen to walk for St. Jude, but Mike wasn't really a part of that. I had to hand it to him, though. He had lasted a month with me, and we'd just claimed our three hundredth mile. Carrying fifty pounds on your back all day is pretty hard work, especially when there's no reason behind it.

After taking a break for about thirty minutes, Mike stood up and said, "Sorry, man. I can't do it anymore. When I went to hold that sign, I planned on using the money to get a bus home. I just didn't know if I really wanted to give up or not, so I thought I'd keep trying. I'm just over it, man. My body hurts, I'm dirty, and I miss my bed. I miss being able to take a shower. I don't know how you've done this for so long, but I'm going to go get that bus ticket home. Good luck, man." He then shook my hand and began walking back towards Vicksburg. I knew I'd miss his company, but I was no stranger to being alone. However, on the positive side, I would be able to set my own pace and not have to worry about someone else.

Once Mike and I had parted ways, I continued hiking west, enjoying the cool, dreary weather and lack of traffic. About five hours later, I received a message from Mike. He wanted to let me know he had safely boarded a bus and was on his way to Tennessee. He then asked where I was, to which I replied, "Just got into the town of Delhi. Found a dog running around, so I'm taking a break to play with it." "Delhi? How far is that from Vicksburg," Mike asked. "About forty miles," I answered. He messaged back a few minutes later, "I had a feeling I was slowing you down. That's not why I stopped, but I could tell you were on another level. You're crazy, man. Keep me posted and take care of yourself out there."

<u>Alone</u>

As I made my way farther into the town of Delhi, Louisiana, I decided to stop by at a small park to grab a seat and have some dinner. As I was chewing away at my dried beef strips, I noticed a sign next to me that read, "Tim McGraw was raised here." I wasn't too interested in country music, but I still thought it was cool to see he had been born and raised in such a small town and how random it was for me to be there. After enjoying a short break, I still had about two hours left of daylight. Since I still had quite a bit of energy, I decided to get back to walking and found a place to camp between towns, sometime around midnight.

The next day, which was December 12, 2015, I'd made my way into the town of Rayville. It looked as though some dangerous weather was on the way, so I decided to rent a cheap motel room. There were several tornado warnings that night and again in the morning, so I felt I'd gotten my money's worth. Although there didn't appear to be too much destruction in the area, I still felt like I'd made a good decision to take the shelter while I had it. Thankfully, the weather had cleared up by the time I had to check out of my room, and I was back on the move again.

I'd made it into the town of Monroe just before dark and decided to stop by at a gas station. I was starting to run low on funds, so I walked around the parking lot and began searching for any loose change. Surprisingly, I had collected about four dollars' worth before one of the workers came out and told me to leave. I was satisfied with what I had, though, because that would be enough to get a couple of coffees. I thought about camping in Monroe, but I still had quite a bit of energy left and decided to do some night walking.

As I was making my way through the town of Claiborne, two teenage boys ran over to me from their house. The curly-haired brunette then held up a small wad of cash and said, "Here you go." When I asked him what the money was for, the apprehensive blonde boy standing behind him muttered, "We just thought you were homeless and could use the help." I laughed and said, "Well, technically, I am homeless, but I'm walking across America for St. Jude. How's about I take these four dollars and make a donation from my bank account?" They didn't seem to believe me at first, so I showed them my Facebook Page. They began laughing and thought it was so random to meet someone who was walking across the country. After getting a picture with them, I thanked them for their contribution and continued hiking into the night.

It wasn't long after I had left the two young men when a flash of lightning lit up the sky. The weather was supposed to be clear, so it caught me off guard. I then checked the weather on my phone and noticed a tornado had touched down just a few miles away and was headed in my direction. I didn't know where to go, but I knew I had about fifteen minutes to find some kind of cover. After jogging for about ten minutes, I came across a funeral home just as the rain began to fall. I made my way to the side of the building and took refuge underneath the carport. Not that it would offer much protection, but there was a wooden wheelchair ramp leading up to the side door, which would help keep things from falling on top of me. I tossed my sleeping bag underneath the ramp and crawled inside to wait for the worst part of the storm to pass. Just a few minutes later, the rain had begun to fall so heavily that the carport was flooding, and I was forced out from my cover. I then sat on top of the ramp and waited to see if it would get so bad that being soaked was worth it. The wind's strength then picked up and began blowing the rain sideways into the carport, soaking me anyway. The storm finally calmed after an hour, so I laid my sleeping bag on the ramp and crawled in to try and get some rest. Just before falling asleep, I opened my eyes and noticed a sign that read, "Live life like you mean it." I wondered what kind of living the person who made it had in mind. I got a chuckle out of that because that's what I was trying to do, but I was sore and soaking wet.

Although I'd only gotten about three hours of sleep the night of the storm, I'd made it sixty miles into the town of Arcadia by the next afternoon. Since I'd spent half of those miles trudging through the rain, I was so exhausted that I was wobbling with each step. Thankfully, without having to do much searching, I came across an old building to camp behind and was able to turn in early. As soon as my head hit the pillow, which was a tightly sealed bag of clothes, I fell straight into a deep sleep and slept like a rock throughout the night.

I woke the next morning feeling rested and sat out for a twenty-mile hike into the town of Homer. I had put down a lot of miles the day before, so I figured I would take it easy and try to enjoy myself. Just as the sun was going down, I had made it into the city limits. I didn't want to be scrambling around, searching for a place to stealth camp, so I decided to hike on through and look for a place to sleep on the opposite side of town. As I was passing through the heart of the city, a police officer pulled up next to me and yelled to get my attention. I looked over at him, wondering what his intentions were. He then smiled and asked, "Are you Jake?" Feeling a bit confused, I replied, "Yes, sir. My name's Jake. How's it going?" The officer's smile grew larger, "My wife is following your Facebook Page. She said you were making your way through here. We thought we'd offer you a hotel for the night. How does Best Western sound?" Since it had been a few days since I'd had a shower, my clothes were a bit ragged, and I wasn't too excited about looking for a place to camp. I then accepted his offer and hopped into the front seat.

I didn't know the area, but I assumed he was headed towards the hotel. However, after driving around for a few minutes, we pulled into the police station parking lot. I looked at him kind of funny, wondering why we were there. Without having to ask, the officer said, "I have to run some business real quick. Go ahead inside and have a seat. I'll be back in about thirty minutes to take you over to the hotel." I got out of the vehicle, grabbed my pack from the trunk, and limped into the police station. It felt like I could walk forever, so long as I didn't stop but starting back up after taking a break was a slow and painful process.

After taking a seat in the waiting area, all the workers began giving me the strangest looks. It felt as though they were waiting for me to provide them with some troubling news, so I tried breaking the ice, "I'm just waiting for an officer to come and get me." As soon as those words fell out of my mouth, I knew I should have explained things a little more clearly. The dispatcher then came out of her room and asked, "Excuse me, but what do you mean you're waiting for an officer to come and get you?" I began laughing and said, "Sorry. What I meant to say was, I'm walking across the country for St. Jude and one of the.." "Oh! You're that guy," she interrupted, "I thought you were just some homeless person. Well, there's water and coffee if you want some. Feel free to help yourself."

The officer arrived back at the station just as I was finishing my coffee, and we made our way to the hotel. It felt kind of strange being escorted in by an officer. I could tell by the look on the clerk's face that it was especially unusual for her. The officer checked me in without any explanation, which I thought was kind of funny. I then thanked the officer for his help and made my way up to my room.

The next morning, I made my way over to the post office to pick up another care package from Jody. Inside, there were fourteen packs of tuna, six cans of potted meat, four cans of spaghetti, one can of chicken soup, one bag of corn chips, one can of smoked oysters, a bag of dried fruit, two cans of spam, a handful of instant coffee, and two five-dollar bills. That was a pretty typical care package from Jody, which I appreciated, but at the same time, I would roll my eyes because of all the added weight. However, I was feeling a bit famished at the time, so I sat around and ate as much as I could before leaving town.

I ended up staying in Homer for another night and pitched my tent behind a church. When I woke the next morning, I heard someone vacuuming inside. Since it was freezing cold, I decided to go inside and ask if they had any hot coffee. As I made my way into the church, I was greeted by an older heavyset man with short white hair and a long beard. After explaining that I was walking across America for St. Jude, the man introduced himself as Jerry and began to share his story of how he had lost his wife to cancer. He appreciated my efforts and showed me to the kitchen area, where I was able to fill up a small foam cup with a freshly-brewed, dark roast.

For some reason, I stuck around Homer until about 5:00 p.m. before deciding to get back on the move. Just as I was leaving town, a van pulled over just up ahead. A woman and three young girls got out and began walking towards me. They had been following my blog for a few years and wanted to give me a bag of food to help with the cause. Although I was already bursting at the seams with food, I accepted their gift anyway and strapped it to the outside of my pack. I figured the noisy plastic might help to deter any wild animals as I continued my hike through the night. Although it was only thirteen miles to the next town of Haynesville, I was a bit skeptical since I had forgotten to charge my headlamp.

Shortly after leaving Homer, I found myself in complete darkness with dense forests and murky swamps on either side of the road. It was one of those situations where I was locked in, and my only option was to make it all the way through. Since it was pitch black, cold, and my pack was heavier than usual, I was probably only moving at about three miles per hour. About halfway between towns, two police officers pulled over to see what I was up to. After explaining to them my business, they got back into their vehicles, and I watched as their taillights disappeared into the night. Once they were out of sight, I took a few steps and heard something rustling in the woods nearby, but I just shrugged my shoulders and continued walking. After covering about fifty yards, it was obvious that whatever it was, was following alongside me. I finally turned to yell at it, and it began wandering away deeper into the forest. I assumed that it was either a bear or a boar, although I never actually saw it, and it made no distinct sounds. Either way, it spooked me enough to pick up my pace, and I safely made it into Haynesville around 9:00 p.m.

As I made my way into town, I entered a gas station to use their restroom and fill up on my water. As I was on my way out, I was approached by two women who had been following my blog. Their names were Stephanie and Taylor, and they insisted I let them buy me a hot meal. I appreciated that since it was quite cold that night, and I knew having some warm food in my belly would help me sleep. I then found a place to camp not too far from the gas station.

The next morning, I was making my way into Arkansas when I ran into a fellow Army veteran named Glen. We talked for several minutes before he made a small donation on my behalf. He then said he hadn't followed my Facebook Page for a while but knew it was me because of the green bandanna. We both had a good laugh about that, but I wondered why he had stopped following my posts. I didn't bother to ask, but I was curious as to how many others had stopped following me as well. I then thanked him for his contribution and continued making my way west.

Not long after parting ways with Glen, I had reached the Arkansas border. I then sat my backpack on the ground and propped my phone on top of it, preparing to get my usual picture with another state sign. After adjusting my camera's view, I set the timer and ran over to pose with the sign. Just as the camera's flash went off, a car pulled over next to me, and a large black man stepped out. He then walked up to me and introduced himself as Al, a pastor at a church in the town of Magnolia. He then asked if I needed any help. I smiled a little and replied, "No. Well, not exactly. I'm walking across America for St. Jude. You can make a donation if you'd like." He seemed rather skeptical about what I'd said but decided to give me five dollars anyway. Before I had the chance to show him proof of what I was doing, he had already begun walking away with his head shaking in what felt to me as disbelief. As he hopped back into his car and drove away, I put the money into my wallet and then donated that amount from my bank account, which had dwindled to about one hundred dollars.

Not long after claiming my Arkansas sign, I'd made it into the small town of Emerson. As it was mostly a rural area with a dense forest behind the few houses that were there, I came across a family who was grilling in their front yard. The man standing at the grill yelled across the street, "Hey, man! Ya'll wanna come eat? We got plenty!" I wasn't exactly hungry, but they all seemed so inviting that I decided to accept his offer anyway. I walked up and introduced myself to everyone. There was the older man who called for me, his wife, his wife's female friend, a teenage boy and his girlfriend, and a few small children. They seemed like your typical, down to earth, southern black family, which was very entertaining and enjoyable. As we were eating dinner, I tried to fill them in on as many stories as I could think of from my travels. I then brought up one of my bear encounters, and the wife said, "There's a bear that comes around here just about every night. We've been leaving our scraps out for it for about five years or so." I had planned on camping in the area but figured I'd probably best put down some more miles, so I wouldn't end up getting caught in that bear's way.

Since it was starting to get late, I thanked the Emerson family for having me over and got back to walking.

It was about midnight once I'd made it into the next town of Magnolia. I spotted a church just off the highway before making it all the way into town and figured it looked like a good place to get some rest. I then noticed a power outlet next to the front door, so I plugged in my electronics and slid down into my sleeping bag while waiting for my things to charge. I then heard the footsteps of a person walking on the sidewalk next to my head. Once they'd entered the church, I popped my head out and realized it was already morning. The church door then opened back up, and an old black lady stepped out, "I was wondering who it was sleeping out here, but I just figured I'd let you sleep. We're cooking breakfast in here if you want to come and get you something." Rubbing the crust from my eyes, I replied, "Do you guys have any coffee?" The old lady laughed and placed her hands on her hips, "Yes, we have coffee. Come on inside. It's cold out here."

I followed the lady into the church and was greeted by her husband, who was also the pastor. They quickly resumed their normal conversations and didn't pay much attention to me. I don't mean that in a bad way, though. It just felt as though they were comfortable with me being there. They were just a laid-back couple that made me feel at home. The lady then went into the kitchen area, where I watched her prepare breakfast and listened to her ramble on about whatever popped into her head. She finally turned and asked, "What were you sleeping outside for?" Shocked that neither of them had asked yet, I filled them in on what I was doing. They didn't really seem to care too much about it but thought it was for a good cause. The lady then turned to hand me a small plate of food and a cup of coffee.

After I'd left the church, I received a message from one of my followers, Rayanna. The message read, "I booked you a room at the Hampton Inn in Magnolia. There's a package waiting for you there as well." I didn't necessarily want to take a day off, but I couldn't say no to a free room. I then made my way to the hotel and took the package up to my room. Inside of the package, there was some ointment for a rash I had been complaining about, which was all bloody and appeared to be close to infected, and two new pairs of underwear that were designed to prevent chaffing. After thanking Rayanna for the gifts, I went straight to the bathroom and let my body soak in a hot bath. I didn't realize how sore I must have been until I noticed how much better I felt after getting out. I then threw all my clothes into the bathtub and went to lie down for the rest of the day, hoping the rash inside of my thighs would be healed by the time I had to check out.

The next morning, I packed up my gear and made my way down to the hotel lobby to enjoy my continental breakfast. After helping myself to a couple of plates and nearly drowning myself in orange juice, I took off for another day of walking. I decided to take some back roads on my way to the next town because I was sick of dealing with all the traffic on the highway. After a few miles of walking aimlessly through the neighborhoods, a truck passed by and came to an abrupt stop. The truck then quickly pulled into a nearby parking lot, and a woman jumped out from the driver's door. "Hey! I've been looking all over for you," she shouted. I wasn't sure how she'd found me since I was quite far from my planned route. She then continued, "My son wants to meet you. He's a cancer survivor and has been following your blog. He thinks you're the coolest!" The little blonde boy then climbed down out of the truck and made his way over to us. He had a huge smile on his face and wanted to thank me for trying to help raise money for St. Jude. We then got a picture together, which really seemed to make his day. For the past few days, I'd been wondering if anyone actually cared about what I was doing, so having the little boy stop and show his appreciation helped to put my negative thinking aside.

I continued walking after parting ways with the little boy and found myself ending my night in the town of Stamps. I had planned on doing some night walking, but another storm was headed my way, so I began searching for a place to seek shelter. Ironically, I found myself under another carport of a funeral home. I then pulled out my sleeping gear and laid it next to one of the side doors. If the storm got too bad, I figured I'd just kick the door down and see myself inside. As I was lying there, listening to the thunder get closer, I heard what sounded like tiny feet plopping against the pavement. I looked up and noticed an opossum had come up to check me out. I just watched it for a few minutes but finally said something when it tried nipping at my backpack. Startled by my voice, it hopped away and scurried under the fence into someone's back yard. The storm hit shortly after that. While there weren't any tornadoes that night, the wind and lightning got so bad that I was glad to have found a way out of it.

Christmas Break

I made it to the outskirts of Texarkana just after the sun had gone down. There was still about a mile left before I got into the city limits, so I decided to go ahead and set up camp in the woods. I woke early the next morning, which was Christmas Eve, and finished making my way into town. After reaching the center of the city, I'd finally claimed my Texas sign. Normally, I would have just kept walking, but I received a message from a girl I'd been talking to for a few weeks. Her name was Jessica, and she was living nearly four hundred miles away in the town of Meridian, Mississippi. She asked if it would be okay if she purchased me a bus ticket for Christmas, so I could come and spend a few days with her. Since I was feeling down about spending the holidays alone, I accepted her offer. However, my bus wasn't scheduled to leave for two more days, so I began searching for a place to sleep for the night. I then came across a church that looked safe enough, so I spent the rest of the day sitting and relaxing in a nearby graveyard, waiting for it to get dark before setting up camp.

Once the sun had finally set, I made my way to the back of the church and opened the gate of a fenced-in area. Inside, there was an air conditioning unit and just enough space to fit my tent. Although I felt safe because I was well-hidden, I barely got any sleep because the unit created so much noise throughout the night. The next morning, I went ahead and made my way to the bus station. My bus was supposed to leave early the next day, so

282

I wanted to see if I could find a place to camp nearby. As I approached the bus station, I passed by a hotel and could see the coffee pots inside, waiting to serve the groggy guests on their way out. I then noticed a family who was leaving, so I pretended I was with them and went in to grab a cup. I then went back outside and sat on a concrete slab where a light pole used to be. As I was sitting there, enjoying the dull, gray sky and the aromatic steam rising from my cup, an older man pulled up next to me in a station wagon. He signaled for me to come over and held out his hand to give me something, so I reached out to take whatever it was. As the small, lightweight item fell into my hand, the man said, "Merry Christmas. Jesus loves you." I hadn't looked down at what it was yet, but I replied, "Thanks. Merry Christmas to you too." As the man drove away, I turned to see what it was he had placed into my hand. I laughed when I realized it was a large plastic coin with a bible verse on it. Even though I wasn't religious, I still appreciated the fact that the man cared enough to give me something, so I decided to keep it anyway and tucked it away in my wallet. After enjoying my cup of coffee, I made my way into the woods behind the bus station to see if it looked like a good place to camp. Although it appeared someone had camped there recently, I had my doubts they would return because of how cold it was. I then sat there for the rest of the day, waiting to see if anyone would come around that might pose a threat to me staying the night there. As the day went on without any incidents, I decided to set up my tent after dark and crawled inside to get some sleep.

I climbed aboard my bus the next morning and was on my way to meet up with Jessica. It was only a six-hour ride, so I made it there in time for lunch. However, Jessica said she was still busy with her family's holiday shenanigans and wouldn't be free until the next day. I didn't mind waiting another day, especially since I'd noticed a large wooded area to venture into. After hiking up into the forest-covered hills for about an hour, I came across the perfect place to set up camp. It was still quite early, though, so I decided to kill some time by making a few survival-type videos for my Facebook Page.

Jessica was ready to pick me up the next morning, so I told her to meet me at the store that I'd passed by on my way into the hills. When she got there, she said she needed to have her oil changed, so we dropped her car off with a nearby mechanic and went back to walk around in the store. Since she had planned on renting us a motel room for three days, she decided to purchase a couple of board games, a DVD player, and a few movies to help keep us occupied. We then made our way to the motel, and I quickly realized how much I had missed having someone's company. Although we had known each other for a while, physically being with her gave me something that I didn't know I was missing. After spending the afternoon laughing and enjoying one another, we fell asleep wrapped in each other's arms, and I felt so comfortable and loved.

The next morning, Jessica decided to take me to one of her favorite hiking spots. After driving down several country roads, we came to a stop in a secluded area, deep in the woods. We then began walking along a trail that was covered with dead leaves and outlined with aged oak trees. We finally came across a large tunnel that passed underneath a set of train tracks, so we made our way inside and made our way through. Once we had reached the other side, there was a small pond and an old campsite with logs for us to sit on. Jessica then took a seat while I continued standing to share some stories from my travels. She then asked if I could show her how I went about setting up my traps. I always carried a strand of paracord in one of my cargo pockets, so I began searching for a few sticks and taught her some of my techniques.

After spending a few hours in the forest, we made our way back to the motel and quickly became intimate. Although we had relations the night before, the way we were holding and kissing each other this time was more like making love. We then ended the night by cuddling and watching movies, and I began to feel like I had made a huge mistake. It wasn't that I had necessarily caught feelings for Jessica, but I was terrified of missing her company. I didn't want to go through the ordeal of trying to convince myself that I was happy with being alone when I wasn't. Instead of worrying about the days to come, I decided to just enjoy the moment and fell asleep wrapped in her arms again.

Jessica had some business to take care of over the next two days, so I decided to look for some work while I waited for her to return on New Year's Eve. To pass the time and make a little money, I began walking around the neighborhoods, knocking on everyone's door and asking if they had any work I could do. Over the next two days, I raked a few yards, fixed one lady's plumbing, insolated someone else's pipes in the crawl space, cut and stacked another person's firewood, and patched a leaky roof over another man's shed. After I'd made about two-hundred dollars, I returned to the motel and waited for Jessica. However, she said she wouldn't be able to make it until around 8:00 p.m., so I figured I'd just lie in bed and watch some television while I waited. As I was sitting there, I began to feel overwhelmed with horrific memories, so I decided to go for a walk and see if it would help clear my head. Once my anxiety seemed to be under control, I began making my way back to the motel and stopped to purchase a bottle of spiced rum. I wasn't much of a liquor drinker, but I figured it would be nice to celebrate the new year with.

10:00 p.m. finally rolled around, and I still hadn't heard anything from Jessica. Feeling a bit worried, I sent her a message and asked if something had happened. About thirty minutes later, I received a message back, "I'm sorry, but I don't think we should continue seeing each other." I replied, "I understand, but I was still hoping to have you over to celebrate the New Year. We can just hang out as friends. I've been feeling a bit down today and would really appreciate the company." I never heard anything back from her, though. As I watched everyone on the television counting down the seconds to New Year, celebrating with a loved one, I threw my head back and swallowed a shot of rum. I then continued drinking until I fell asleep - lonely and depressed.

I woke sometime later and felt this insatiable urge to end my life. I wasn't sure why I felt it so strongly, but I did. It was an uncontrollable state of mind- as if someone or something had power over my thoughts. I then reached over for my pants and removed a long strand of paracord from one of my side pockets. It was still done up in a noose from when I had shown Jessica how I set my traps, so I carried it over to the closet and tied it to the steel bar between the empty clothes hangers. I then placed the noose around my neck and prepared to let my body drop. Once I felt ready, I heard a knock at the door. I didn't want anyone to catch me in the act, so I hurried out of the closet and went to see who it was. I opened the door and looked around but saw no one in either direction. I shrugged my shoulders and assumed the knocking must have come from somewhere else, so I shut the door and turned around to walk back to my death trap. I then noticed a Bible was sitting on the floor directly in front of the closet. I wasn't religious, but I couldn't help but feel a bit mystified. I then picked the book up, shoved it in a drawer, and crawled back into bed to try and get some sleep.

I woke up again about an hour later and was completely overwhelmed by the idea of how peaceful I remembered death feeling. Strangely, I didn't feel upset. It was more of a feeling of relief than anything. I had settled on the idea, and nothing was going to stop me this time. The room was pitch black, minus a small amount of light peeking in through the curtains. As my feet began to carry me through the dark and back towards the closet, it felt as though everything was moving in slow motion. I then opened the closet door and felt something land on my foot. I reached down and, even though I couldn't see it, I knew it was the Bible. I'd never experienced anything like that, so I immediately turned on the lamp and sat at the foot of the bed with the book in my hand. With my eyes closed, I firmly grasped it and said, "Look, I've never read this thing in my life. I don't know what you're trying to get at, so I'm going to open it to a random page. Feel free to direct me to whatever it is that you want me to know." After flipping through several pages, I opened my eyes and looked down to read, "For I know the plans I have for you, declares the Lord, plans to prosper you and not to harm you, plans to give you hope and a future." I couldn't even remember the last time I had cried, but I did that night. It wasn't that I feared death, but because I felt so selfish for what I had almost done. I had a hard time grasping the reality of the situation, so I stopped trying to make sense of it and placed the Bible on the desk in front of me. I then removed the noose from the closet and went back to bed, where I fell into a deep and peaceful sleep.

I woke the next morning and made my way back into the wooded hills where I'd gone for my first night in Mississippi. I then spent the rest of the day hiking through the forest, admiring all the natural beauty around me, trying to remember my walk's purpose. I soon began to feel like maybe I should try and focus on myself a bit more. No one ever said I couldn't enjoy myself while I was walking for a charity. It just seemed like all the new people who were following my Facebook Page had some sort of expectations for how I should be doing things. I almost felt like stopping the charity and just continuing the walk for some kind of self-healing, but I figured I just needed some practice managing both. Even though it was only noon, I came across a perfect place to camp and decided to go ahead and set up my tent. I then made a small fire and prepared a cup of tea using pine needles, which made me feel a bit more grounded.

Back On Track

I arrived back at the Texas state line on January 3rd, 2016, and I continued heading west. As I was making my way out of Texarkana, a small car quickly pulled over next to me, and the young female driver shouted, "Hey, Jake! I saw you were passing through here and figured I'd bring you some food!" She never introduced herself, but I assumed she must have been following my Facebook Page. I reached into the car and took the bag of food she was holding out to me. I thanked her for her help and peeked over into the bag as she was driving away. Inside, there were two cheeseburgers, two large fries, two orders of chicken nuggets, and a large drink. I probably looked much hungrier than I felt, so I took out the chicken nuggets and drink for myself and gave the rest to another homeless man who passed by as I continued walking down the sidewalk.

By the time I'd reached the outskirts of the city, I had about two hours left of daylight. I wasn't in the mood to do any night walking, so I ventured away from the highway and followed an old trail into the forest. The trail was overgrown and showed no signs of recent human traffic, so I felt like it would probably be a good place to look for a place to camp. Since it was supposed to be in the teens that night, I decided to hike far enough from the road that I could have a fire and not worry about anyone seeing it. After hiking for about half a mile, the trail came to an end at an old abandoned house with a slightly collapsed roof, and the walls had all sunken inward. I didn't think anyone was inside, but I didn't want to know for sure either, so I quietly walked around it and continued deeper into the forest. After hiking another half-mile, I came upon an old cemetery. There were only five tombstones, but all of them were too weathered to make out what they said. I figured they were probably the family members of the house I'd passed by, which was a little sad to think they were all out here alone and forgotten. Although it looked like a great place to camp, I decided to give them some space and walked another half-mile before finding another spot to set up my tent. The sun began to set as I was collecting firewood, which turned out to be a good idea because the temperature was dropping rapidly. It took quite a bit of work to get the fire going that night because everything was soaking wet, but the extra work seemed to be worth it once the flames began to dry the sweat that had frozen over my clothes. After about an hour of warming up, the fire began to die out, and I slipped into my sleeping bag before the heat could be wiped away by the cold wind.

The next morning, I packed my things and sat out for a twenty-mile hike to the next town of New Boston. It had been a slow day, and by the time I'd made it, the sun had just gone down. The temperature was already in the teens by then, so I decided to stop by at a fast-food restaurant to grab something hot to fill my stomach. The restaurant had an outdoor seating area from which to order your food, and as I was waiting for mine to be brought out, I could feel the sweat on my body turning into ice. Although there were several people parked in their cars around me, I immediately stripped down to my underwear and put on a fresh pair of base layers. I had completely stopped worrying about what people thought of me a long time ago, although I was sure they probably thought it was strange to see a half-naked man in public. A restaurant worker then walked out with my food and began asking about my backpack, "A little cold to be going camping, isn't it?" I laughed and replied, "Well, most people would probably think so. I've hiked and cycled the country a couple of times, though, so I'm pretty much used to it." He then gave me a strange look and shouted, "Oh! You're the Jake Does America guy! I remember reading about you walking across America a couple of years ago! Wait here!" He then ran back into the restaurant, and I could see him through the window, explaining who I was to his coworkers. They all began looking me up on their phones, and I could see their faces popping up on my screen as my notifications began going off.

Everyone began smiling, laughing, and giving me a thumbs-up through the window. The young man who had brought my food out then came back outside and said, "Don't worry about the check, man. We'll take care of it for you. Try to stay warm out here!" I thanked him for his help and finished my dinner before looking for a place to set up camp. I then noticed a building about a hundred feet from the restaurant and decided to check it out. As I made my way to the front of the building, I looked over their business hours. I noticed they wouldn't be open until 9:00 a.m., so I figured it would be safe to sleep there, so long as I was gone before then. I then made my way to the back of the building and sat up my tent on the frozen grass. Before turning in for the night, I spent about thirty minutes doing pushups, jumping jacks, and running in place to get my body warmed up.

The next morning, I packed my things and prepared to continue making my way west. Just before getting on the highway and leaving New Boston, I saw a park across the street with a few benches in it. I then made my way over to one of them and took a seat, where I enjoyed a small snack and a pack of instant coffee for breakfast. As I was getting up to leave, I noticed a sign that read "East Texas Trail." I didn't know anything about it other than it ran east to west, but I figured it would be better than walking along the highway. I then entered the forest and began following the muddy trail. After taking only a few steps, snow had begun to fall and made it much more serene. I could hear cars on the highway nearby, so I assumed the trail probably just followed it the whole way. However, after a few minutes of walking it, it was hard for me to convince myself that it was any better than dealing with traffic because the mud continued getting worse. By the time I'd made it to the next town of DeKalb, which was only fourteen miles, my feet were freezing and soaking wet. I didn't want to continue walking in those conditions and risk hurting my feet, so I went ahead and ended my day early. Even though I probably had five hours left of daylight, I went ahead and sat my tent up in the forest next to the trail, tossed some powder into my boots, and slid into my sleeping bag. As I was lying there, I decided to check and see how well my campaign for St. Jude was doing. I then realized I was the only person who had made any donations in the past two weeks. I didn't have a lot of money left, but I went ahead and sent in another twenty dollars, hoping it would encourage people to step up and show their support.

After slowly continuing my way west over the next few days, battling boredom, the cold, a meaningless birthday, and one monstrous storm, I'd finally made it into the town of Paris. There was a lady there, Delores, who had invited me over to her house so I could get a shower and do some laundry. She offered to toss my clothes into the washer while I was taking a shower, and after I got out, she had a bowl of hot soup waiting for me. She was working from home as a dispatcher and seemed rather busy, so I fell asleep on the couch while waiting for my clothes to finish drying. I woke up a few minutes later and noticed I had received a message from a solar panel company who was wanting me to try out one of their latest designs. Since I was having a hard time keeping my things charged with all the recent overcast, I figured I would give them a try and told them to send it to the post office there in Paris. My clothes had dried by then, so I gathered my things and thanked Delores for having me over. The solar panel was being shipped with next-day delivery, so, after leaving her house, I began searching for a place to camp for the next day or two.

As I was walking around Paris, looking for a place to camp, I made a post on my blog to let everyone know what I was up to. Shortly after making the post, I was contacted by someone from the Holiday Inn and was offered to stay there until my solar panel arrived. After making it to the hotel, I discovered several of the workers there had set up the whole thing and had pitched in to pay for my room. Although I did appreciate their help, I felt kind of bad for taking it. I would rather they had donated to St. Jude, but I couldn't tell them that and just appreciated what they had done for me.

The next morning, I checked the tracking number on the solar panel to see where it was. It was supposed to be in Paris by that afternoon, so I went ahead and prepared to make my way over to the post office. As I was checking out of the hotel, all six of the ladies who had pitched in to buy my room had followed me outside to get a picture with me. Because no one had made any recent donations to my St. Jude campaign, I didn't feel like I was worth the attention, but I tried to look enthusiastic for them anyway. I then made my way over to the post office and collected my package just before they closed. After opening the package, I realized there was more inside than just a solar panel. I'd also received two battery packs, two extra charging cables, and a card that had been signed by all their employees.

Since it was starting to get late, and I had a ton of energy left, I decided to do some night walking. After hiking twenty miles through the dark, I'd made it into the town of Honey Grove. Thankfully, it was a small town that seemed rather safe, so I decided to camp behind one of the churches there. By noon the next day, I'd made it another twenty miles into the town of Bonham. As I was making my way through, a young woman with dark hair pulled up next to me in a small car. She waved at me to come closer to her and said, "Hey, Jake! My name is Emily. I've been following your travels for about a year now.

I'm headed down to Dallas right now to watch a friend perform at a comedy club. Do you want to go? I'll be coming back to Bonham tonight, and we can get you a motel room." I thought it might be fun to do something different and spontaneous, so I tossed my pack into the trunk and hopped into the passenger seat.

Once Emily and I had made it to Dallas, she looked over at me and said, "I think maybe we should get you some casual clothes for the show. Would that be okay with you?" I guess she could tell by my expression that I wasn't comfortable with her wasting any more money on me, so she continued, "Oh, don't worry. I'll keep the receipt and return them to the store tomorrow. Just don't spill anything on them." I figured that would be okay, so we made our way to a clothing outlet. Once we were in the store, Emily picked out a few shirts and pants that she thought would look good on me and told me to pick a pair. None of them looked like anything I would normally wear, so I just grabbed a pair without thinking and took it into the dressing room. I felt more out of place wearing those than my normal clothes, but Emily seemed to be impressed, and she was the one paying for everything. We then made our way to the comedy club and enjoyed the show. We were both tired after the show, so we ended up getting a hotel in Dallas and then drove back to Bonham the following morning.

Wanting to get away from the highway, I took some backroads out of Bonham. After passing through a few small towns, I decided to stop in one of them called Sherman. I still had about five hours of daylight, but the weather was so nice and dreary that I couldn't resist the urge to stop and enjoy it. As I was searching for a good place to get some privacy, I walked by a harvested cornfield and noticed a patch of woods in the center of it. I thought that looked promising, so I made my way over to it and found an old, blue couch sitting within the trees. No telling how dirty it actually was, but at least it wasn't wet, and it looked clean enough that I decided to sit on it. As a matter of fact, it was so comfortable that I sat there for the rest of the day, enjoying the cold breeze blowing from across the wide-open field. As the day was coming to an end, I put my tent up next to the couch and turned in for the night.

The next morning, as I was making my way out of Sherman, a white truck pulled over next to me. Two older women then stepped out and introduced themselves as Christina and Lisa. They were friends who had been following my journey for a while. They then asked if I'd be interested in having lunch with them, which, of course, I agreed to. As we were sitting there enjoying our meal, Christina asked if I'd like to stay the night at her family's house. She assured me that I would be able to do my laundry, get a shower, and would have a bedroom all to myself. Although I was really hoping to put down some miles that day, I felt like it may be worth the experience if I just gave it a chance. I was still trying to change how I did things and wanted to start taking opportunities as they presented themselves instead of passing them up. So, after we finished eating, I hopped back into Christina's truck, and we began making our way for her house.

Once Christina and I arrived at her house, her husband and two sons greeted me. They all seemed to be friendly, so I was glad I had accepted the invitation. After I had gotten all cleaned up, everyone gathered in the living and began talking about my travels so far. At some point, it got brought up that I played guitar, so Christina's husband went back into his room to get his. I then sat and played for a few hours as they went on about their daily lives. As the day was coming to an end, Christina and her husband began preparing dinner while their two sons sat in the living room and played video games. They almost seemed like the perfect family, which made me wish I had one of my own.

The next morning, after saying my goodbyes to the family, I decided to call around for any doctors that might see me before leaving town. I'd noticed a couple of bumps had appeared in my mouth a few months ago and showed no signs of going away, so I was feeling a bit concerned. Luckily, after explaining my situation, one of the doctors in the nearby town of Denison agreed to look at them for me. However, I wouldn't be able to be seen until the next day, so I slowly began my ten-mile hike towards the clinic. As I was walking along, I received another message from Emily. She had a couple of days off work and would like to get us a hotel so I would have a place to rest in case I needed surgery. I figured that sounded like a good idea, so I accepted her offer and continued making my way for the hotel she had already rented in our names. After making it to the hotel, Emily said to enjoy the rest of my day, and she would be there tomorrow to keep me company.

The next morning, I made my way to the doctor and found out that the bumps in my mouth were benign tumors. Although they weren't cancerous, the doctor recommended that I had them removed. It was a simple procedure to have them burned away, but I was glad to see Emily waiting for me in the parking lot because the shot of adrenaline had made me quite anxious. I also knew the pain medication would be wearing off soon, so getting a ride back to the motel was much appreciated. Once we made it back to the motel, the pain from the surgery was worse than I thought it was going to be, so we decided to lie in bed for the rest of the day and just take it easy.

The next morning, Emily and I decided to go out and do some exploring. We weren't too far from the Red River, which separated Texas and Oklahoma, so we decided to check that out. There were a few hiking trails near the parking lot, but I had to explore them alone because it was just too cold for Emily's liking. She missed out on some great views, though. The trail followed along the river through the forest, and once I'd made it around one of the bends, I looked back to admire the steep, rocky cliffs being battered by the raging river below. I could have stayed out there all day, but I didn't want to leave Emily sitting in the car for too long.

Soon after leaving the river, we passed by a large statue of a man's head. I wondered what it was about, so I had Emily stop the car. As I approached the gigantic statue, I discovered that it was a sculpture of President Eisenhower. It turned out that he was from Denison, and the park I'd just been exploring had been dedicated in his honor. After having Emily get a picture of me sitting on one of his shoulders, we made our way to a local distillery. They were doing tours that day, which we thought sounded fun. Not only was it interesting to see how they went about making all their alcoholic beverages, but they also gave out free samples, which helped to soothe the stinging sores in my mouth. We then made our way back to the hotel, and I was able to show Emily how I did my laundry while traveling. We then took it easy for the rest of the day and just kicked back to watch a few movies and enjoyed each other's company.

We checked out of our hotel the next morning, and Emily and I parted ways. I then continued walking west and made it fifty miles into the town of Muenster two days later. It was about noon as I was passing through when a car pulled up next to me. A middle-aged man then stepped out and said, "Never seen anyone walking through here with such a large backpack before. Where you headed to?" "Just walking across America," I replied. The man laughed, "Just walking across America? Well, I just so happen to run a radio station! It sounds like you might have a heck of a story! Would you mind if I recorded a conversation for my show?" Although I was beginning to feel like it wouldn't make any difference, I figured I'd humor the man and said, "Sure. I guess I can take a minute to talk." The man then reached over into his car and pulled out a tape recorder. Without any warning, he hit the record button and began asking all the same questions as everyone else, "Why are you walking across America? How long have you been at it? What do you eat? Where do you sleep? How many miles do you walk each day?" After talking with the man for about an hour, he felt he'd had enough for his show and wished me well for the remainder of my trip. However, the long break I'd taken to talk with him left me feeling lazy, so I made it just to the outskirts of town and wandered off into the hills to find a place to set up camp. Snow began to fall shortly after setting up my tent, so I began gathering sticks to have a fire that night. After feeling confident that I had enough wood to last a couple of hours, I crawled into my tent and slid down into my sleeping bag, leaving the door open to watch the snow falling around me.

After lying in my sleeping bag for a couple of hours, an opossum walked right in front of my tent and began sniffing at my backpack. I'd never felt like eating an opossum before, but it was like an animal instinct came over me, and my mouth began to water. I slowly sat up and reached over for my hunting knife, which I was very confident with throwing. Just before releasing the knife from my hand, I decided to pull out my phone and show my followers what I was about to have for dinner. I took a picture of the opossum and said, "I'm going to let you guys be in control of this opossum's fate. Should I eat it or no?" Notifications began flooding my phone, and, surprisingly, most people wanted to watch me eat it. Then, I received a message from a lady, "Don't eat the opossum! I just heard your story on the radio. I'm in Muenster and will bring you some food!" I didn't know my interview was going to be on the radio that evening, but it definitely saved that opossum's life.

I told the lady where she could meet me, and I began hiking back towards the highway. A van pulled up next to me just after dark, and a lady stepped out. She started laughing and said, "I can't believe you were about to eat an opossum! I think you might enjoy this a bit more!" I smiled and reached out to take the paper sack, which had steam escaping from the top and corners. Before I had the chance to open it, the lady continued, "There's two cheeseburgers, some fries, and a milkshake. I know it's a little cold for ice cream, but I thought you might like it anyway!" I laughed and replied, "Oh, yeah! I'm enjoying it already! Haven't had a milkshake in forever!" The lady then hugged me and began walking back to her van. Before she got in to drive away, she asked, "You weren't really going to eat that opossum, were you?" Although I would have, I laughed and yelled back, "Of course not!" I then took the food back to my campsite and began preparing my fire. Once I was ready to enjoy my meal, I pulled out my phone and realized people were still wondering whether I had decided to eat the opossum or not. To humor my followers, I posted a picture of my cheeseburger with the caption, "Best opossum burger I've ever had!"

The next morning, I continued west, and by that afternoon, I had made it into the small town of Saint Jo. I hadn't yet eaten anything that day, so I stopped when I came across a restaurant. I stood there for about ten minutes, asking myself if I thought spending money on food was worth it or not. I finally decided I'd rather hang onto what little money I had and could probably find a place to catch a fish or something. Just after I'd taken a few steps, a police officer pulled over and asked what I was up to. He didn't seem to believe me when I said I was walking across America for St. Jude and demanded that I let him look through my things. I knew he had no right to do that, but I decided to let him anyway since I had nothing to hide and could tell he was on a power trip. He then asked if it would be okay if he cuffed me for his safety, so I rolled my eyes and said, "Whatever makes you feel better, I guess." He then shoved me up against his vehicle and grabbed my arms from behind. "Stop resisting!" he shouted.

Feeling a bit confused and not wanting to escalate the situation, I calmly said to the officer, "What are you talking about? I'm not resisting." I then realized he was trying to pull my hands behind my back, but my shoulders were just too broad for his scrawny muscles to do anything with my arms. I began laughing and said, "Oh, sorry. Let me help with that." I then put my hands together close enough for him to put the cuffs on and turned around to watch as he went through my things. "What's this for?" he asked as he pulled my machete from its sheath. I

298

rolled my eyes again, "That's a machete. I use it for chopping wood, digging holes, and protection against dangerous animals." He looked up at me and said, "If you want to be a wise-ass, I can take you to jail for carrying a dangerous weapon. How's that sound?" Right about that time, another officer pulled up to see what was going on. Thankfully, the second cop was a bit more understanding and had his partner remove my handcuffs. He then told his partner to get back into his car and apologized for how he had overreacted. Since the second officer seemed to be on my side, I told him not to worry about it and picked up my things to continue on my way.

Once I'd made it to the other side of Saint Jo, I came across an old store and decided to go inside to fill up on my water. As I was leaving, the older man who was standing behind the cash register yelled out, "Be careful walking through here. We have some crooked cops. They will probably give you a hard time if they see you walking through here." I began laughing and yelled back, "Oh, I think it's too late for that! Pee-Wee stopped me on my way in. I'm headed out of here now." The old man began laughing and said, "Don't take it personally. He's a new cop that got relocated here after getting into trouble at his last station. He gives everyone in town a hard time." The man's wife then walked out from one of the aisles and added, "Oh, not that scrawny fucker again! I'm too scared to drive because of him. He's been pulling everyone in town over just to give them hell. I've been letting my husband do all the driving since he's been here. Which way are you heading? We can give you a ride to the county line if you don't mind waiting around for a few minutes. Otherwise, he will probably stop you again." I didn't know how far I'd make by the time they got off work, so I decided to start walking. However, I'd only made it about two miles before the couple pulled over next to me in their truck.

The lady then rolled down the passenger window and said, "Come on. Let us take you up to the county line. It's only a couple of miles." I really didn't mind walking, but I figured I'd take the ride anyway, at least to help the old couple feel better for getting me out of Saint Jo. After driving for about five minutes, we entered the next county, and the truck pulled over. Before driving off, the old man leaned across his wife and said, "Now, all you have to worry about are the mountain lions." As I began adjusting my shoulder straps, I laughed and replied, "Well, I'd rather deal with them than pigs."

I got back to walking after the old couple had dropped me off and was able to make it just outside of Nocona before nightfall. I'd planned on hiking into town but decided to stop and try to catch a fish after I'd passed by a pond. I walked around to the other side of it, out of view from the road, and sat my tent up behind a large tree. I then pulled out my fishing gear, which was just some line, hooks, and fake corn, and tossed it out into the water. Surprisingly, I only had to sit there for about thirty minutes before catching two bluegills. I then took my machete and prepared a safe place to have a fire. I then tossed the fish down onto the dirt while I went out to the tree line to gather some sticks. Shortly after I got a fire going, I tossed the fish in and sat back to enjoy the warmth and solitude.

The next day, I'd made it about fifteen miles and just passed through the town of Ringgold, when I began to have a sharp, stabbing pain in one of my big toes. It was the nostalgic sting of a toenail on the verge of falling off, which I hadn't experienced since my military days. My pace quickly dropped to about a third of what I had been doing, and the overwhelming pain forced me to take several breaks. If I wanted to save it, I would have had to stop walking for about a week, and that was out of the question. I would just have to hobble and grit my teeth for a few days while I waited for my toenail to fall off. As the sun was beginning to set, I had made it about two-thirds of the way to the town of Henrietta when I noticed a small white car had pulled over about fifty yards ahead. Since I was pretty much in the middle of nowhere, I figured it was probably someone wanting to offer me a ride. However, as I made my way closer, I noticed the car was full of passengers and knew there was no room for me. I then began to think it may be some people wanting to start trouble, but I continued walking towards them anyway. Once I'd made it about thirty feet from the parked car, the doors flew open, and six teenage girls jumped out. As the girls began running up to me, I couldn't help but laugh and looked to the sky in relief. It turned out they had heard my interview on the radio and wanted to get a picture with me.

It had been dark for about three hours once I'd made it into Ringgold, so I prepared to start looking for a place to camp. Seeing as how the town had a population of only one hundred people, I wasn't too worried about finding my own space. As I continued making my way through, I walked by a house and noticed a woman sitting on the tailgate of a truck parked in the driveway. She then yelled over to me, "Hey! Are you hungry? I just made dinner!" I was so tired that I was stumbling, but I figured I could keep myself together long enough to grab a bite to eat. Once I'd made it up to the lady, I realized she was talking on the phone, which made it kind of awkward because I wasn't able to introduce myself properly. She then yelled over to her young son, who was sitting on the front porch and shaving down a stick with his pocketknife, "Run in the house and fix this man a plate!" The lady then looked back at me, placed her phone up to her chest, and asked, "Where are you heading? You need a ride?" I replied, "No, ma'am. I'm actually walking across America. I was just getting ready to find a place to set up camp." "Walking across America!" the woman shouted. I could hear another woman's voice coming from the phone, "What? Who's walking across America?" The woman replied, "This gentleman was just walking down the street, so I offered him dinner. He just said he's walking across America. Got a big ole' backpack and everything." The woman's son then walked back outside and handed me a plate loaded with pasta and mashed potatoes. As I was sitting next to the woman and enjoying my food, I heard the female voice on the phone ask, "Is he cute?" I acted like I didn't hear anything as the woman turned to look at me, "I'd say so. A little too young for me, though!" I finished eating shortly after that and thanked the lady for her help. She then wished me luck on the rest of my trip as I disappeared back into the night.

Not long after leaving the woman's house, I turned down a side road and sat up my tent behind a concrete foundation of where a house used to be. The spot worked out well for the night, but when I woke the next morning, I stuck my head out and saw a man walking around my tent. Neither of us said anything, which made the situation even more awkward, but I assumed he was just curious to see who was camping across the street from his house. Being that it was such a small town and pretty much in the middle of nowhere, I was sure they weren't used to seeing too many travelers. I then gathered my things and sat out for a thirty-five-mile hike, destined for the next town of Wichita Falls.

After hiking for a few hours, I received a message from Emily. She said she would like to hang out one last time before she had to go back to work. We both seemed to enjoy each other's company, and I felt that it would be a good idea to give my foot a break. I then accepted her offer and asked if she could meet me in Wichita Falls. Knowing that I would be hanging out with Emily helped to speed up my walk, even though it felt like someone was hitting my toe with a hammer with each passing step. I finally reached the city around 3:00 p.m. and made my way to the hotel to meet up with Emily. Since I'd made it there before her, I went ahead and took a shower so I'd be cleaned up by the time she got there. Emily arrived about an hour later, and we made our way to Lucy Park, well-known for its man-made waterfall, standing fifty-four-feet high. The natural waterfall, which the city was named for, had been washed away during a flood in the 1800s.

After spending one last night with Emily, I was ready to continue heading west. By late that evening, I had passed through the towns of Electra, Harrold, and almost made it into Oklaunion before deciding to call it a day. After hiking nearly forty miles on a busted toe, I sat up my tent behind a large pile of wood, stacked beside some train tracks. Although there was plenty of peace and quiet out there, I barely got any sleep because my toe was hurting so badly. I thought about heating a needle and pushing it through my toenail to relieve some pressure, but I'd already waited too long. There was nothing I could do except take some ibuprofen and wait for it to rupture on its own.

The next morning, as I was making my way through Oklaunion, my toenail finally lifted from the skin, and blood began to fill my sock. After taking an hour-long break to let my foot air out, I put my boot back on and continued hobbling west. I had a care package waiting for me just fifteen miles away in the town of Vernon, which was what kept me motivated for the time being. However, with my foot being in such bad shape, it took me all day to make it only ten miles. Just as I'd made it to the top of a hill that overlooked Vernon, I immediately noticed a massive storm was quickly approaching from the east. Ominous black clouds filled the horizon, and thousands of bolts of lightning began darting across the sky. Although the sun hadn't completely set yet, the darkness of the storm enveloped the remainder of light, and fast-moving winds began whooshing across the plains. I knew there was no way I could make it to Vernon before the storm hit, but I could see a cemetery about half a mile away with concrete walls surrounding it. Although the four-foot-high walls wouldn't offer much protection, I thought it would surely be better than being out in the open and would help to keep the wind from blowing me away in my tent.

As I was setting up my tent next to the cemetery walls, I continuously checked over my shoulder to see where the storm was. By the time I had finished getting everything ready, I could see the storm had just begun to pummel the town below. As the wind speed began to increase and the lightning became more frequent, I crawled into my tent and slid into my sleeping bag, anticipating the storm. Within the next ten minutes, I was directly under the worst of it. Both rain and hail were falling so hard that all I could hear was white noise like someone had turned up the volume on a staticky radio channel. I knew the wind had picked up to about eighty miles per hour, but the wall behind me was stopping most of it. My greatest fear was the lightning, which was hitting all around me without hardly any breaks. Thankfully, there were several tall trees in the cemetery that took most of the strikes, which sounded like bombs going off when they got hit. I knew there was nothing else I could do, so I rolled over onto my stomach and closed my eyes, trying to ignore nature's fury.

Surprised to still be alive, I woke the next morning and began making my way down the hill and into the town of Vernon. After leaving the post office with my care package from Jody, the postal worker, Alyssa, came outside and said, "Are you walking across America?" I replied, "Yes. How did you know?" The lady began laughing and said, "My daughter told me you were coming through here. I didn't know what you looked like, though. She said she wanted me to get a picture with you." As small of a town as Vernon was, I surprised anyone there knew about me, so I happily took a picture with her and continued making my way west.

After making it about six miles outside of Vernon, I came across a small electrical building and decided to go behind it to urinate. As I was standing there, relieving myself, I noticed some kind of animal was making its way towards me through the tall, gold-colored wheatgrass. As I could see a house about a hundred yards away, I thought it might be a dog and whistled out to it. The animal then ducked down into the brush, and I noticed a long skinny tail go down behind it. I immediately realized it was a mountain lion, so I forced myself to stop peeing and pulled out my bowie knife and bear spray. I then shouted for it to get out of there, but it just kept sitting and staring at me. I took a deep breath and began screaming and running towards it. Luckily, it turned to run off before things had to get physical. I then made my way back to the road and could see a man walking around by the house just up ahead. As I passed by the house, the man walked out of a nearby shed, and I shouted over to him, "Hey! I just saw a mountain lion run off behind your property! Thought you might want to know in case you have any children or pets running around!" The man yelled back, "Thanks for letting me know! I had a dog disappear last week! I had a feeling that's what it was!"

I continued making my way west after seeing the mountain lion and ended my night just outside the town of Chillicothe. After setting up my tent in an open field just off the highway, I crawled inside and decided to see how far I'd made it since leaving Fort Walton Beach. I then realized I was right at my one-thousandth mile and had only reached five percent of my goal for St. Jude. I then began to question whether I should even continue to try and raise money for them since no one really seemed to care. Although, I kind of felt like my lack of support may have been because Texas was so boring. There just wasn't much for me to post about and keep people entertained. I figured I would keep trying, but I could feel my motivation drop significantly.

I woke the next morning, and it was the coldest it had ever been during my travels. It was the only time I'd felt the urgency to put on all of my clothing, which was three pair of medium-weight wool base layers, two shirts, two pants, a waterproof pant and jacket, a fleece jacket, three pair of wool socks, waterproof gloves, and a waterproof balaclava. Although I could barely move, my backpack had never felt so light, which helped alleviate some of the pain from my knees and busted toe. The winds coming down from the mountains of New Mexico had brought the temperatures down to minus fifty degrees, cold enough that all my water had frozen into solid chunks of ice. To

305

thaw one of the canteens, I placed it underneath my jacket and continued hiking west.

Since it was the dead of winter and the cold was causing my knees to hurt more than usual, I was only able to make it ten miles before it got dark. Feeling exhausted, I ended my night at a rest area between Chillicothe and Quanah. However, I was unable to get much sleep because I had to get up and exercise every thirty minutes to keep my body temperature up. Otherwise, I probably would have died due to hypothermia. Thankfully, by the time I'd made it into Childress the next night, the strong, bitter-cold winds had calmed significantly. Just as I entered the town, I put my tent up behind the large welcome sign and was finally able to get some rest without having to worry about freezing to death.

Although not nearly as bad as it had been, it was still cold the next morning. However, since I felt hidden enough, I decided to stay in my sleeping bag until about 9:00 a.m. before making my way into town. As I passed through, the temperatures were back into the mid-forties, so I made my way behind some of the businesses and began removing my excess clothing. As I was stuffing the extra gear into my backpack, I looked across the fence in front of me and saw an older woman picking up pecans in her back yard. I then noticed a ton of them around me, so I began picking them up to give her a hand. After filling up one of my extra bags, I walked up to the fence and said, "Here you go. I think that's all of them from this side of the fence." Surprised, the old lady laughed and said, "Thank you! I was wondering why I didn't see that many. Guess they all blew over there. That wind was crazy yesterday!" She then poured the bag of pecans into her bucket and said, "Here. Take you a handful." For some reason, I was starting to feel depressed again and didn't care for her offer, but she seemed so nice that I reached in to take some anyway.

After leaving Childress, I continued hiking west. By the time the sun was going down, I had made it forty miles into the town of Hedley. Normally, I would've been ready to get some sleep by then, but I could tell my depression was going to keep me awake. Not wanting to waste a full night of just lying around, I continued walking through the night and made it another forty miles before reaching the town of Claude. It was about 3:00 a.m. by then, and I was finally feeling tired enough to get some sleep. Thankfully, I came across a bunch of shipping containers right off the highway, where I would be able to set up my tent and not have to worry about anyone seeing me. I knew I would need to get some rest, though, because Amarillo was coming up, and I wanted to make sure I had the energy to get through there before dark.

Desert Sirens

The next morning, as I was making my way into Amarillo, a grey SUV pulled up beside me. I turned to focus on the people inside and saw two beautiful ladies. The passenger window rolled down, and a girl with dreads stuck her head out, "Hey! We're on our way to a concert in Tucson! You need a ride?" It looked like they were having a lot of fun, which made it very tempting to hop into the car with them, but I declined their offer. As they drove away, I made a post on my blog about how I'd just turned down a ride from two fine-looking hippie chicks. Everyone began commenting on the post, asking if I was crazy. Since I hadn't made a single dollar for St. Jude in weeks, I was really kicking myself for not taking off with them. Not that I needed the ride, but I knew being in their company would have gotten me out of that depressing funk I was in. It was too late to do anything other than to fantasize about what it would have been like if I had said yes, so I continued to daydream as I limped my way into the city.

Once I finally reached Amarillo's city limits, I noticed a gas station across the street and decided to make my way over to it so I could fill up on my water. As I was about to walk into the store, I looked over towards the fuel pumps and saw the two girls who had offered me the ride earlier. My mind began to race because I knew I only had a few seconds to speak up, or they would be gone again. I felt like the whole purpose of my walk had failed, and I was sick of being alone and depressed, so I ran over to them just before they drove off. "You girls still have room for one more," I asked with a huge smile on my face. The passenger stuck her head out of the window again and yelled, "Yeah, man! Let us pull up, and we'll make room for your pack!" After parking in front of the store, the two girls jumped out to introduce themselves. The dread-head introduced herself as Sara and the driver, whose beauty really grabbed my attention, said her name was Caylee. I then began telling them about how I was walking across America for St. Jude, but it had become a total bust, and I was just done with it. In my mind, since I'd already walked half of the country twice and cycled half of it twice, it just felt like the time to do things a bit differently. Although a part of me did feel bad for abandoning my walk, it felt great to be on the road with a couple of young, attractive women who seemed like they knew how to have a good time.

After driving about halfway through New Mexico, we began to take some shortcuts towards Phoenix, Arizona. A few hours later, we had made it deep into the backcountry canyons and decided to stop to set up camp. We had driven a couple of hours away from any major highways, so I wasn't sure where we were exactly, but it was very peaceful. Caylee and I then began working together to set up our campsite while Sara wandered off to explore the rocky terrain.

Later that night, as we were all gathered around the campfire, I asked, "What made you guys decide to stop and ask if I needed a ride?" Caylee began laughing and replied, "Well, honestly, I thought you were cute. Otherwise, I probably would have kept driving." I began laughing with her and said, "Same here. I'd still be walking if I hadn't thought you were babes. I just couldn't pass up the opportunity." Sara then joined in, "But you did! You said no! Caylee and I almost felt offended!" Sara then walked back to the truck to turn on some music, and they both started dancing around the fire. I fell into a sort of trance while watching them. It was so surreal to me how I had been feeling so alone and depressed, and suddenly I had found myself in such a magical moment. Caylee then reached out for me to stand up and began leading me towards the tent. My pulse began to race because I was pretty sure what she had in mind. Sara started laughing and said, "Don't make a mess! I'm sleeping in there tonight, too!"

Caylee laid down on top of my sleeping bag and began reaching out for me. My eyes grew to the size of the moon that night as I began inching closer to her. Just as her lips pressed against mine, I recanted all the times I'd said a woman was the most beautiful before. I never dreamed anyone could be as gorgeous as Caylee was, and I was beyond excited that she was mine, even if it were only for the moment. Her long, soft, brunette hair spiraled around my heart, and I was instantly seduced.

The next morning, the three of us loaded everything back up into their SUV and made our way for Tucson. Since we made it a point to stop at several sites along the way, we didn't reach our destination until dark. Caylee and Sara decided to get a motel and said I could stay with them if I wanted. No way was I going to pass up spending another night with them. Plus, I'd be able to get a shower, so we took our things up to our room and began making ourselves comfortable. Sara seemed preoccupied with her phone, so Caylee and I decided to take advantage of the shower. Having such a beautiful woman's soft hands washing over my achy body sent me over the top. It's hard to describe the feelings I had at that moment, but I suppose you could imagine that it was pure bliss, and I'm sure she knew how much I appreciated it. After being in the shower for nearly an hour, Sara knocked at the door, "Hey! Save some of that hot water for me!" We then traded rooms with her and made our way to the bed to pick up where we left off. By the time Sara was finished with her shower, Caylee and I were snuggled up in the blankets, near the point of exhaustion.

After parting ways with Caylee and Sara the next morning, I began my one-hundred forty-mile hike north towards Phoenix. I figured I would try to spend a little time with Jody since I was in his neck of the woods, and then I could continue hiking west from there. After hiking through the desert for one and a half days, I'd made it about halfway when a semi-truck pulled over up ahead. As I approached the passenger door, a man leaned over from the driver's seat, "Jake! What's up, man? Do you need a lift? I'm heading into Phoenix!" I figured since the man knew my name, he was probably a trustworthy character, so I climbed into the truck, and we began rolling down the highway. The middle-aged man then stuck out his hand for a shake and said, "Name's Kevin. I've been following your travels for a couple of years now. I wasn't expecting to see you out here, though. I thought you were still back in Texas." I began laughing and said, "Oh, well, you know, women can make men do crazy things." He began laughing and replied, "Oh, I hear you! I'm guessing you ended up taking a ride from those girls after all, huh?" I then pulled out my phone to show him a few pictures I'd taken with them, hoping he'd understand why it had been impossible for me to tell them no. "Oh, man! I get it! That's some temptation on another level, man!" We both began laughing in agreeance, and then he asked, "So, what are your plans in Phoenix?" I replied, "I'm hoping to meet up with an old friend, but he doesn't even know I'm on my way. I should probably message him now." Kevin nodded his head and asked, "Old friend, huh? Are you talking about Jody? I can give him a call for you." I looked over with a confused look on my face, "You know Jody?" He began laughing and replied, "Oh, sure! We've been friends for about ten years now. Great guy!" I couldn't believe I had just been picked up by a friend of the person I was on my way to meet. Anyone could have stopped to give me a ride, but it just so happened to be Kevin. He then whipped out his phone to give Jody a call and put it on speaker mode as it began to ring. "Yellow," Jody answered instead of saying hello. "Jody! How's it going, brother? So, I picked up a hitchhiker who says he's on his way to meet up with you. You know anything about that?" Jody began laughing and replied, "Not that I can recall. Did they give you a name?" "Says his name is Jake," Kevin replied with a smirk. After having a few laughs and explaining everything to Jody, he said he would swing by to pick me after Kevin dropped me off at the truck stop. I was glad to know everything was going to work out on such short notice.

After being dropped off at the truck stop in Phoenix, I sat at one of the benches outside and waited for Jody to arrive. He quickly pulled up next to me about thirty minutes later and yelled, "Come on! Get in!" I didn't really understand the urgency, but I threw my pack into the back and jumped into the backseat as fast as I could. Putting my seat belt on, I asked, "What's the rush?" Jody's wife, Lisa, then looked back and said, "We were supposed to be at our family reunion ten minutes ago." Jody then began laughing and said, "Hope you're hungry!" Feeling like I'd annoyed his wife, I replied, "Oh, man! I didn't know you guys had a family reunion today! I could have waited to hang out tomorrow!" Jody replied, "Heck, no! I'm showing you off to my family! I wasn't about to pass that up!" Thankfully, I'd taken the time to get a little cleaned up while I was back at the truck stop. Although it was only the middle of February, the desert temperatures were already on the rise. And all the dirt in the air had clung to my sweaty clothes.

After spending a few hours at Jody's family reunion, where I was included in the family photo, we made our way back to their house so I could get cleaned up. After getting a shower and doing my laundry, I went out with Jody and Lisa, searching for a place to do some karaoke. Once we found a bar that had an open-mic night, we made our way inside and began drinking beer to help us loosen up. I was a much better singer when I was sober, but I wasn't so comfortable performing in front of so many people. Not only did I have poor vision, to begin with, but the alcohol made the words on the screen appear to be wobbling all over the place, so I backed off the stage after only one song. After taking my seat back at the table with Jody and Lisa, Jody challenged me at an arm-wrestling competition. I may not have been sober enough to win anything with my voice, but I had been doing nearly three-hundred pushups each day for the past few years, so I was excited to put my arms to the test. Seeing as how Jody was such a large biker guy, about three times my size, I figured he would be a worthy opponent. We thought it would be a quick, friendly game, but it turned into a long, raging battle between two sweating bulls. As time went on, nearly everyone in the bar had gathered around to be spectators. Nearly ten minutes had gone by, and we were both stuck in the middle, shaking, growling, and turning red. I'd never been in such a long arm-wrestling match in all my life! Finally, just as I was about to back off, Jody began to show some signs of tiring. For all I knew, the weight of my arm was all that was left. Just as I thought I was about to lose, his hand slowly fell to the table. The crowd then went wild, as they'd probably never seen such an intense arm-wrestling competition.

After making it back to their house, I said to Jody, "I still can't believe I beat you. Did you let me win?" Jody began laughing and said, "No way, man! I used to do some serious arm-wrestling, and it feels like you may have broken my arm!" I then reached up to see if mine was sore to the touch and realized there was a huge knot on it. I began laughing with him and said, "Oh, man! We're gonna be feeling that tomorrow!" There wasn't a whole lot of life left to us at that point, so I pulled out my sleeping bag and tossed it onto the couch in the living room. Jody then took a seat in his recliner next to me, and we quickly drifted off to sleep with the ambient sound of his television playing in the background.

Jody and I woke the next morning to the sounds of Lisa and their grandchildren playing in the kitchen. We then realized it was close to lunchtime, so we jumped up and began making plans on where to eat. After shaking off our hangovers, we all hopped into his truck and made our way to one of Jody's favorite restaurants. As we were sitting there enjoying our meals, Jody suggested that we take a ride into the mountains once we'd finished eating. I wasn't interested in hiking out of Phoenix after dark, so I was down to do pretty much anything after confirming I could stay with them another night. We then loaded back into the truck and made our way through the desert, driving through the winding canyons. After riding along for nearly two hours, we came to a stop at Theodore Lake, which was a pretty good-sized body of water to be sitting in such an arid climate. About fifty boats were riding around out there, some of which had skiers on the back, and the shore was lined with people who were fishing. We then found a place to park and began walking along a nearby trail, just enjoying ourselves and the beautiful scenery.

After spending a couple of hours exploring around the lake, we made our way back into Phoenix and picked up a couple of pizzas and some beer before making it back to their house. Jody and I then settled down in the living room, where I shared some of my more inappropriate stories of life on the road. After having a few laughs from my more private moments, Jody excused himself for a moment and came back with a mason jar filled with some sort of liquid. As I removed the lid and leaned in to take a whiff, my head jerked back from the intense smell of alcohol. Jody began laughing and yelled out, "Cherry pie moonshine! A little bit of that ought to last you a while!" I took a small sip to see just how strong it was, and my lips began to tingle, "Oh, yeah! That'll come in handy if I have any problems getting to sleep!"

As I was shoving the jar of moonshine into my backpack, my phone began to ring. My heart stopped when I saw that it was Caylee. Not knowing what to expect, I answered with some hesitation in my voice, "Hey, what's up?" "Hey, man!" Caylee screamed with excitement, "Sara and I decided to drive all the way across the country before heading back home. You want to meet up with us tomorrow and catch a ride to San Diego?" "Yeah! That sounds great! Where are you now?" I asked. "We're still in Tucson. Where are you?" Caylee replied. I could tell by the way she sounded when I told her I was in Phoenix that they didn't have time to drive an extra four hours out of the way. Jody must have understood the situation and cut in, "Do they want to meet back up with you? The interstate from Tucson runs straight into Gila Bend, just a few miles southwest of here. I don't mind driving you down there tomorrow." Caylee overheard Jody and said, "Gila Bend? Sounds perfect! We'll meet you there tomorrow around noon!" I was so excited about getting to see Caylee again that I barely got any sleep that night.

The next morning, Jody, Lisa, and their two grandchildren gave me a ride down to Gila Bend. Once we made it into town, we pulled into a restaurant, where Jody offered to buy me lunch one more time before Caylee and Sara got there. Just as I was finishing my chicken sandwich, the girls pulled up in their SUV, and I thanked Jody for having me over for the past couple of days. It had been a real pleasure visiting with him, but I was sure it wouldn't be our last. I then opened the back window of the SUV to toss my pack inside, and Caylee said from the driver's seat, "Do you think you can drive? We haven't slept in almost two days." I hadn't driven in forever, so I smiled back and said, "Oh, yeah! Put your seatbelts on!" Since I was so used to walking everywhere, I knew I was going to enjoy being behind the wheel of a vehicle, covering the distance I'd normally make in a day in just a few hours.

Since Caylee and Sara slept for most of the six-hour drive across the desert, I was able to reflect on all that I'd been through. I began to wonder what I was going to do once Caylee and Sara went back home. I no longer had a reason or motive other than making it across the country again, and that was only about two hours away. I had no desire to go back to Tennessee, or anywhere at all for that matter. I figured I would continue heading north along the coast again, but I didn't know why or for how long. As the sun began to go down behind the mountains of Southern California, a feeling of emptiness came over me. I then realized this was the reason I had been feeling depressed for the past couple of weeks. I subconsciously knew that once I reached the coast that it would all be over. As much as I would love to wander the country forever, I knew that was impossible. My body was already showing signs of slowing down. Most of the pain was in my knees, which were swollen and continuously popped in and out of place with every step. I had no idea where my future was going to take me. I was scared that I was so beaten up that I wouldn't even be able to work again. And for what, the three hundred dollars I'd raised for St. Jude? I'd seen drug addicts begging on the side of the street make more than that in a day. I felt like such an idiot. I wished I'd just stayed in Alaska and took the chance of dying in the winter.

Caylee finally woke up as we were making it into El Cajon, about an hour from San Diego. I suggested we find a parking lot somewhere to stay the night since finding somewhere to sleep would be much more difficult in San Diego. She agreed with me, so we pulled into a shopping center and cut the engine off underneath all the streetlights. I pulled the lever to recline my seat and tried to get some sleep, but I gave up after a few minutes and said, "I think I'm going to go set my tent up behind the store." Caylee replied, "That sounds like a good idea to me. Do you mind if Sara and I join you?" I smiled back and said, "No. No, of course not." Although, I was a bit surprised that she'd asked because why would someone so beautiful want to sleep with a homeless man? Because, at that moment, that was all that I saw in myself.

After setting up my tent behind the building, Caylee climbed inside with me while Sara decided to sleep on the ground next to us, all wrapped up in a couple of thick blankets that she'd brought. We then fell asleep for a couple of hours

316

before we were woken up by the sounds of people screaming. At first, we tried to ignore it since we assumed it was just a couple of drunks yelling at one another. However, just a few minutes later, a man and woman came running down the hill towards us, so we jumped up to see what was going on. As the couple approached us, the woman said, "You guys need to be careful camping back here. There are a couple of people fighting up there, and they're acting all kinds of crazy. I think they're on those bath salts." Caylee, Sara, and I all looked at each other and rolled our eyes. Seeming annoyed, Sara laid back down and said, "Well, if they come down here, we'll fuck em' up." Caylee looked at me as if waiting to hear my input. I shrugged my shoulders because I figured Sara was right. Caylee and I then crawled back into my sleeping bag and fell back to sleep.

The next morning, we packed up our things and continued driving into San Diego. Caylee and Sara had never seen the Pacific Ocean, so I recommended the beach I had gone to the last time I'd been there. Although it was pretty much just another day for me, Caylee and Sara were really excited about it, so I was happy for them. We spent the rest of the day sitting on the sand and watching people play with their dogs. Then, after watching the sunset, Sara pulled out her phone and said, "Oh, Caylee, Ryan said we can come over to his house now!" Curious about what she was talking about, I cocked my head and dropped my eyebrows. Before I could ask, Caylee said, "Oh! Sorry, Jake! I forgot to tell you! Sara met some guy back in Tucson. He invited us to stay at his house while we were here. I'll ask if he minds you coming over later!" I then gave them both a hug goodbye and said, "Well, have fun and be safe. I'll just be hanging around here, I guess."

Shortly after Caylee and Sara had gone to meet up with their other friend, I began walking along the beach and scoping out a place to sleep for the night. I didn't make it too far before deciding to toss my sleeping bag down on the sand, hidden amongst a patch of weeds and small dunes. I lied awake for a few hours, hoping to see a text from Caylee, but I fell asleep before ever receiving anything. I'm not sure if it was because I was sleep-deprived, felt concealed enough, or just didn't care if I got caught stealth camping anymore, but I didn't wake up until the sun had made my sleeping bag uncomfortably hot. As soon as I sat up, I saw two police officers walking over towards me. "Fuck," I mumbled under my breath. With a big stupid grin on his face, one of the officers asked with an attitude, "How's it going?" I began laughing and said, "Well, I just got a good night's sleep, so I guess it could be worse." After directing me to stand up, the officer said, "You aren't being detained, but I'm going to put these cuffs on you so we can make sure you don't have any dangerous weapons." I calmly put my hands behind my back and said, "Have at it. I don't have anything." After digging through my things for a few minutes, completely ignoring the jar of moonshine, the officer pulled out his ticket book and began writing a citation. "What's that for," I asked as the second officer began removing my restraints. As the other officer handed me a pen to sign the ticket, he replied, "There's no sleeping on the beach." As I was signing my name, I noticed it was a hundred dollar fine and began shaking my head. I only had about fifty dollars to my name and had no idea how I was going to come up with the extra funds to pay for that ticket.

The Last Coast

After receiving a hundred-dollar ticket for sleeping on the beach in San Diego, I began to think of ways of how I could come up with the money to pay for it. Since I'd left the cold weather back in Texas, I figured I'd put my tent up for sale and finally put my tarp to use. Within an hour of posting my tent online, I'd already received an offer from a local and went to meet up with them. It was kind of strange to me how happy the person was to be buying my tent. They were so oblivious to the fact that they were taking the house I'd lived in for years. I guess it felt kind of like being evicted, but on the bright side, my pack was nearly three pounds lighter, and my knees seemed to appreciate it. I then made my way over to the courthouse to pay for my ticket and stood with everyone else in a long waiting line. As I was standing there, thumbing through the five twenty-dollar bills, I began to consider using it for a bus ticket out of there. I really didn't care if I had a warrant in San Diego. I just wanted out of there and had no intention of ever going back. I then shoved the money back into my wallet and tossed the shredded-up citation into the trash on my way out. I then made my way to the bus station and purchased a ticket to Long Beach for only fifteen dollars.

I didn't know what to expect out of Long Beach, but it was the farthest north I could go and still have some daylight left to find a place to sleep. As I exited the bus, I received a message from one of my followers, Andrea. She said she was living in the area and that I was welcome to stay with her and her husband for a couple of nights. I was very grateful to hear that because Long Beach already felt like a huge mistake. There were just way too many people for my liking. Andrea then gave me her address, and I made it to her house just a couple of hours later. There wasn't much of an introduction when I got there because we had been friends online for so long that it seemed quite casual. Of course, maybe that was just how I felt, but it seemed we were all on the same page. They were just so relaxed about me being there that all I heard for the first hour was, "Make yourself comfortable" and "Help yourself."

After resting up at Andrea's house for two nights, I was back on the move again and began walking north along the coast, trying to avoid the busy inner city. After hiking thirty miles, the sun began to set just as I'd made it into the city of Redondo. Before searching for a place to camp, which I thought would be easy enough, I decided to look for a place to grab a bite to eat. As I began passing by all the small restaurants along the main street, I couldn't help but notice all the people inside were wearing expensive clothes and jewelry. I then noticed all the cars parked outside were probably worth more than the average persons' home. I didn't have to look over any menus to know it was all more than I was willing to pay, so I figured I'd just go to bed hungry and turned to make my way towards the beach.

Once I'd made it to the beach in Redondo, I noticed a bench that looked like it would keep me hidden well enough until morning, so I tossed my sleeping bag down between it and the concrete wall behind it. After lying there for about thirty minutes, a couple came and took a seat on the bench. I didn't know if they'd seen me or not, but I decided to lie as still and quiet as possible, trying not to disturb or surprise them. After sitting there for about twenty minutes, patiently putting up with them being loud and annoying, they finally got up to leave. I began falling asleep shortly after they'd left, but I was quickly

320

awakened by another group of people who decided to loiter near the bench. And after dealing with several more people over the next couple of hours, I decided to look for somewhere else to sleep. Since the beach was being patrolled, I made my way into town, with no idea where I would go to get away from everyone. I then looked up towards the top of a building and knew that would be my best bet. Gripping the jagged bits of concrete with my cold, numb hands, I slowly pulled myself high above the city. Once I reached the top, I looked over the edge and huffed at all the people below. I then tossed my gear down onto the roof and slid into my sleeping bag, enjoying my hidden treasure of solitude.

It was nice being able to get some sleep without having to worry about people seeing me. However, as I was making my way back down from the building the next morning, a group of people gathered around to watch my descent. As soon as my feet hit the ground, I turned towards the crowd to take a bow for giving them a show. Within the two seconds it took to lift my head, everyone had looked away, and it was like I had turned completely invisible. People had just become so strange to me, so I thought I would give them a dose of their own medicine. They didn't mind putting me in the spotlight, especially when I was trying to sleep, but they couldn't handle my socially awkward confidence and sense of humor that only a homeless person could laugh at. I thought the situation was funny anyway.

After continuing my hike north for a few hours, I'd made it into Manhattan Beach, when I passed by a beach house full of partying rich people. I noticed a handful of them were standing outside with beers in their hands. I then heard one of the men yell out, "Hey, man! You look like you could use beer!" As I turned to see if it was me the man was talking to, I overheard the woman standing next to him, "Don't call that homeless man over here." I wasn't interested in stopping until I heard the lady say that, but then I decided to take the man up on his offer and made my way over. "Sure! I could go for a drink!" I replied with a huge smile on my face. I then took the ice-cold beer from the man's hand and drank nearly half of it in one sip. "That's a heck of a hiking pack you got there," the man said, "Where you headed to?" I quickly finished the beer with a second sip, "Don't know. I was walking across America for St. Jude, but I don't know what I'm doing now." "You walked across America?" the man asked excitedly. "Well, half and half. Half one time and half another. The other halves were on a bike. I kind of hitchhiked another half. It's a long story." I could tell he didn't believe a lick of what I was saying as he handed me another beer. As I finished that one, a small group of people approached him and asked if they were still going out on his boat. "Yeah! Let's go," he yelled back at them. As he turned to walk away with the crowd, he smacked me on the back and said, "You too, man! Come on!" Since I didn't have any other plans, I figured I'd tag along just to spice things up.

After driving a few miles back south to the man's boat in Redondo, the seven of us climbed aboard, where we all began drinking and dancing to the music on the radio. The rest of that day is pretty much a blur, but I was still on the boat when I woke the next morning and had no idea where I was. I began calling out but quickly realized I was alone. I then remembered everyone had gone to a bar the night before and must not have made it back. After spending a few minutes trying to figure my way out, I finally got the door open and climbed out of the sleeping quarters. I then realized we were tied down to a port, and although I still had no idea where I was, my anxiety was pretty much gone because at least I knew we were on land. However, my stress was quickly re-elevated once I realized I had lost my wallet. After searching all around the boat, I finally saw it sitting in one of the deck chairs and felt a huge sense of relief. Once I was sure everything was still inside, I vowed never to do anything like that again and grabbed the rest of my things to leave. After making it back to the beach, I checked my phone to see where I was. As it turned out, I was still in

Redondo, but we had docked in a different area than when we first got there.

After rehydrating from a night of drinking, I continued hiking north and made it into Venice just as the sun was beginning to set. There were so many interesting people all along the beachfront that I was able to melt into the crowd. It felt great to blend in, or at least not to be the main attraction, which several hundred people were fighting for. For example, a Jamaican man was riding roller skates in his underwear while playing an electric guitar with a small amp strapped to his waist. Oddly enough, even he had a hard time getting noticed in Venice. I couldn't help but take several pictures and share them on my Facebook Page. Not long after posting them, I received a message from Cynthia, a girl I had gone to high school with. She had moved to East Los Angeles a few years back and asked if I'd like to stay the night at her place while I was making my way through.

I had a feeling that finding a safe place to sleep in Venice might be rather challenging, so I took her up on her offer and made my way to a restaurant where she would be able to find me easily. She pulled up about an hour later with her three kids and asked if we'd all like to grab a bite to eat before heading back to their house. For some reason, I wasn't hungry, but her kids began jumping up and down for pizza. As her kids took their time eating, Cynthia and I began to do some catching up. As she was squeezing a lemon into her tea, she began smiling and asked, "So, you basically disappeared after high school. You were completely off the radar, and all of a sudden, you were walking across the country. What did I miss?" I couldn't help but laugh because nearly everyone I'd grown up with had asked me something along those lines. I took a deep breath and replied, "Well, I dropped out of school when I turned eighteen and went to get my GED. As soon as I was finished with that, I went straight to see a recruiter about joining the Army. I was sworn in about a month later and arrived at basic training on my nineteenth birthday." With a surprised look on her face, Cynthia asked, "What made you decide to join the Army? You never took me as that type." I took another deep breath, "Well, I was engaged at the time, and it just seemed like a quick and solid career path that would provide us with a lot of benefits to start a family. However, she ended up cheating on me before I even finished training, so I spent the next four years lugging around a machine gun for nothing." Cynthia's eyes grew larger as if she wanted to say something, but nothing came out.

After riding with Cynthia back to her house in West Covina, she took her kids upstairs to her room and said I could have the downstairs to myself. Feeling exhausted, I flopped down on the mattress that was lying on the living room floor and fell straight to sleep. By the time I'd woken up, Cynthia had already taken her kids to school and left work. I knew she wouldn't mind if I'd stuck around for a few days, but I was so used to being outside and on the move that being left alone in her house made me feel claustrophobic. I then walked outside and noticed a large, snow-capped mountain probably fifteen miles away. It looked like a great place to get away from all the people of the city and be able to relax, so I pulled out my phone and began searching for any nearby trails that would lead me to the top. I then found out the mountain was named Mt. San Antonio, but it was currently off-limits. A man had recently died up there, and the park rangers were issuing fines to anyone caught hiking in the area. The conditions were just too dangerous for them to allow people up there.

Since I was unable to venture out into the mountains near Cynthia's house, I hopped onto a bus and took an hour-long ride back towards the coast. Once the bus reached Santa Monica, I grabbed my pack and continued following the beach north. Finally, after spending the day hiking through all the rich neighborhoods, I'd found myself in the Topanga State Park. My anxiety had been building up over the past few days, so finding a trail that led me into the forested hills was a great sense of relief. After spending two nights alone in the wilderness that overlooked the city of Malibu, I decided to follow a dirt trail that appeared to be heading north. I didn't know which trail it was or where it would take me, but I wasn't too worried because I still had plenty of water. After hiking through the mountains for two more days, I finally exited the forest and found myself in the town of Oxnard. There were only a couple of hours of daylight left once I'd made it into the city, so I quickly began searching for a place to sleep. I tried to make it to the beach, but there had been an unusual amount of rain, and all the fields that I needed to cross were flooded. I then followed a service road that ran alongside one of the fields for about an hour and pitched my tarp behind a mound of dirt.

The next morning, I made my way back into Oxnard and hopped aboard a train to catch a forty-mile ride north into Santa Barbara. Once I arrived, I immediately made my way for the ocean pier and noticed a small crowd of people had gathered near the entrance. I made my way over to see what had caught their attention, and I saw a homeless man who was making sculptures out of the sand. As I looked closer, I realized he was working on a couple of soldiers, where one was dragging the other away after he'd had his legs blown off. I then noticed a large bucket hanging up that had "No donations, no pictures" written on the side of it. I looked back over towards the crowd and saw everyone taking pictures and walking away without leaving any tips. I shook my head at everyone and tossed a five-dollar bill into the bucket. I then took a picture for myself and shared it with my Facebook followers. I then walked out onto the sand and asked the man, "How long does it usually take you to make a sculpture like this?" There was so much detail that I expected him to say it took him several days. However, the man replied, "I usually spend a day working on them and come back in the morning to start on something new." "Wow! Something new every morning," I asked, "How come?" As he continued working, the man replied, "Well, the first few times I tried to preserve them, someone came out during the night a kicked them over. I then realized that I had nothing better to do anyway, so I decided to just keep coming back and making new ones." I thought for a minute and asked, "Every day? Is this your only source of income?" The old man nodded, "Yep. This has been it for about eight years now." I was intrigued by the fact that he'd been surviving off his art for so long. Another group of people then walked by to take a picture. I waited to see if any of them were going to leave a tip, but none of them did. I then shook my head and looked back over to the man and said, "Metaphorically speaking, you know what's funny? People will spend a hundred dollars on perfume and think the world owes them something because they smell good. Then they come strutting around with their heads up their ass and think it's our fault they smell shit." The man started laughing and nodded his head as I left him to his work.

After parting ways with the homeless sand sculptor, I made my way back across the street to look for an outlet to charge my phone. It didn't take long before I passed by a building and saw a place to hook up on the outside of it. After sitting there with my phone plugged in for about five minutes, a man walked around the corner on the sidewalk and began screaming at me for stealing the electricity. I looked at him like he was out of his mind before asking, "Are you the manager of this business? Because I will pay you to charge my phone." Instead of answering my question, the man pulled out his cellphone and called the police, "Yes, I'd like to file a complaint. There's a homeless man out in front of the Best Western Hotel, stealing electricity." After hanging up with the police, the angry old man began walking away and said, "Man, I am so sick and tired of all these homeless people!" Not wanting to deal with the cops, I rolled my eyes and began collecting my things to get out of there. Just as I was about to walk away, a young man took a seat where I had just stood up from and said, "Man, what was that guy's deal? He was tripping because you were charging your phone?" I shook my head as I began walking away, "Not because I was charging my phone. Because I'm homeless."

After leaving the motel, where I'd tried charging my phone, I made my way into a nearby park and came across an interesting homeless man. He was standing next to an old mountain bike with a large trailer hooked to the back of it. Curious about his setup, I walked up to him and began asking questions about it. He then began to tell me about how he'd been homeless in Santa Monica for twenty years but had been living in the trailer on the back of his bike for most of it. He was proud of the fact he'd built the trailer himself from a bunch of scrap parts and showed me the inside of it. Amazingly, there was a bed, shower, sink, toilet, heater, and even a small stove. There were even locks on the door to help keep people from breaking in at night. I couldn't help but ask, "The cops don't bother you for sleeping in this?" The man began laughing and replied, "Nothing they can do! I've designed it for it to be completely legal! Any time they make changes to the law, I make changes to my bike!" I couldn't help but be a bit envious of his trailer and wished I'd had something like that while I was on a bike.

Shortly after admiring the homeless man's elaborate trailer, I began walking the streets, searching for something to eat. Although I had some money left, I didn't want to spend any of it, so I began digging through every garbage can that I could find. I finally came across a half-eaten bag of cereal and pulled it out to inspect it. As I was holding it up to get a closer look, a bunch of ants began climbing up my arm, and I dropped it onto the sidewalk. Thousands of little black ants began scurrying out of the bag and made their way for the nearby grass. I then looked over at a group of pedestrians who were walking past me and began laughing. I then said out loud, "I don't know why I just wasted all that protein!" I then reached down to pick up the bag of cereal and began shoving handfuls into my mouth.

I could hear people around me making gagging sounds and saying things about how disgusting I was, but I didn't care. All I wanted was to stop feeling hungry, and I knew it would get the job done. I then took my bag of cereal back to the park and began searching for a place to sleep. I noticed a group of bushes next to a fence, so I made my way over to them and crawled inside. I wasn't surprised to see another homeless man had already claimed that spot, but I was surprised when he said, "Don't mind me. There's plenty of room." Since he didn't mind, I decided to go ahead and take a seat next to him.

After talking with him for about an hour, we heard someone walking up to us, and the branches began to separate. Another man came crashing through, and I immediately recognized his face. It was the guy who had sat next to me when I was getting yelled at for charging my phone. After settling in and making himself comfortable, he looked over at me and yelled, "Hey! You're that guy who was charging his phone this morning! I got arrested because of you!" I gave him a confused look and asked, "What do you mean you got arrested because of me?" He began shaking his head and added, "Remember that guy who called that cops on you? Well, they thought I was you and didn't believe me when I said they had the wrong guy. They took me to the station for questioning but let me go about an hour later." The odds of him being arrested because of me and then crashing into the same bush was just too weird. I apologized for what had happened, but he didn't seem to be too bothered by the incident. He actually seemed to have a good sense of humor about it and just kind of laughed it off. However, the bush began to feel too crowded for me, so I decided to part ways with them and left to search for another place to sleep.

Since it was almost 3:00 a.m., the entire beachfront was pretty much void of human life. Then I realized there was a jetty with no people on it, so I decided to walk out and enjoy having it all to myself. Once I'd made it to the end, which was about fifty yards from the beach, giant waves began slamming into the walls and splashing up on me. I decided to head back before a rogue wave came and swept me out into the ocean. As I was making my way back to land, I noticed a few people walking towards me with fishing poles. As they got closer, I stepped to the side so they could go around me, and then one of the men started yelling at me, "What the hell is this? I can't even come out here at 3:00 in the morning without running into some homeless piece of shit. You need to get the fuck out of here, dude!"

I wasn't in the mood to fight, so I kept my mouth shut because what I wanted to say would have only escalated the situation. I then continued walking, and one of the guys shoved my backpack from behind, causing me to fall forward. Every bit of anger that had been boiling inside of me came out, and I jumped back up in a fit of rage. I can't remember what all I said, but I still remember the mixed look of fear and anger on their faces. I then jumped in front of the guy who shoved me and dared him to try and hit me. I could see that he was yelling at me, but it was like everything went silent. I could then see the man standing next to him take a swing at me from the corner of my eye. I dodged his left hook, which left him stumbling over his friend. I immediately took my opportunity to land a solid blow just behind his ear, and he dropped to the concrete. The woman with them began screaming for us to stop fighting, so I slowly began walking back to leave. The man who had started the whole thing then came charging at me and got himself knocked out as well. I then picked up my backpack off the ground and started to walk away when the woman yelled, "I'm calling the police!" I turned back to her and screamed, "Good! Do it! You guys started This! I was just minding my own business! It's called self-defense!" With my adrenaline still pumping, I stomped away and began searching for a place to hide. Although I knew I hadn't done anything wrong, I was worried the cops would side with them because they lived there, and I was just some homeless traveler. It didn't take long before I found a place to sleep within another group of bushes.

329

Although I hardly got any rest because my blood was still boiling, and it felt like I may have broken one of my hands.

When I woke the next morning, I immediately made my way over to the bus station and bought a ticket for Santa Cruz. It was the closest any bus could get me to Half Moon Bay, which was where I had my sights set on. The severity of my depression had been creeping up on me again, so I figured if I could meet up with Jennifer or Bill and they would help to elevate my mood. Once I'd made it to Santa Cruz, I filled up my water and began hiking north. Uneventfully, I passed through all the small coastal towns as I had before and finally reached Half Moon Bay three days later.

As I began making my way through town, I decided to head over to the coffee shop where I'd ran into Bill the first time I'd come through. After grabbing a cup and taking a seat at one of the outdoor tables, I was secretly hoping Bill would come by and help cheer me up. I knew he walked by the coffee shop every day, so if I waited long enough, I was sure that I would run into him. However, after sitting there for a few hours, the only person to stop and talk to me was some old, half-blind homeless man named Black Wolf. Although I didn't ask, I was fairly certain that he was a Native American, so the name didn't surprise me. However, what did surprise me was that it was only 10:00 a.m., and he was already drunk and continuously taking sips of vodka from a flask he kept in his jacket pocket. He kept going on about how much he hated everyone and everything, and he would occasionally look at a passerby to yell something along the lines of "Fuck you" and "What are you looking at?" I don't know why he decided to sit with me if he hated everyone so much, but I guess maybe he could sense I wasn't too far from understanding the way he felt. He finally got up to leave after about an hour of talking, so I asked, "Before you go, you wouldn't happen to know of an old homeless man that hangs around here by the name Bill, would you? He's kind of heavyset and has a big white beard." Before turning to walk away, he casually replied, "Bill? Yeah, I knew Bill. He died a few months back." My head dropped to the table.

Although I hadn't spent much time with Bill, I was sad to know he had passed and felt like I'd lost a great friend. I wasn't sure of the circumstances that led to his death, but I hoped he hadn't gone out feeling like no one would miss him because I surely did. I then felt like I needed more cheering up than I did before, so I sent Jennifer a message to let her know I was in the area. A few minutes later, I received a reply that read, "I have a boyfriend now. Please don't talk to me." I was hoping to explain that I just wanted someone to talk to and that it didn't have to be romantic, but she blocked me before I had the chance. I felt my heart being ripped out because I would have given anything to be with her, but I had stupidly lost that opportunity when I had chosen to go to Alaska. I then picked my phone back up to message the lady who had invited me over for dinner, but she too had a boyfriend and said she couldn't talk to me. I couldn't believe how opposite Half Moon Bay was from the last time I'd been there. What was once my favorite town had become a symbol of where everything went wrong. How I'd once loved the cold, dark, and dreary weather that seemed to linger over the city now felt like the perfect setting for some sad poem.

After realizing I'd lost my friends of Half Moon Bay, I decided to try and help myself feel better by occupying my time crafting bows. After hanging around my favorite spot on the beach for a week, I'd made four bows and sold each of them for fifty dollars. I then went back into town and bought myself a new pair of clothes and paid for a nice haircut. After feeling more socially acceptable, I decided to head over to the San Benito House, the bar and grill I'd gone to before with the firepit in the back. I had gone in with high hopes of making some new friends, but shortly after ordering a beer and some fries, I tripped over an empty base for an umbrella and fell onto it with all my body weight. The steel pipe almost went through my torso like a giant hole puncher, so I had to cut my chances of

331

making any friends short and walked six miles north to the nearest emergency room. After getting a couple of x-rays, the doctor informed me that my abdominal muscles had some tears, but none of my organs had been damaged.

After leaving the hospital, I decided to set up camp in the dense forest nearby. The next morning, I gathered my things and figured I might as well continue hiking north since Half Moon Bay didn't seem to have anything for me. I'd finally made it into San Francisco around noon and had a hard time making it through because of all the steep hills. My knees were popping in and out of place, and the torn muscles in my stomach caused a sharp stabbing pain that took my breath away with each difficult step. When I finally had a good view of the Golden Gate Bridge, I imagined how nice it would be to leap over the side and just fly away. As I continued to make my way closer to the bridge, all the pain I had felt seemed to disappear because I knew it would all be over soon. Every mistake I'd ever made, everyone I'd ever let down, every nightmare that kept pushing me across the country, that I no longer had the strength to fight, would all be washed away into the ocean.

As the sun was beginning to set, I made my way into a wooded area close to the bridge and set up my tent for the night. As the night went on, I began to feel unsure of my abilities to throw myself over the bridge, so I started to think of some backup plans. I then remembered I had nearly a full bottle of Klonopin in my backpack, which I knew would take away all my worries. I then reached into my bag and pulled out two of them to help me relax. About an hour later, the medication had really taken hold of me, so I did something I wouldn't have done otherwise. I pulled out my phone and created a detailed post on Craigslist of everything I'd been through and my plans of jumping off the Golden Gate Bridge. At the end of the post, I pleaded for someone to bring me an unmarked pistol, loaded with a single bullet so I could shoot myself in the head just before leaping into the bay. Shortly after clicking the submit button, I drifted off to sleep with the ominous sounds of the bay nearby.

I woke the next morning and noticed someone had responded to my advertisement. I had a feeling that it might be a police officer trying to set me up, so I deleted the post from Craigslist and never responded to them. I then began to gather my things to make my way up to the bridge, when my phone began to flood with hundreds of messages from people who were looking for me. Hoping to conceal my identity, I removed everything from my Facebook Page and changed the privacy settings so no one could see it. I then turned off my phone and made my way back into the city, where I could lay low for the rest of the day. I eventually passed by an empty tennis court and tossed my sleeping bag underneath one of the benches on the side. I laid there for the rest of the day and into the night, hoping everyone would just forget about the post I'd made.

I woke the next morning around 5:00 a.m. to the sound of people playing tennis. I peeked my head out of my sleeping bag to get a look at them when I realized it was pouring down with freezing rain. I thought the two men were crazy to be out playing in it, but then I began laughing because there I was lying soaking wet in my sleeping bag. I crawled out from underneath the bench and began shoving my things back into my backpack. As I was walking away, I stopped to look over at the two men who were still happily playing tennis. I wondered why they had never said anything to me or even looked at me, for that matter. Although I was sure it was because they were probably used to seeing so many homeless people that they just ignored them, I couldn't help but feel strange by their lack of concern. Being from a small town, I knew no one there would ever just pass by someone sleeping outside in the rain. It wasn't that I expected things to have gone any differently or that it phased me at all, but it certainly made me stop to consider how unimportant all the homeless people who lived on these streets must feel. That one day didn't bother me, but I couldn't imagine waking up to be treated like a ghost every day.

As I began walking back towards the bridge, I decided to stop at a fancy restaurant and have one final breakfast. I was certainly out of place since I was all dirty and dripping wet, but I didn't care what anyone thought of me. About halfway through my meal, I pulled out my phone to see what was going on in the area. I then read an article about another veteran who had been walking across America and was about to finish his hike just a few blocks away. I scarfed down the rest of my food and began making my way in his direction. As far as I knew, the police had no idea what I looked like, and I thought this other veteran might have been the perfect scapegoat.

After locating the other cross-country hiker, who was pulling along a cart down a blocked-off street, I began walking alongside him on the sidewalk. As we got closer to the beach, reporters began running up to him with cameras, so I listened carefully to see if any of them asked if he was planning to jump from the Golden Gate Bridge. I couldn't make out what any of them were saying, though, because he had gathered a large crowd of people who were just too noisy for me to hear over. Once we'd made it to the beach, I saw several police officers waiting for him. I stood back at the intersection to see if any of them would interrogate him about the craigslist post, but they just began slapping him on the back and shaking his hand. I figured the police had either spoken to him already or that they had given up on their search. I then began to wonder if the police knew what I looked like. It was possible, but I thought it was unlikely because I had deleted all my pictures from my Facebook Page. I then shrugged my shoulders and turned to make my way up to the bridge.

Once I'd made it up to the bridge, I took a seat on a large concrete structure next to it and pulled out my bottle of pills. After chewing and swallowing all of them, I began walking across the bridge. My knees began to shake like crazy, and I wondered if it was the pills or the traffic that was making their way across. Then, just as I'd reached the middle of the bridge, my knees completely gave out, and I fell against the railing. Not wanting to cause any extra attention, I gritted my teeth to stop myself from screaming and pulled myself up by one of the beams. I then looked up at the fence I'd have to climb over to make the jump and dropped my backpack onto the ground. I'd carried it as far as I could, but I wasn't going to be able to take it with me. As soon as my pack hit the concrete, I was approached by several police officers. As they grabbed me and spun me around, I realized there were no other cars or pedestrians. They'd had the whole bridge blocked off, and I was so focused on jumping that I hadn't even realized it. After placing me in handcuffs, one of the officers asked, "Is your name Jake? Are you the veteran we've been looking for?" I was so ashamed of myself that I couldn't even answer to the sound of my own name, and I dropped my head. They then helped me across the railing and loaded me into one of their police cars, when I finally began to feel the pills kicking in. The officer then looked back at me and asked, "Are you on something? You look a little loopy."

I woke the next day and realized I was in the VA hospital. Although they had pumped my stomach and assured me that I was going to be okay, they had me sign several papers stating that I would be admitted to their psychiatric care for being suicidal. I fell back to sleep after giving them my information and woke up for only a few minutes at a time over the next couple of days. Each time I woke up, a different nurse was there to help me eat, drink, and use the bathroom. I couldn't do anything else anyway because I was still tied down to the bed, waiting to be evaluated by a psychiatrist.

Three days after being admitted, I was transferred to the psychiatric unit that was housing about twenty other veterans who were also struggling with post-traumatic stress disorder. I was then shown to my room, which was already occupied by three other guys who had been there for about a month. They seemed to be in a much better state of mind than I was, as they were laughing and joking amongst themselves. However, other than introducing themselves, they seemed to respect my personal space and left me alone when I decided to lie in bed for the rest of the day.

As the days went on, I began to feel more comfortable with my surroundings and finally decided to join them in their group therapy. I was a bit surprised by some of the stories they were sharing since they sounded very similar to those I'd sworn to take to my grave. Although I wasn't as open as they were, it felt great to know I was surrounded by people who wouldn't judge me if I'd chosen to talk. However, I finally let everyone know why I was there, and opening up about it did make me feel a little better. They were all blown away by the amount of traveling I'd done, though. Even the doctor who was sitting in the room with us didn't know my full story until I'd told everyone. She then asked, "How many miles have you traveled altogether?" I shrugged my shoulders and replied, "I'm not really sure. I've thought about mapping it out but never really had the time." One of the patients then said, "You've got all the time in the world right now. I want to know!" Everyone seemed interested, so we all pulled out our phones and began connecting the dots. Another patient held up his phone and shouted, "Ten thousand miles! Holy shit, brother! No wonder your knees hurt!" After hearing about my knees, the doctor recommended that I get an x-ray on them. It turned out that I had developed a severe case of patellar tracking disorder that caused my knees to slip out of place every time I bent my legs. The doctor then gave me a set of resistance bands to do some exercises with but said I'd likely need surgery if I couldn't walk within the next month. I was a bit skeptical about having knee surgery or even being there for that long, so I took the bands and made sure to use them every chance I had.

The next day, I was having a one-on-one conversation with my psychiatrist when she asked, "What are your plans for when you leave here?" I had no idea what I was going to do, but I knew it was time to find something else. I then replied, "I haven't had the time to think about it, but I suppose I need to start looking for some work. I don't want to go back to Tennessee, though." After leaving the doctor's office, I remembered this woman, Elizabeth, had messaged me a few months back and said her dad was looking for a ranch hand in Wyoming. I decided to send her a message to see if the position was still available. She replied immediately, "Yeah! He still needs help! We have fourteen horses that need looking after. You think you can handle that?" Fourteen horses sure sounded like a handful, but she had sent several pictures of the ranch that was located within the Wind River Range, and it was so beautiful that I thought any amount of work would be worth living there. I replied, "When's the soonest I can be there?"

Epilogue

Shortly after leaving the hospital in San Francisco, I took a bus to Wyoming, where I began working construction while keeping up as a ranch hand at home. Within three months of being there, Elizabeth and I got married. However, we ended up getting a divorce after being together for only one year. I then lost everything I had and took a bus to Tennessee. Since I had nowhere to go, I decided to stay with my parents until I could figure out my next move. Over the next two weeks, I grew increasingly tired and weak. Since I'd just separated from Elizabeth, everyone thought I was depressed and just needed some time to get over it. However, I knew something wasn't right, so I made an appointment with my doctor and was diagnosed with liver cancer.

Since my doctor was too far away from my parents' house to walk, and I had lost my vehicle in the divorce, I was forced to live in the woods behind the hospital. To occupy my time, I bought a laptop and began working on a book about my travels. Finally, after a grueling three months, I received results saying that my cancer was in remission. The very next day, I'd finished working on my book and submitted it for printing. I then gathered my things from behind the hospital and headed to my parents' house to share the good news.

After staying with my parents for two weeks, one hundred printed copies of my book arrived at their doorstep. I then loaded twenty of them into a backpack, strapped across my chest, and walked to every library I could find, asking each of them if I could set up a book signing. Within the next month, I'd sold all my copies and used the money I'd made to take a bus back to Los Angeles. I then began walking up the coast, promoting my book online, and selling autographed copies on the streets to anyone interested. By the time I'd made it back up to Half Moon Bay again, I'd sold nearly a thousand copies and met back up with Black Wolf. I then used all the money I'd made from my book sales to purchase him a small RV, hoping it would restore his faith in humanity.

I then began making my way back south, hoping to sell enough books to get myself a vehicle. However, I didn't have the same amount of luck as I did when I was heading north. By the time I'd made it back down to Los Angeles, I'd only sold about a hundred copies. I then met back up with my old friend, Cynthia, who said I could stay with her until I sold enough books to get what I needed. Three months later, I was able to purchase myself a used Jeep for five thousand dollars. However, I soon realized I had been ripped off and was tricked into buying something with a bad transmission. Sympathizing with me, Cynthia decided to let me use her car for work, so long as I could make the payments on it. Since my knees were starting to hurt again, I took her up on her offer and quickly found a job with a business that allowed me to work my own hours. By the time I'd made enough money to leave, Cynthia and I had fallen in love. That was three years ago. We're still together and living in Los Angeles.

Adjusting to life in the city was difficult at first, but I eventually found a passion for photography that helped to balance living there. I still travel the country, though now by car, and spend a few weeks out and a few weeks at home. Since my main focus in photography is wildlife and landscapes, I have continued to pursue my gift of giving by donating a percentage of my print sales to The Nature Conservancy and local homeless shelters. I no longer battle with depression and was finally able to let go of my troubled past. I continuously reassure myself that everything happens for a reason and that it will all work itself out in the end. Until that day comes, I will remain content and keep searching for all the beauty this life has to offer. As it turns out, it was worth it after all.

CPSIA information can be obtained
at www.ICGtesting.com
Printed in the USA
LVHW041551180723
752688LV00003B/704